TOURISM AND HOSPITALITY INDUSTRY: Status and Development

Editors

R.K. Gupta
Anish Slath
Arun Singh Thakur

NEHA PUBLISHERS & DISTRIBUTORS
DELHI

Publisher

NEHA PUBLISHERS & DISTRIBUTORS

4832/24,Prahlad Lane,S-207

Ansari Road, Daryaganj,Delhi-110002

Ph.: 43570976, 23278261

Email: nehapubdistributors@gmail.com

Edition: 2014

ISBN : 978-93-80318-51-6

Laser Typesetting

JEE-VEE Graphics

Delhi

Price : Rs. 1495.00

Printed by **Vikas Computers**

PREFACE

"Human nature will not change. In any future great national trial, compared with the men of this, we shall have as weak and as strong, as silly and as wise, as bad and as good. Let us therefore study the incidents in this as philosophy to learn wisdom from and none of them as wrongs to be avenged."

Abraham Lincoln

According to the UN Green Economy Report, the greening of tourism, which involves significant investment in efficiency improvements in energy, water and waste systems, would stimulate job creation, especially in poorer communities, with increased local hiring and sourcing, and have a positive spill-over effect on other areas of the economy. The direct economic contribution of tourism to local communities would also increase; maximizing the amount of tourist spending that is retained by the local economy. With adequate policies and investment, the tourism sector can be at the forefront of the transformation to a green economy. Greening the growing tourism sector would strengthen its capacity to generate economic growth, jobs and development worldwide, while protecting the environment for future generations. Tourism can impact on all aspects of people lives - economic, social, cultural, and environmental - simultaneously. For example, a tourism initiative aimed at enhancing local/rural economic development through nature-based tourism can have the added benefits of empowering the local/rural people through their involvement in decision-making, contributes to a sense of ownership over the resource and an associated sense of pride, which in turn can improve conservation of the natural resources through increased protection and reduced harvesting. Tourism activities can also result in improved access to infrastructure, which is beneficial for the community.

Sustainable tourism recognizes that the future of tourism and hospitality sector depends on protecting life in all its diversity. It integrates economic and ecological concerns by, for example, conserving a natural area which, in turn, generates increased revenues from tourism for future conservation. Given tourism's importance in the global economy, the sector has a responsibility to take the lead on the path towards sustainable development. At the same time, with cultural and natural resources at the core of its business, tourism has a vested interest in doing so. Thus, sustainable tourism and hospitality industry should make optimal use of environment resources, respect the socio-cultural authenticity of host communities and provide viable, long-term socio-economic benefits to all.

Over the past years, and particularly since the start of the global economic crisis, a widespread consensus has emerged on the need to build a new economic paradigm. Multiple crises - in climate, biodiversity, fuel, food, water and the economy as a whole - have led to calls for a new development model: a "green economy". A green economy is one which is low carbon, resource efficient and socially inclusive. The United Nations Environment Programme (UNEP) defines a green economy as one that "results in improved human-wellbeing and social equity, while significantly reducing environmental risks and ecological scarcities". The UN Green Economy Report demonstrates that the greening of economies is not a constraint on growth, but rather a new engine of development, able to create decent jobs, reduce poverty and address major environmental challenges. Tourism, finds the Report, is one of the ten economic sectors best able to kick-start the transition to a sustainable and inclusive green economy. Making tourism businesses more sustainable will foster the industry's growth, create more and better jobs, consolidate higher investment returns, benefit local development and contribute to poverty reduction, while raising awareness and support for the sustainable use of natural resources.

As Tourism is one of the most promising drivers of growth for the world economy, but is accompanied by significant challenges. Green tourism has the potential to create new jobs support the local economy and reduce poverty. Investing in the greening of tourism can reduce the cost of energy, water and waste and enhance the value of biodiversity, ecosystems and cultural heritage. Tourists are increasingly demanding the greening of tourism. Much of the economic potential for green tourism is found in small and medium-sized enterprises (SMEs), which need better access to financing for investing in green tourism. Destination planning and development strategies are the first step towards the greening of tourism. Government investments and policies can leverage private sector actions on green tourism. Green innovation in tourism can trigger major economic, social and environmental benefits.

The present book 'Tourism and Hospitality Industry: Status and Development' organised itself as per the spirit of the introductory quote of this preface. Editors are feeling very happy to bring this book on the occasion of 'HOSTOCON 2014' at Panjab University, Chandigarh.

This book is a collection of assorted researches that addresses a large vista of tourism related issues. The research articles are all, in their own part, notable scholarly contributions documenting diverse aspects and studies related to the tourism. This book offers an inclusive glance into issues related with the status and development of tourism and hospitality industry. The tourism and hospitality industry is well on its way to becoming one of the most powerful growth engines in the coming time, thus these research studies are relevant for a number of stakeholders like governments, destinations, tour operators, travel agents, tourism workers, developers, tourism researchers, students and travellers themselves. This book seeks to fulfil the needs of planning for the industry.

Editors acknowledge the valuable research of the contributors and believe that this publication is a significant contribution towards future development and planning purposes not only for tourism industry but also for other tourism related activities and those who are interested in the tourism research. Editors sincerely believe in the standards of academic integrity and highest levels of scholastic conduct, thus declare that the respective authors would be responsible for any kind of plagiarism found in their contribution.

LIST OF CONTRIBUTORS

Abhishek Ghai	Assistant Professor, University Institute of Hotel Management & Tourism, Panjab University Chandigarh, abhishekghai87@ gmail.com
Amit Kumar Uppal	Assistant Professor in Tourism Department, Aditya College Gwalior (M.P.) uppal.it@ gmail.com
Amrik Singh	Assistant Professer, School of Hotel Management and Tourism, Lovely Professional University, Jalandhar, amrikmhm@gmail.com.
Anjali Khanna	Associate Dean, School of Hotel Management and Tourism, Lovely Professional University Phagwara, Punjab, Pin - 144401. anjali.khanna@ lpu.co.in
Anushree Banerjee	Research Scholar Institute of Tourism Studies University of Lucknow. 08anushree@ gmail.com
Arun Sharma	Research Scholar Tourism Management, School of Tourism Travel and Hospitality Management Central University of Himachal Pradesh Dharmshala TAB - Shahpur sharma.arun84@gmail.com
Arun Singh Thakur	Assistant Professor, University Institute of Hotel Management and Tourism, Panjab University, Chandigarh. arun.tourism@gmail.com
B. Srinivas Rao	Project Manager Shailja's Organic Products Pvt. Ltd. Bidyanagar, Mahura, Janla Bhubaneswar - 752054 Orissa srinivastevia@gmail.com
Bharat B. Sharma	Research Scholar, Centre for Mountain Tourism and Hospitality Studies, Hemwati Nandan Bahuguna Garhwal University Srinagar, Garhwal. bharat4sai@gmail.com
Bharat Kapoor	Assistant Professor, School of Hotel Management and Tourism, Lovely Professional University, Jalandhar, bharatkapoor22@gmail.com.
Daleep Kumar	Research Scholar of Hotel & Tourism Management, Pacific Academy of Higher Education & Research University, Udaipur-Rajasthan (India)
Dinesh Dhankhar	Assistant Professor, Department of Tourism &

	Hotel Management, Kurukshetra University, Kurukshetra dd.dhankhar@gmail.com
Divoy Chhabra	Lecturer, School of Hotel Management and Tourism Lovely Professional University Phagwara, Punjab, Pin - 144401. divoychhabra@gmail.com
Gaurav Garg	Associate Professor Amrapali Institute of Hotel Management, Shiksha Nagar, Haldwani gary281178@gmail.com
Goldi Puri	Assistant Professor, Institute of Hotel & Tourism Management, Maharishi Dayanand University, Rohtak-124001 drgoldipuri@gmail.com
Himanshu Malik	School of Hotel Management & Tourism, Lovely Professional University. himanshu.18051@lpu.co.in
Imosongla Jamir	Dept. of Tourism, Hotel, Hospitality and Heritage Studies, Jamia Millia Islamia, New Delhi 110025, India amyxjamir@yahoo.com
Javeed Ahmad Teeli	Research Scholar, Department of HRM & OB, Central University of Jammu, J&K, jaaslords@gmail.com
Kumar Nilmani	Academic Associate, Economics at Indian Institute of Management, Kashipur. kumar.nilmani@iimkashipur.ac.in,
Lakhvinder Singh	Research Scholar, Department of Tourism & Hotel Management, Kurukshetra University, Kurukshetra lakhvindersingh.kuk@gmail.com
Lipika Guliani	Assistant Professor, UIHMT, Panjab University lipika_b@yahoo.com
Mahendra Kumar Khuntwal	Trainee, Regional Level Tourist Guide Training Program, Indian Institute of Tourism and Travel Management, Gwalior(M.P.) mahendra_kumar21@hotmail.com
Mahesh Kumar	Research Scholar, Institute of Hotel & Tourism Management, Maharishi Dayanand University, Rohtak-124001 mahesh972000hm@gmail.com
Mahesh Sharma	Research Scholar, Institute of Hotel & Tourism Management, Maharashi Dayanand University, Rohtak mahesh972000hm@gmail.com

Manik Arora	Research Scholar School of Hospitality and Tourism Management University of Jammu manikarora1986@gmail.com
Manpreet Arora	Assistant Professor, School of Business & Management Science, Central University of Himachal Pradesh, Dharamshala, Kangra, Himachal Pradesh arora.manpreet3@ gmail.com
Mou Roy	Lecturer, Ranjita Institute of Hotel Managemnt, Bhubaneswar. (Affiliated to National Council for Hotel Management & Catering Technology, Noida) Bidyanagar, Mahura, Janla Bhubaneswar - 752054 Orissa dutta_mou@yahoo.com
Nurmahmud Ali	Assistant Professor, School of Hotel Management and Tourism Lovely Professional University Phagwara, Punjab, Pin - 144401 Contactnur23@ lpu.co.in
P. Aparna	Associate Professor (English), GNITS, Hyderabad
P.Siva Sankara Reddy	Principal, GVRS Govt Degree College, Dhone, Kurnool
Parul Mathur	Director, Pacific Institute of Hotel Management, Pacific University Udaipur & Ahmedabad. mathur.parul@rdiffmail.com
Prashant K Gautam	Assistant Professor, University Institute of Hotel Management and Tourism, Panjab University, Chandigarh. Prashant.k.gautam@gmail.com
Puja Mathur	Assistant Professor, Pacific Institute Of Management & Technology, Pacific University Udaipur. puja11@rediffmail.com
Ranu Chauhan	Assistant Professor, Indian Institute of Tourism and Travel Management (IITTM), Gwalior. chauhan.ranu7@gmail.com
Sanjeev Sharma	Assistant Professor, School of Hotel Management and Tourism Lecturer, School of Hotel Management and Tourism Lovely Professional University Phagwara, Punjab, Pin - 144401.
Saurabh Rawat	Research Scholar Institute of Tourism Studies University of Lucknow. vicious_saurabh@ yahoo.com

Sidharth Srivastava	Assistant Professor, School of Hotel Management and Tourism
Lovely Professional	University Phagwara, Punjab, Pin - 144401. sidharthsrivastava2011@yahoo.in
Sonia Sharma	Assistant Professor, School of Tourism and Hospitality Services Management, Indira Gandhi National Open University, New Delhi. soniasharma@ignou.ac.in
Suvidha Khanna	Assistant Professor School of Hospitality and Tourism Management University of Jammu urs_suvidha@rediffmail.com
Syed Ahmad Rizwan	Assistant Professor, UIHMT, Panjab University syedahmadrizwan@gmail.com
Vikash Prasad	Assistant Lecturer Dr. Ambedkar Institute of Hotel Management Chandigarh vikash.ihmghy07@gmail.com
Vikrant Kaushal	Lecturer, School of Hotel Management and Tourism, Lovely professional University vikrant.kaushal@lpu.co.in

CONTENTS

Preface 3

List of Contributors 7

1. ENVIRONMENTAL SUSTAINABILITY IN THE FOOD SERVICE INDUSTRY: A REVIEW 15
Abhishek Ghai

2. RURAL TOURISM: SCOPE AND DELIVERANCE SPECIAL REFERENCE TO VILLAGE BASSI IN RAJASTHAN 27
Amit Kumar Uppal
Mahendra Kumar Khuntwal

3. BROADENING THE IDEA OF CSR FROM CORPORATE TO INSTITUTIONS-SUCCESS STORY OF A UNIVERSITY 36
Anjali Khanna
Vikrant Kaushal

4. MEASURING THE IMPACTS OF ECO-TOURISM 43
Anushree Banerjee
Saurabh Rawat

5. TOURIST PERCEPTION OF A RELIGIOUS TOURISM SITE: A CASE OF MANSA DEVI TEMPLE PANCHKULA IN HARYANA, INDIA 54
Prashant K Gautam
Arun Singh Thakur

6 BARRIERS IN SUSTAINABILITY: A TOURISM PERSPECTIVE 71
Arun Sharma

7. ECOTOURISM: A VIABLE SOLUTION TO DEVELOP GREEN PRACTICES AT TRIKUTA HILLS IN JAMMU & KASHMIR, INDIA 91
Bharat B. Sharma
Sonia Sharma

8. GUEST SATISFACTION IN THE HOSPITALITY SECTOR: A STUDY OF HOTELS IN PUNJAB 108
Bharat Kapoor
Amrik Singh

9. ENVIRONMENT FRIENDLY PRACTICES ADOPTED BY THE HOTEL TO PROMOTE SUSTAINABLE TOURISM: A CASE STUDY OF THE HOTEL CABBANA, PHAGWARA, PUNJAB 121
Divoy Chhabra
Sanjeev Sharma

10. PROMOTING CULTURE: A STUDY OF HOSPITALITY MANAGEMENT INSTITUTES OF UTTARAKHAND VIS-À-VIS BY REGIONAL CUISINE AND ITS DEVELOPMENT 133
Gaurav Garg
Vikash Prasad

11. A REVIEW PAPER ON MANAGING AND DEVELOPING ORGANISATIONAL CULTURE IN HOSPITALITY INDUSTRY 150
Himanshu Malik

12. CONVERTING INDIAN NUPTIALS INTO TOURISM PRODUCTS 162
Imosongla Jamir

13. THE ROLE OF HUMAN RESOURCES EMPOWERMENT IN THE SUSTAINABLE DEVELOPMENT OF TOURISM INDUSTRY 170
Javeed Ahmad Teeli

14. OPPORTUNITIES & CHALLENGES FOR ECOTOURISM IN VALLEY OF FLOWER (UTTARAKHAND) 181
Lakhvinder Singh
Dinesh Dhankhar

15. FOOD SAFETY AND PERCEIVED RISK: A STUDY OF HARYANA TOURISM COMPLEXES SITUATED ON NATIONAL HIGHWAY-1 193
Lakhvinder Singh
Dinesh Dhankhar
Mahesh Sharma

16. DOES GREEN TOURISM SPEAKS BUSINESS? 212
Lipika Guliani
Syed Ahmad Rizwan

17. AYURVEDIC CUISINE: A WAY TO UNDERSTAND AHAR AND ANNA ACCORDING TO YOUR OWN CONSTITUTION 231
Mahesh Kumar
Goldi Puri

18. IMPACT OF GREEN IMAGE ON GUEST SATISFACTION IN HOSPITALITY INDUSTRY 244
Manik Arora
Suvidha Khanna

19. FOREIGN EXCHANGE EARNINGS THROUGH TOURISM IN INDIA 255
Manpreet Arora

20. ORGANIC FOOD AND HOSPITALITY 264
Mou Roy
B. Srinivas Rao

21. TERRORISM AND TOURISM: AN INDIAN PERSPECTIVE 279
Kumar Nilmani
Ranu Chauhan

22. BLENDING YIELD WITH TECHNOLOGY: A STUDY OF LOW-COST CARRIERS IN REFERENCE TO SCENARIO OF INDIAN AVIATION INDUSTRY 298
Nurmahmud Ali
Sidharth Srivastava

23. RURAL TOURISM; KUCHIPUDI DANCE -A CULTURAL HERITAGE 308
P. Siva Sankara Reddy
P. Aparna

24. TRAINING NEEDS FOR THE HOSPITALITY INDUSTRY A STUDY OF HOTELS IN RAJASTHAN 319
Parul Mathur
Puja Mathur

25. FLOURISHES THE TOURISM SECTOR AND ITS TRENDS IN STATE OF QATAR 329
Parul Mathur
Daleep Kumar

ENVIRONMENTAL SUSTAINABILITY IN THE FOOD SERVICE INDUSTRY: A REVIEW

Abhishek Ghai

Assistant Professor, University Institute of Hotel Management & Tourism, Panjab University Chandigarh, abhishekghai87@gmail.com

Abstract: Service sector being a star performer in Indian economic scenario and hospitality being a major component of this sector, which is related to food production, service, issues of green and sustainability will be a cause of major concern in this sector. The consumer choice is also titling towards organizations that support sustainability. The paper discusses the concept of environmental sustainability in the food service industry and reviews the practices that could yield positive results.

Keywords: Environment, Sustainability, Food Service Industry, Energy, India.

Introduction

Today, economy has emerged as a big giant globally and India is no exception in this context. The Indian economy predicts 8.6% GDP growth in 2013-14. With agriculture and services continuing to perform well, the slowdown can be attributed almost entirely too weakening industrial growth. The services sector continues to be a star performer as its share in GDP has climbed from 58% in 2010-11 to 59% in 2011 12 with a growth rate of 9.4%. Similarly, agriculture and allied sectors are estimated to achieve a growth rate of 2.5% in 2011-12 with food grains production likely to cross 250.42 million environmentally responsible practices has been the focus of some studies, with a common conclusion that a barrier to further adoption is the lack of hoteliers awareness and market research about consumer attitudes and behavior towards green practices.

Vieregge et al. (2007) stated that loyal customers of the globally branded restaurant do appreciate the use of local products usually. He also explored the consumer perceptions of eco-friendly behavior in a fast food restaurant chain in Switzerland. Further Choi and Parsa (2006) conducted a study of manager attitudes towards green practices in the US restaurant industry, and revealed that to engaging in green practices can tip to strengthened customer relations and increased harmony with the community. In spite of the positive attitude or behaviour towards green practices, only 15 per cent of respondents were willing to pay extra for environmental creativities, while the remaining consumers felt that costs should either be paid for by the hotel or shared (Manaktola and Jauhari, 2007).Harris & Crane (2002), analyzed that during the last few decades it has become a common phenomenon to focus on the environmental impact of the hotel industry with each hotel striving to achieve environmental sensitivity even though there is no universally agreed upon definition of a green hotel. He also suggested that generally the term "green facility or hotel" can be used interchangeably with "an environment friendly hotel," "an eco-friendly hotel," or "a sustainable hotel." Kasim (2004) opined that tourists were knowledgeable and cared about the environment but they did not consider a hotel's environmental strategy as a foundation for their hotel choice. That is not to say that they would not approve of room attributes that were environmentally friendly. Now a days tourist are willing to accept rooms with water saving features, recycling bins, fire-safety features, energy saving features, and information on local ecotourism attractions. Green hotels are "environmentally-friendly properties whose managers are eager to institute programs that save water, save energy and reduce solid waste-while saving money-to help protect our one and only earth" (Green Hotel Association, 2007).

Aspects of Sustainability within Industry

Hotels are constantly becoming greener and environment friendly. These days many big players of the world are adopting various green practices. Sustainable and environmentally responsible practices are becoming part of the daily business process across the industry as restaurant owners understand that waste reduction, energy efficiency, water conservation, and recycling are beneficial for their business and their community. From the help of past review the present study focuses on the major categories of things that may be used as the aspects of environmental sustainability.

Food

A responsible food production model must be reinstituted if any measures of control over food quality and safety are to be regained. The "Buy Local, Buy Organic" and "Fair Trade" concepts are now familiar to many of us; however, there still appears to be a sizeable gap between comprehension and action for most businesses-most likely maintained by the industrial efficiency and cost economics of large, centralized food producers and distributors, as well as intentionally misleading marketing campaigns. Organic foods can include fruits, vegetables, grains, dairy foods, eggs, and to some extent, meats and poultry. Organic foods are defined as those foods that are grown without the use of synthetic fertilizers, sewage sludge, irradiation, genetic engineering, pesticides, or drugs. It is made according to the definite production standards. The USDA, United States Department of Agriculture, defines organic foods as products grown without the use of pesticides, synthetic fertilizers, sewage sludge, or genetically modified organisms (Dahm et al., 2009). The market for organic foods continues to grow, and is driven by a number of factors. According to Knudson, 2007; the establishment of a USDA standard has increased consumer acceptance and there is also an increasing interest in healthy foods. The OTA, Organic Trade Association, estimates that the total global organic food and beverage sales were $13.8 billion in 2006. From 2004 through 2006, sales of organic food increased by 38.4 percent. Upon that it is estimated that sales of organic foods will increase by 71 percent from 2006 through 2011. Further Knudson, 2007; revealed that customers these days are increasingly interested in products which are free of pesticides and other health risks. Clearly, organic food has become mainstream. According to the Organic Foods Productions Act of 1990, to be organic a product must have been made through organic production, which involves using renewable resources, lack of antibiotics and growth hormones for animals, and without most conventional pesticides. It also requires that fertilizers are not made with synthetic ingredients and there is no bioengineering or ionizing radiation.

Seyfand, 2006; Weatherell et al., 2003 stated that local food, although more or less impervious as a concept, is thus seen to represent environmental concerns, local livelihoods and economies embedded in place, as well as citizens' local involvement and good social relations. Within the globalized food system, re-localization efforts celebrate the local vis-à-vis "the global" (Morgan & Sonnino, 2008), whereby the local is understood as "radical and subversive" in contrast to the global, which is "hegemonic and oppressive" (Born & Purcell, 2006, in Morgan &Sonnino, 2008).

Energy

According to Kasim, (2007); and Deng, (2003); apart from seasonality, location and number of guests a hotel operation requires energy for 24 hours on daily basis. Gossling, (2002); opined that energy is required to maintain the tools which are used to carry out the functions efficiently to maintain the flow of guests. Dascalaki and Balaras, (2004); demonstrated that the energy consumed by hotels is used for space heating, cooling, ventilation, hot water, lighting, laundry and kitchen recreation and miscellaneous uses and further found that the energy consumption patterns for hotels are different around the world. Further Becken et al., (2001), analysed that it is important to know the fuel type that is used to generate energy. They revealed that coal (12%) and LPG (9%), are the major fuel types used to generate energy, whereas petroleum fuel (3%), natural gas and wood (1%) play a very slightpart in producing energy. Further

Bohndanowicz, (2005); stated that the use and consumption of different forms of energy by hotels leads to the release of harmful gases into the atmosphere and leads to air pollution.According to Ernst and Young, 2008; The Otani Hotel in Japan installed a new air conditioning and kitchen system, through which it achieved a 14% savings in energy and a 30% carbon emissions reduction. From the report of Willard InterContinental Hotel Washington D.C., 2009 found that the hotel is now running on 100% wind energy power resulting in a 12% decline in energy consumption over the past five years.

Plastics and Paper

Kirk (1996) demonstrated from the study that production and service of food operations produce more waste than other areas of hotel operations. In the UK hospitality Industry a report on food waste conducted in 1980 indicated that 15.5% of edible food was wasted by the hotel and restaurant, compared with an average of 11.4% of the catering industry as a whole. Further Alexander (2002), stated that in hotel there is variety of waste is generated during operation and it consist of paper, food, various metals, plastics, aluminum and glass. The hotel has visible effects on the environment by the generation of waste. The generation of solid waste depends upon the size of the hotel. Kasim (2007) revealed that it is not the size of the hotel that makes the difference but also the type of functions being held at the hotel and any important events taking place at a particular time. He further opined that waste created by hotels not only increases the cost of the industry but it is also important to manage that waste to help save resources, energy and money.China recycles and makes most of the world's plastics and most of the post-consumer plastic comes from the west. This creates concerns about how much shipping these plastics overseas actually costs, which turns out to be small since so much is being shipped at a time. According to Duraiapah et. al., (2002); the five major side effects that processing of recycling has on the environment are: global warming potential, eutrophication, human toxicity, solid waste, and acidification. Further Tacey, (1996) stated that so much of the US plastic recycling can't be recycled and gets brought to the waste dump in China, there have been issues of the US being accused of using China as a place to dump their waste.According to the ISO15270 Guidelines for the recovery and recycling of plastics waste, the selection of methodologies and processes for the management of plastics waste (2008) can be firstly divided into material recycling, chemical or feedstock recycling, and biological or organic recycling); and secondly in energy recovery in the form of heat, steam, or electricity generation using plastics waste assubstitutes for primary fossil fuel resources.

Water

Water has been described as one of the major resources in the hotel industry.Restaurants use hundreds of thousands of gallons of water every year. Water conservation encourages food service industry to better manage how and when water is being used, addressing both the technical and human side of water management issues.Looking for ways to reduce these can be a big step towards environmental sustainability. Changing some of the practices throughout the restaurant can help as well. Only refilling water upon request is one good way to cut down on the water use, however it may not be the best business practice. Previous studies indicate high level of water consumption among hotels. According to the report of RBR, 2002 discovered a water consumption rateamounting to 440 liters per guest per night.There are lot of changes luxury facilities can do for water conservation. To help conserve water resources in the hotel, water management practices in now being implemented. According to Mensah, 2006; Brodsky, 2005; Sherman, 2008; the major practices in water management include the use of low-flow or infrared activated faucets, low-flow showerheads, low-water volume toilets, regular fixing of toilet lacks, and the use of water-efficient laundry equipment and dishingwashers. Furthermore, the reuse of towels and linens by hotel guests not only helps hotels inreducing the water consumption but also reduce the cost ofrunning the hotel. The implementation of these practices will enable hotels to save some quantities of water for the hotel.

Conclusion

India being a rising star cannot afford to ignore the sustainability aspect of the food production and service. If it has to keep the graph going up then its focus has to be consumers who are sustainability conscious and this includes sustainability in food service too. Green hotels, organic foods, water conservation and recycling, use of eco friendly materials and practices are initiatives that will rule the consumer's choice. The replacement of fossil fuel is also one of the steps. All efforts have to be concentrated on being sustainable irrespective of the fact how small the step is. It is the cumulative of the action taken towards sustainability that will count.

References

Alexander, S. (2002). Green hotels: Opportunities and resources for success. Zero Waste Alliance, 2-9.

Álvarez, M., Burgos, J., Ce´cspedes, J., 2001. An analysis of environmental management, organizational context and performance of Spanish hotels. Omega 29,457-471.

Becken, S., Frampton, C., & Simmons, D. (2001). Energy consumption patterns in the accommodation sector-the New Zealand case. Ecological Economics, 39(3), 371-386.

Bohdanowicz, P. (2005). European hoteliers' environmental attitudes: greening the business. Cornell Hotel and Restaurant Administration Quarterly, 46(2), 188.

Blanco, E., Rey-Maquieira, J., Lozano, J., 2009.Economic incentives for tourism firmsto undertake voluntary environmental management. Tourism Management 30(1), 112-122.

Bohdanowicz, P. (2006) Environmental awareness and initiatives in the Swedish and Polish hotel industries - survey results. International Journal of Hospitality Management 25 : 662 - 682.

Bohdanowicz, P., 2009. Theory and practice of environmental management andmonitoring in hotel chains. In: Gössling, S., Hall, C.M., Weaver, D.B. (Eds.),Sustainable Tourism Futures: Perspectives on Systems, Restructuring and Innovations.Routledge, New York, pp. 102-130.

Choi, G. and Parsa, H. G.(2006) Green practices II: Measuring restaurant managers' psychological attributes and their willingness to charge for the 'green practices. Journal of Foodservice Business Research 9 (4) : 41-63.

Dahm, Molly J., Aurelia V. Samonte, and Amy R. Shows. "Organic Foods: Do Eco-Friendly Attitudes Predict Eco-Friendly Behaviors?." Journal of American College Health. 58.3

Beaumont, Texas: (2009).

Dascalaki, E., &Balaras, C. A. (2004). Xenios- a methodology for assessing refurbishment scenarios and the potential of application of RES and RUE in hotels. Energy and Buildings, 36, 1091-1105.

Deng, S. (2003). Energy and water uses and their performance explanatory indicators in hotels in Hong Kong. Energy and Buildings, 35, 775-784.

Duraiappah, Anatha Kumar, Zhou Xin and Pieter J.H. Van Beukering. "Issues in Production, Recycling and International Trade: Analysing the Chinese Plastic Sector Using and Optimal Life Cycle Analysis (OLC) Model." Environmental and Development Economics 7 (2002): 47-74.

Eiadt, Y., Kelly, A., Roche, F., Eyadat, H., 2008.Green and competitive?An empiricaltest of the mediating role of environmental innovation strategy. Journal of WorldBusiness 43 (2), 131-145.

Enz, C.A., Siguaw, J.A., 1999. Best hotel environmental practices. Cornell Hotel andRestaurant Administration Quarterly 40 (5), 72-77.

Green Hotel Association (n.d.). Retrieved October 30, 2007 from http://www.greenhotels.com/whatare.htm

Goodman, A., 2000. Implementing sustainability in service operations at Scandichotels.Interfaces 30, 202-214.

Gössling, S. (2002).Global environmental consequences of tourism. Global Environmental Change, 12(4), 283-302.

Gössling, S., Hall, C.M., Weaver, D.B. (Eds.), 2009. Sustainable Tourism Futures: Perspectives on Systems, Restructuring and Innovations. Routledge, New York.

Han, H., Hsu, L. T., & Sheu, C. (2010). Application of the Theory of Planned Behavior to green hotel choice:Testing the effect of environmental friendly activities. Tourism Management. 31(3), 325-334.

ISO15270: 2008. Plastics - Guidelines for the recovery and recycling of plastics waste. PDF document. http://www.tehranstandard.org /pr/news/Draftfile/ISO_15270_2008(E)-Character_PDF_ document.pdf.Referred 16.05.2013.

Kasim, A. (2004). Socio-environmentally responsible hotel business: Do tourists to Penang Island, Malaysia care? Journal of Hospitality & Leisure Marketing, 11(4), 5-28.

Kasim, A. (2006). The need for business environmental and social responsibility in the tourismindustry. International Journal of Hospitality & Tourism Administration, 7(1), 1-22.

Kasim, A. (2007). Towards a Wider Adoption of Environmental Responsibility in the Hotel Sector. International Journal of Hospitality & Tourism Administration, 8(2), 25-49.

Kasim, A., 2009. Managerial attitudes towards environmental management among small and medium hotels in Kuala Lumpur. Journal of Sustainable Tourism 1 (6), 709-725.

Kassinis, G., Soteriou, A., 2003. Greening the service profit chain: the impact of environmental management practices. Production and Operations Management 12 (3), 386-403.

Kirk, D. (1996). Environmental Management for Hotels. Oxford: Butterworth-Heinemann Ltd.

Knudson, William A. "The Organic Food Market." Business Innovation in Agriculture, Food and Natural Resources. Michigan State University: 2007.

Krozer, Y., 2008. Innovations and the Environment. Springer-Verlag, London.

Le, Y., Hollenhurst, S., Harris, C., McLaughlin, A. and Shook, S. (2006) Environmental management: A study of Vietnamese hotels. Annals of Tourism Research 33 (2) : 545 - 567.

Lui, Z. (2003). Sustainable Tourism Development: A Critique. Journal of sustainable Tourism (Vol.11, No.6), pp. 459-475.

Manaktola, K. andJauhari, V. (2007) Exploring consumer attitude and behaviour towards green practices in the lodging industry in India. International Journal of Contemporary

Hospitality Management 19 (5) : 364 - 377.

M. Sherman. "Green lodging program helps revive Florida hotels", Hospitality Construction, (2): 66-70, 2008.

O'Brien, C. (2002, August/September). Organic beer and wine. Co-op America .

Organic Foods Production Act of 1990. Public Law 109-07, 10 Nov 2005.

Radisson SAS. "Responsible Business Report, 2002.Radisson SAS Hotels & Resorts", Brussels, Belgium.

S. Brodsky. "Water conservation crucial to energy savings", Hotel & Motel Management, 220(13): 12, 2005.

Tacey, Lis. "US Companies Accused of Dumping' Waste Cargoes." Nature 382 Aug. (1996): 484.

Vieregge, M., Scanlon, N. and Huss, J. (2007) Marketing locally grown food products in globally branded restaurants: Do customerscare? Journal of Food Service Business Research 10 (2) : 67 - 82.

RURAL TOURISM: SCOPE AND DELIVERANCE SPECIAL REFERENCE TO VILLAGE BASSI IN RAJASTHAN

Amit Kumar Uppal

Assistant Professor in Tourism Department,
Aditya College Gwalior (M.P.) uppal.it@gmail.com

Mahendra Kumar Khuntwal

Trainee, Regional Level Tourist Guide Training Program,
Indian Institute of Tourism and Travel Management, Gwalior (M.P.)
mahendra_kumar21@hotmail.com

Abstract: Tourism growth potential can be harnessed as a strategy for Rural Development. The development of a strong platform around the concept of Rural Tourism is definitely useful for a country like India, where almost 74% of the population resides in its 7 million villages. Promoting rural tourism means promoting and protecting local customs and tradition to protect cultural identity and providing support to local people to improve their economy. The paper is based on rural tourism and its scope. An analysis has been done to understand the attitude of the rural population towards tourism. Rural tourism realities have also been discussed in the paper. The paper tries to investigate the existing framework of the rural tourism and the gap in the channel of deliverance.

Keywords: Rural Tourism, Tourism Scope and Deliverance, Promotion, Tourism Realities, Channels

Introduction

India is a multi - destination country with a variety of tourism resources. Its rich cultural heritage has created magnificent architectural buildings & monuments. The snowcapped mountains, the beautiful beaches of coastal states offer the world tourist community some of the best & unique tourist destinations, which rejuvenate the mind, body & soul. Tourism is the third largest foreign exchange earner after gem, jewelry& ready-made garments. Tourism generate more jobs than any other sector for every rupee invested.

In spite of all types of tourism resources & potentialities in India we are unable to fully explore the tourism products & services to attract a size able number of International tourist. Now it is the right time to identify the right market & right consumer in this era of fierce competition among the tourism generating countries. So that India can be real Incredible India as a destination in the map of World tourism.

As the perceptions, attitude, is changing very fast of the present tourist communities & today's tourists are also very keen to enrich & experience about the unique features of a country. In view of the above changing pattern of the tourists steps are, therefore being taken to develop the alternative strategy to promote Rural tourism in domestic & as well as International market.

Rural Tourism has emerged as a new mantra for alternative tourism development. This concept has been already tested in the developed country & proved the best results. Our country & its villages have so many things to cater the needs of the tourists. The rural people, its culture, tradition, arts, handicrafts, scenery, landscape can attract the tourists irrespective of its taste, perceptions & attitudes. Rural tourism has been defined as ***'a variety of visits away from home to locations outside main towns and seaside resorts, be they holidays, day trips, business trips or to visit friends & relatives'***.

According to **Ganon, 'Rural tourism'** covers "a range of activities provided by farmers and rural people to attract tourists to their area in order to generate extra income for their business." Rural tourism has been seen as tool though which many problems in rural areas can be addressed in the countries like Sub Sahara, afflicted by debilitating rural poverty, tourism is perceived to be one of the few feasible options for development. (Brideham and Wickens, 2004).

Any form of tourism which highlights the rural life, art, culture, heritage, at rural sites, thereby supporting the Hosts (Local) community socially, economically as well as enabling interaction among the Guests (tourists) and the Hosts (Locals) for more experience & enrichment can be called as rural tourism. This type of tourism takes place in rural sites.

Bassi

Bassi one of the most prominent rural village of Chittaurgarh districts on *Chittorgarh - Bundi* Road. which is very well known for its artistic handicrafts, Ancient temples, Rural culture and a wildlife sanctuary. It is also known for the famous Bassi Fort which was built in 16th century by the Thakur Jaimal of Sisodiya Dynasty known as (Chundawat) cousin of MaharanaPratap. The Chundawat family fought for Mewar and the Famous Chittorgarh Fort.

Presently Mr. Janak Singh (Chundawat family) is the head of the village. People of every cast lives here like Rajput, Muslim, Brahmin, Lohar, Sutar and also the schedule cast etc. Different colonies are there for different cast of people like Sutar lives in KhairadiBasti, Rajput in Rajput Basti, and Muslims in Muslim Bastivise versa. The main occupation of people is agriculture but also the do their parental business like Khairadi (Sutar) use to make wooden crafts, Lohar (Blacksmith) would do iron work etc.

Bassi, itself is a versatile place for every kind of tourist, means whether the tourist is history lover, nature lover or interested in cultural activities everything can be experienced here. Though there are many things Bassi is famous for like: Wild Life Sanctuary, Bassi dam, Old Temples, Bassi Lake, Heritage Hotel (Bassi Fort Palace), Sculptures and Handicrafts.

General information of bassi

- Location 24 kms from Chittorgarh
- Longitude 74 47' East
- Latitude 24 25' North.

- Area — 20 square km
- Population — above 100,000
- Climate
  - o Summer — Maximum 48 c Minimum 32 c
  - o Winter — Maximum 18 c Minimum 10 c
- Annual rainfall — 750mm
- Rainy season — July-September
- Language — Hindi and Mewari

Bassi on Map

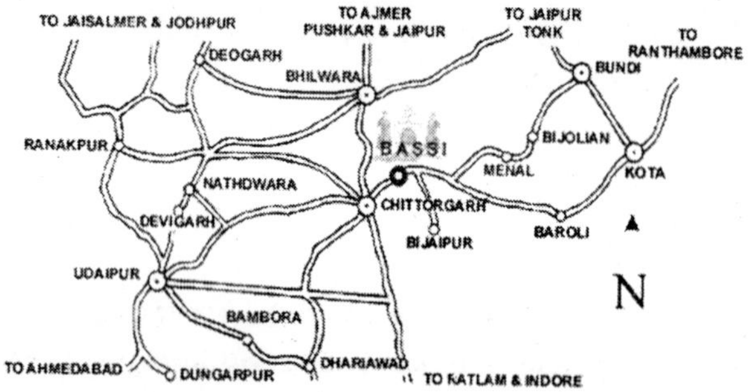

Bassi heritage treasure

Bassi is full of heritage treasure which includes its fort and palace, laxminath temple,kavad, wooden crafts of Isaargangaur and very important opium farming.

The treasure of bassi is explained below-

1. Bassi Fort and Palace

   Famous BassiFortand palace was built in 16th century by the Thakur Jaimal of Sisodiya Dynasty known as (Chundawat) cousin of MaharanaPratap. The Chundawat family fought for Mewar and the Famous Chittorgarh Fort.

2. LaxminathTemple and Step well

   According to the villagers this temple is near about 450 years old means it was built in 16th Sanctuary. In temple, Lord Vishnu and his wife Goddess Lakshmi Worshiped. Near the temple a Kund

(Reservoir) is there which also has its own specialty; all the four sets of Stairs of Kund are begins from the same height or even in height. So here we can see a very wonderful piece of architecture.

3. Kavad

   Kavad is 500 years old craft which can be defined as traveling temple or shrine. These are used to tell the stories. The Khairadi people make them and Kawadiya or Bhats use them to tell stories in the marriages or any such functions. There are many stories like Ramayana, Shree Krishna, MeeraBai, Marwari and more are made on Kawads. It is believed that listening to the stories purifies the soul. Kawadiya or Bhat tribes have shifted to Kishangarh Village now.

4. Wooden Crafts ofIssarGangaur

   Gangaur is a festival celebrated in Rajasthan and on that festival people would worship God Shiva and his wife Goddess Parvati. So people use these crafts to worship.

5. Opium Farming

   The government has given the fixed land for the opium farming to the villagers in fixed rate for lease and then the villagers are expected to sell it back to the government in the pre-fixed price which creates the employment in the village. But the opium farming is not easy to do. There is always a threat of the harvest decay and its stealing. Sometimes people illegally start black marketing of the opium. So there is need of continuous observation of this kind of activities.

Methodology

The present study consists of several parts. Primary data was collected through interviews and observations method. The respondents are the members of NGOs, villagers of Bassi, Researchers, academicians & tourists. The source of this study is based on the data published by Ministry of Tourism and other information available through Internet. On the other hand the secondary data was collected from various Books, research papers, brochures etc.

The following studies have been compiled through the studies-

1. Scope of rural tourism
2. Attitude of rural population toward tourism
3. Rural tourism realities
4. Existing channel of rural tourism and the gap in the deliverance

Study results

Bassi have not gained the popularity as a rural tourism destination although it has treasure of tourist spots and archeological sites. After interviewing the key players of the village following studies are investigated-

Scope of rural tourism

In the fast moving life where we are facing the problem of culture degradation. Village Bassi has given us the hope to promote and save our culture and rural life for a better livelihood by means of tourism activity. The traditional parental practices of Bassi people such as Agriculture with major emphasison Opium farming, culturally decorated fairs and festival like - fair of Tejaji and Gangore festival, the unique art of wooden handicrafts such as "Kavad" and the tribes living along circumference of the village, makes it most desired rural destination of Rajasthan.Bassi ishelping in widen the scope of rural tourism with safeguarding the culture, tradition and ethics of the real India which lives in the village.

Attitude of rural population toward tourism

Lack of awareness can be felt in the rural population toward the tourism and its economic benefits. The tourist inflow in the bassi is not up to the mark, so the interaction between the tourist and villagers does not happen to desired extent. The villagers are forced to leave their parental occupation i.e. handicraft making as they don't find it sufficient money yielding to support their livelihood. But on the positive side after the initiative of the government and NGO's the rural tourism has reported growth in the past few years. The initiative includes renovation of step well, wildlife sanctuary and Bassi fort.

Rural tourism realities

Although the initiative taken by the government to protect this heritage treasure is praiseworthy but at the same time some anti-social elements have their direct or indirect negative impacts on the rural people. The fund has been raised by the government to protect the wildlife sanctuary was great initiative which resulting to it, taking wood from within the protected area became prohibited for the villagers, which affected their handicraft business and for the survival of their parental business and to support their livelihood, the villagers are forced to buy the wood through black marketing which is more than their affordability.so it indirectly encouraged the black marketing of the handicrafts.

The excess interference of the middleman discouraging the handicrafts business.it enforcing the villagers to leave their handicraft work and shift to agriculture to support their livelihood. To avail the handicrafts for the tourist the villagers take the help of middleman as the tourist inflow is not much in the Bassi which results less profit to the handicrafts maker which is creating sense of dissatisfaction in them.

Existing channel of rural tourism and the gap in the deliverance

The key players like travel agents, tour operators, hoteliers etc. are not aware about Bassi perhaps the reason could be lack of marketing which never promote the Bassi as a rural tourism site. The tourists many times accidently visit Bassi as a reason of lack of good accommodation facilities in Chitaurgarh which is 25 Km away from Bassi. They visit Bassi as it has good heritage property to accommodate tourist. Therefore, the bassi is identified as an alternative destination instead of a prime one.

Suggestion

On the basis of the interviews and the interaction of the locals which includes the head of the village and NGOs, some of the problems been identified and keeping it as base, following are the suggestions that can be given-

1. To create awareness the familiarization tour should be organized specially for travel agents, tour operators, journalists, travel writers, academicians and travel scholars. It will help Bassi to gain popularity as a rural tourism destination which will increase the tourist inflow.
2. Craft fair should be organized to showcase the crafts and culture of the villagers. For this the initiative should be taken by the NGO's, local authority and the head of the village along with Rajasthan tourism department.
3. The art school should be opened in Bassi which educate and train the manpower to safeguard the age old art of handicrafts.
4. As the wildlife sanctuary has been established and resulting lack of availability of sufficient amount of wood for making the crafts. To solve this problem the government should step forward to avail the wood in appropriate price which will over throw the problem of black marketing of the wood and will make the wood affordable for the villagers.
5. Policymakers should ensure the public involvement and public participation in the policymaking and the implementation of it, which will result the tourism awareness among the villagers and will help in realizing its importance for them.
6. Renovation of Step well is also one of the requirements of Bassi. This will lessen the chances of accidents during the local gathering on the special occasions.
7. The mud houses should be constructed with the modern facilities with rural ambience for accommodation for the tourist, which will give chance to tourist to live the rural life.

Conclusion

The rural tourism is always meant to showcase the country's heritage, customs, culture, handicrafts and much more. After investigating the case of Bassi, the scope of rural tourism can be assured but there are number of hurdles to cross as discussed in the study.

Therefore, the key players, stake holders, policy makers, locals and the government should ensure the above mentioned suggestion's implementation while thinking of making rural tourism as the back bone of the industry. This will surely bring the change in the local's and tourist's perception toward the rural tourism and strengthen their social and economic status.

Referenece

Briedenhann, J. and Wickens, E. (2004), Rural tourism?-?meeting the challenges of the new South Africa. Int. J. Tourism Res., 6: 189-203. doi: 10.1002/jtr.484

Gannon, A. (1994), 'Rural Tourism as a Factor in Rural Community Economic Development for Economies in Transition', Journal of Sustainable Tourism, vol. 2, pp. 51-60. Hjalager, A.M. (1996)

Sofique, M. Abdul, Rural tourism a new mantra for alternative tourism development: A case study of West Bengal with special reference to Ballavpurdanga near Santiniketan.

http://tourism.gov.in/

http://www.bassifortpalace.com

http://www.rajasthantourism.gov.in/

BROADENING THE IDEA OF CSR FROM CORPORATE TO INSTITUTIONS-SUCCESS STORY OF A UNIVERSITY

Anjali Khanna

Associate Dean, School of Hotel Management and Tourism, Lovely Professional University Phagwara, Punjab, Pin - 144401.

anjali.khanna@lpu.co.in

Vikrant Kaushal

Lecturer, School of Hotel Management and Tourism, Lovely professional University Vikrant.kaushal@lpu.co.in

Abstract: Corporate social responsibility can be understood as a concept through which an organisation attempts to attain a balance in its approach toward business, environment and society. This concept is frequently being used in corporate jargons and the companies that are known to be trend settlers and path definers for others in the industry, apart from their business commitments, place efforts by focusing on their corporate social responsibilities. Institutions on the other hand are known for their research contributions in various fields and are mostly credited for proposing a theoretical framework for various projects. Institutions can also play a significant role in the groundwork contribution. This paper studies the drive of a university towards society by the provision of training in a state prison to impart skills in the inmates. The area that the institution identified after a thorough research to focus was a prison and the experienced minds of the university have instilled the necessary skills to make the inmates capable enough to sustain themselves post imprisonment term.

This paper investigates the approach towards the social responsibility, the impact towards personal improvement of inmates and development of a brand from within the 'otherwise tabooed' boundaries. The study focuses on a north Indian university- Lovely Professional University, which offers a variety of programs in various disciplines and this paper concentrates on university's 'school of hotel management and tourism', that made an effort to connect society with academics and research. The paper holds the scope of enrichment of further research that could be applied for the society betterment, as these initiatives may have implications that can be analysed with a multidisciplinary perspective.

Keywords-Corporate social responsibility, society, institution, prison, improvement

Introduction

A significant part of our population remains in the enclosed walls of prisons located in various parts of the country and termed for various durations. The investment on prisons for the sustenance of the charged inmates is often contended. The jail authorities have much more to think and consider. The primary objective of imprisonment is the punishment for the inmate's wrong doings and meanwhile reducing the crime from the society. The imprisonment term is not all for the authorities. The next big challenge lies in retention of the inmates on the right path once their term completes. Post imprisonment survival has been a critical area of research in social studies and it has been realised that making them self sufficient in carrying on with their livelihood is important if we do not want to see them repeating their deeds again. Why some people might choose criminality above other forms of income generation has been a subject of debate for many centuries, with Campbell and Ormerod (1998) suggesting that the general population can be broadly divided into three groups. The first group consists of those people immune to the temptations of crime; the second consists of active criminals, while the third represents the 'floating voters'. The final group are those who might be susceptible to becoming criminals under a particular set of circumstances, but who may instead decide to live lawfully. The founder of Prison Entrepreneurship Program in Texas found similarities among entrepreneurs and prisoners as many of them have been part of organised crimes of producing illegal products. Gottschalk (2009), consider potential business opportunities can be found in human trafficking, money laundering, the narcotics trade, slavery, piracy, smuggling, 'protection' and other illegal markets. Hormant (1984) highlight the importance of employment in preventing or reducing reoffending. Lockwood and Teasley (2005) argue that the economic cost to society and to those directly affected by criminal activity is certainly growing.

The concept

Like most of the premier institutions globally the university (under study) has attempted to connect its society with its message to improving lives of individuals through education and research. This university is known for its academic approach of engaging its students in various live projects in all the offered streams. 'School of Hotel Management and Tourism' within the university, on the similar grounds have been active in various live projects since its inception. The skills obtained in this university's school are considered to increase the employability of the students. This project was taken up by the this school to impart the skills of production among inmates, and more importantly to project the contemporary approach of institution as premises that provide both theory and practical orientation to the learners.

Training and imparting sustenance skills is slightly challenging in case of inmates completing their respective terms. The program ought to be designed in such a way that it matches the capabilities of the trainees, imparts the necessary skills, increases their employability, and uses appropriate resources. The concept was narrowed down to 'Bakery' and 'Namkeen' preparation training that could help individuals after their term, and simultaneously a vision of a brand originating from within the boundaries of prison could be realised.

Trainers from the institution with active involvement of students that would assist the classes in the whole process were decided. The vocational program was thus initiated within the enclosed premises of the prison with all necessary security and learning equipment and tools in place.

Training

Training the inmates differs from regular skill development programs. The trainer needs to be well verse with fact that he is dealing with individuals with different psychological orientations. A schedule of one and half months was prepared that would cover vital 'Bakery' and 'Namkeen' products among inmates. The equipment and necessary tools were provided by the organising authorities and space was allotted for the production setup. Forty inmates were trained categorically specialising in 'Namkeen' making (eleven trainees) and bakery production (nineteen trainees). To ensure that the engagement of the released inmates in future remains unquestioned due to their tenure in prison, the certification has been done by the institution.

The brand and product

The success of the project was well received and the next phase was to bring the product to the market and get it identified. The 'bakery' and 'Namkeen' products are being introduced in the market under the brand name 'Anand'. The brand has been positively acclaimed and has now been established in the market. The prominent products that are being introduced include various types of bakery products and a variety of 'Namkeens'. The necessary food certifications have also been obtained for food quality assurance, which also builds a positive brand image of the products in the market.

Challenges

Marketing and selling a product to the customers becomes a challenge when the consumers are told about the production centres i.e. a prison for these products. The society is cautious and when they realize theproduction origin they tend to develop apprehensiveness regarding products quality. The major challenge would be to offer the product, satisfactorily convincing the customers not to be ill at ease concerning the quality. The certifications and necessary copyrights and licenses could build a favourable brand image of the product.

The way ahead

The pilot project has been perceived as a success and to extend the scope, the organising authorities have planned to invest Rs 19 lakh on a 'Bakery' plant and Rs 3 lakh on 'Namkeen' plant. Plan to obtain state of the art production equipment, estimated to be worth Rs 15 lakh is in process. The focus has been placed on the inmates who are sentenced to at least eight years of term or more to ensure the continuity of the plant and consistency in quality and quantity of the production. Besides, for quality assurance periodic visits have been scheduled to keep a check on the quality standards during the entire project tenure. Three such visits have already been made by the project team that initiated the execution of the pilot project. Further, the project team has emphasised on continuous periodic-supplementary training in future to induct necessary skills or technology to enhance the products and services.

The case of PEP

Prison entrepreneurship Program was founded by a Wall Street professional Catherine Rohr. The idea struck her mind when she toured a prison and she found similarities among business executives and prison inmates. She found the capabilities of inmates to get a work done, as latent entrepreneurial talent. It emphasises on the entrepreneurial growth of the prison inmates. They are trained in top-tier business class environment, exams are conducted and final exams require them to give oral presentation on their business plans, which is judged by a panel of CEOs and venture capitalists. PEP has now been recognised as one of the most influential prison rehabilitation program.

Case- Brand TJ

The brand TJ stands for 'Tihar Jail', and it offers a variety of products that are being manufactured by the prison inmates in Tihar

Jail Factory. The products range from bakery products, handloom and textile, apparel, furniture, pure mustard oil, recycled hand-made paper products, paintings, designer candles and lamps, Jute bags, herbal products and several others[1]. This project is an epitome of prison rehabilitation programs and beacons hope for numerous prisons located around the country. The Tihar jail factory runs its own website detailing its credentials, products, store locations and other related information for its clients. The prison holds around eleven thousand inmates and is known to be the largest prison complex in Asia. The jail factory employs almost seven hundred inmates in various production units. The project was launched with the idea of rehabilitating inmates after their term, to bring out their creativity and channelizing their energies towards productive works. The project has played a significant role in imparting employable skills in the inmates, and very importantly, financially assisting the families of the victims with almost twenty five percent of the wages earned by the inmates goes towards victim's welfare fund. The concept has evolved and become a success story in itself by achieving milestones in employment generation and jail turnover.The jail turnover achieved the mark of 11 crore in the year 2009-10 from 2.36 crore in the year 2004-05*. The inception of this idea and its present form has also played a crucial role towards the attempts of making the society crime-free. The bakery unit of Tihar Jail, also known as 'Tihar Baking School' has remained a significant inspiration of the pilot project in Ludhiana Prison.

Conclusion

The jail project has been well acclaimed by the institution, jail authorities and media. Future potential of studies and work on similar lines can result in significant changes in the society. Similar projects have been considered in various countries and a project like this offers a scope for various other disciplines for further research. Analysis of psyches of inmates facing terms and their rehabilitation post imprisonment is critical to their betterment and is a gateway to a safer society. Success of this pilot project can also be replicated in

1. Tihar Jail website, URL- http://tihartj.nic.in/the_factory.asp

the smaller jails across the country that also creates the provision of legal consultants and trainer in the prison structure.

References

Cooney, T. Reducing Recidivism through Entrepreneurship Programmes in Prisons. Entrepreneurship and Innovation, Vol. 13, no.2, 2012, pp. 125.133.

Campbell, M., and Ormerod, P. (1998), Social Interaction and the Dynamics of Crime, Volterra Consulting, London.

Gottschalk, P. (2009), Entrepreneurship and Organised Crime, Edward Elgar, Cheltenham.

Hormant, R.J. (1984), 'Employment of ex-offenders: the role of prisonization and self-esteem', Journal of Offender Counselling, Vol 8, No 3, pp 5-23.

Lockwood, F., and Teasley, R. (2005), 'Can entrepreneurship and small business education affect rates of recidivism and the economic prosperity of released inmates?' paper presented at the 2005 Allied Academies Fall International Conference, Las Vegas, Nevada.

Loucks, N., Lyner, O., and Sullivan, T. (1998), 'The employment of people with criminal records in the European Union', European Journal on Criminal Policy and Research, Vol 6, No 2, pp 195-210.

MEASURING THE IMPACTS OF ECO-TOURISM

Anushree Banerjee

Research Scholar Institute of Tourism Studies
University of Lucknow. 08anushree@gmail.com

Saurabh Rawat

Research Scholar Institute of Tourism Studies
University of Lucknow. vicious_saurabh@yahoo.com

Abstract: Ecotourism is an agent of change. The players want the environment to change by improving itself. The customers or the tourists visit a destination to bring change in his lifestyle. The change which has been brought up can be assessed. Research on the impacts has not been cumulative as main attention has not been given towards the major issues which are the reasons for the consequences. It has the potential to create positive social and environmental impacts. On the other hand, it can damage the environment if proper care is not taken place.

Kcywords: ccotourism, impacts, environment, society

Introduction

Ecotourism, in almost every definition, is being defined as an initiator of change. It is impossible that the introduction of tourists to areas seldom visited by outsiders will put demands upon the environment. Ecotourism will foster new relationships between people and environment, and between peoples with different lifestyles. It creates the ambience for both change and stability. Both of these act at a diversity of scales from global to local.

Change is a factor desired by almost all. Majorly the players involved in ecotourism who like to see what they can regard as an improvement of the existing situation. Tourists visit a destination as they want a change from their everyday ambience and wish to acquire special experiences, which are only available in special places. Entrepreneurs in the field of tourism wish to gain a livelihood from the destination. They encourage the tourists to visit the destination and experience altogether a different environment before it is too late. They are often abetted by governments who strive to develop the regions nearby so that they can increase foreign exchange and tax revenues.

Ecotourism destinations can be seen as potential for generating revenues, and enhancing standards of living by the permanent residents living in the destination or adjacent to it. Even the conservationists want changes in resource allocation so that they can ensure the sustenance of the destination and the ecosystem. Almost all the entrepreneurs or players involved in ecotourism desire change. However, there is usually considerable disagreement due to the level of change or concerning which changes are desirable. Contradictions and tensions may emerge between those directly involved and those indirectly affected by its introduction and operation. Hence, compromise must be sought among the players to achieve the target.

Challenges for tourism impact assessments

There are several challenges while measuring the impacts of tourism. They may be summarized as follows:

- There is a difficulty while establishing a level against which change is to be measured;
- Human-induced change cannot be separated from natural change;
- The environmental interactions create complexities. For e.g. primary impacts induce secondary impacts and tertiary impacts and so on.
- There are many diverse activities which are related to tourism.

- The mobile nature of tourism so that impacts may occur on the way and at the destination.

Furthermore, there are three methods through which impact assessments can be done and they are:

- after-the-fact analyses
- monitoring of change through time
- simulation

Each of these three requirements differ with respect to costs of time and money, produce results with differing characteristics and, consequently, different degrees of managerial utility.

Criticisms of Existing Approaches

Much of the work done on the impacts of tourism is simplistic. A more advanced perspective is required to judge perfectly the impacts. Much of the criticism here focuses on inadequate specification of the contexts in which impacts occur. This has two aspects: the adoption of an inappropriate model for analysis of the impact and incomplete consideration of the factors involved.

- **An inappropriate model-**Tourism has been always viewed as an external force imposed upon a static community. It cause change in that community and ultimately leads to the establishment of a balance. This is what Wood (1980) has termed the billiard ball assumption. None of the components of the billiard ball assumption is justifiable. Firstly, tourism is not an external force. It may be welcomed by members of destination areas. In practice, it is extremely difficult to distinguish between internal and external forces of change. Secondly, few communities are static. Vibrant cultures are always in a state of flux for a many reasons. The reason is not the onset of tourism. It is impossible and unrealistic to separate the consequences of tourism from other causes of change which may be occurring in the same place at the same time. It is impractical to study everything at the same time. Thirdly, the residents of the destination areas are not always acted upon: some respond to opportunities and thus play an active role in contributing to and directing change.

- **Factors contributing to and mediating impacts-**The impacts of tourism can be judged by the type or types of tourism involved, the characteristics of the communities in which tourism is taking place, and the nature of resident-visitor relationships. The tourism cycle suggests that with the change in time, the nature of tourists, communities and the relationship between the resident and visitor also changes (Butler 1980). Furthermore, much change associated with tourism may be cumulative as a number of small enterprises develop in sequence and in close proximity, each having a minor impact when viewed alone, but together having far-reaching consequences. Cumulative impact assessment is a challenging topic which is beginning to attract the attention of those charged with conducting and evaluating impact assessments, although it has yet to receive much recognition in the tourism literature (Shoemaker 1994).

While much work has documented the impacts of tourism, often under economic, environmental and socio-cultural headings (Mathieson and Wall 1982), few authors have taken the trouble to document adequately the types of tourism, the community characteristics, or the nature of host-guest encounters which give rise to these impacts. In fact, it would be worthwhile to review the tourism impacts literature in an attempt to establish more precisely the contexts in which authors have documented specific impacts. Failure to provide such information or to take note of it adequately has resulted in:

1. **Communication failures.** If one person is thinking of impacts of downhill skiing, while a second is concerned about sunbathing on a beach, and a third is contemplating visiting a natural area, is it any wonder that they come up with differing evaluations of impacts and talk past each other?
2. **Contradictory findings.** The findings in the literature are not consistent. Thus, for example, some authors lament the destruction of natural areas through tourism whereas others promote the potential of ecotourism to protect such areas.

Who is correct? Of course, both perspectives may be correct but in different circumstances and to varying degrees. However, as suggested above, little attempt appears to have been made to ascertain what types of tourism in what type of community and in what type of host-guest interaction give rise to specific impacts.

3. **Limited policy relevance.** The general failure to specify adequately the contexts in which impacts occur means that the impacts literature provides limited guidance to decision- makers. In general, it fails to indicate how many people, of what type, doing which activities, in communities with specified characteristics, in specific forms of host-guest interaction result in particular consequences. This is not the same as calculating carrying capacities, which has its own problems (Wall 1982). An understanding of use-impact relationships is essential for establishing carrying capacities (if you believe they exist!) and limits of acceptable change (Stankey and McCool 1984), or for implementing concepts such as the tourism or recreation opportunity spectrum (Driver et al. 1987). While this is not the place to review the carrying capacity literature, it is worth pointing out that the determination of appropriate levels of use is as much a value judgment, related to the goals set for the site, as a technical problem. Many researchers have eschewed the search for a magic number which can be approached with impunity and exceeded at peril, recognizing that management is required from the time that the first tourists arrive, if not before, and that trade-offs will be required. However, many managers still seek a simple solution to a complex problem through belief that a single inherent capacity exists and that this number can be determined by technical means. Such a perspective puts power in the hands of consultants who are hired as experts to determine the non existent number. On the other hand, perspectives such as limits of acceptable change have the potential to empower local people if they are permitted to provide input on the acceptability of possible trade-offs.
4. **Culture brokers.** Resident-visitor interactions may be mediated by culture brokers with implications for social, environmental,

directs attention to the problems of equity (who gains and who loses?), which, along with intangibles and incommensurable, are among the more challenging problems with which cost-benefit analysis is not well-equipped to deal. However, it is worthwhile to consider ecotourism briefly in the context of cost-benefit analysis and not only because the importance of intangibles and incommensurable is particularly large in most ecotourism situations.

Cost-benefit analysis is essentially an accounting procedure in which the costs and benefits of an initiative are compared for a specified time period and weighted partially through the application of selected discount rates. If the benefits exceed the costs, then the initiative may be worth undertaking.

In the case of ecotourism, as indeed in many other areas of endeavor, the adding up and comparison of costs and benefits is confounded by the diversity of phenomena to be considered and different ways each is measured. Thus, economic impacts are usually measured in units of currency or jobs. Environmental attributes may be measured through population counts, species diversity, production of biomass, coliform counts, biochemical oxygen demand, the presence or absence of indicator species or using a host of other variables which do not vary together in a linear fashion and whose significance may be debated by lay persons and experts alike. Furthermore, there is no widely-accepted way of converting these into dollars or jobs or, of course, vice versa. Socio-cultural change, similarly, has a diversity of measures, potentially including such items as infant mortality rates, proportion of women in the workforce, or the percentage of respondents answering "perhaps" to a question on a survey. In such situations it is virtually impossible to come up with a single summary measure and to determine whether the benefits exceed the costs.

Fortunately, the above observation, while clearly correct, is, in most circumstances, a red herring (which is not an endangered species!). There are several reason s for this. One is that in most ecotourism situations, the decision to proceed or desist is not made on the basis of a global evaluation of benefits and costs. Rather, it is more likely to be a reflection of access to power, authority, resources and information. Even if it were possible to aggregate the information to arrive at a single measure, such a measure would not be helpful in informing most ecotourism decisions which, as suggested above, involve compromise and trade-offs. To make such decisions, disaggregated information is required. Managers need to know whether the populations of particular species are changing, whether occupancy rates in accommodation for visitors are rising or falling, whether local residents are supportive of the directions which management is taking, and whether tourists are having a good time, as well as many other things, if they are to make wise decisions. Only with such information can the trade-offs and compromises required of decision-makers be made in an informed manner.

Characteristics of desirable indicators

Given that disaggregated information is required for management purposes and a myriad of factors and interrelationships are involved in ecotourism, it will be impossible to measure or monitor everything. Information will never be comprehensive or complete. In such situations it is necessary to select a limited number of indicators of change. It is not possible to suggest exactly what these indicators should be. They are likely to vary with the character of the area, the goals set for the area by the management agency, and the resources and technical expertise available. However, useful indicators are likely to have the following characteristics: they must be sensitive to temporal change and variation, they should have a predictive or anticipatory capability, and they should have conceptual validity and relevance to management problems (Kreutzwiser 1993).

Often relative measures may be more useful than absolute measures. For example, rather than population numbers or habitat area, a measure of population per unit area of habitat may be more relevant. They will also be more useful if references or threshold values for that indicator are established. Furthermore, the range of indicators which are selected should encompass economic, environmental and socio-cultural domains and, if the goals of the management agency are narrow, it may be necessary to extend the indicators beyond their narrow interests to encompass the interests of the neighboring communities and, possibly, other interests as well.

Conclusions

This paper has argued that change is the word to be attached with ecotourism. In fact, the desired changes are debatable. They vary between actors and this necessitates the search for trade-offs and compromises. Assessments of the impacts of ecotourism are not immune from the difficulties associated with measuring impacts in general, as well as those pertaining to tourism in particular. Much research on the impacts of tourism is not cumulative because of the adoption of an inappropriate research paradigm and an inadequate attention to the contexts in which impacts occur. A broad perspective involving economic, environmental, and social indicators is required, and for most purposes, disaggregated information is much more useful than single, summary measures which purport to indicate carrying capacity or whether benefits exceed costs.

References

Butler, Richard. 1980. The Concept of a Tourist Area Cycle of Evolution: Implications for Management of Resources. Canadian Geographer 24: 5-12.

Driver, B.L., Perry J. Brown, George H. Stankey and Timothy G.Gregoire. 1987. The ROS Planning System: Evolution, Basic Concepts and Research Needs. Leisure Sciences 9: 201-212.

Kreutzwiser, Reid. 1993. Desirable Attributes of Sustainablity Indicators for Tourism Development. In Tourism and Sustainable Development: Monitoring, Planning, Managing. Department of Geography Publications Series No. 37, J.G. Nelson, R. Butler and G. Wall (eds).Waterloo: University of Waterloo, pp. 243-247.

Lew, Alan. 1992. Perceptions of Tourists and Tour Guides in Singapore. Journal of Cultural Geography 12: 45-52.

Machlis, Gary E. and Donald R. Field. 1984. On Interpretation: Sociology for Interpreters of Natural and Cultural History. Corvallis: Oregon State University Press.

Mathieson, Alister and Geoffrey Wall. 1982. Tourism: Economic, Physical and Social Impacts. London: Longman.

Murphy, Peter. 1985. Tourism: A Community Approach. New York: Methuen.

Shoemaker, Darryl J. 1994. Cumulative Environmental Assessment. Department of Geography Publication Series No. 42. Waterloo: University of Waterloo.

Stankey, George H. and Stephen F. McCool. 1984. Carrying Capacity in Recreational Settings: Evolution, Appraisal and Application. Leisure Sciences 6: 453-474.

Wall, Geoffrey. 1982. Cycles and Capacity: Incipient Theory or Conceptual Contradiction? Tourism Management 3: 188-192.

Wall, Geoffrey and Cynthia Wright. 1977. The Environmental Impact of Outdoor Recreation, Department of Geography Publication Series No. 11. Waterloo: University of Waterloo.

Wood, Robert E. 1980. International Tourism and Cultural Change in Southeast Asia. Economic Development and Cultural Change 28: 561-581.

TOURIST PERCEPTION OF A RELIGIOUS TOURISM SITE: A CASE OF MANSA DEVI TEMPLE PANCHKULA IN HARYANA, INDIA

Prashant K Gautam

Assistant Professor, University Institute of Hotel Management and Tourism, Panjab University, Chandigarh. Prashant.k.gautam@gmail.com

Arun Singh Thakur

Assistant Professor, University Institute of Hotel Management and Tourism, Panjab University, Chandigarh. Arun.tourism@gmail.com

Abstract: Modern religious tourists are more able to visit holy cities and holy sites around the world. The most famous holy cities are Jerusalem, Mecca and Varanasi. The most famous holy sites are the Church of the Nativity, The Western Wall, Brahma Temple at Pushkar and the Kaaba. Religious tourism has existed since antiquity. A study in 2011 found that pilgrims visited Jerusalem for a few reasons to understand and appreciate their religion through a tangible experience, to feel secure about their religious beliefs, and to connect personally to the holy city.

This paper aims to investigate challenges in religious tourism, what problems occur and difficulties are faced by a tourist on any particular pilgrimage site. The paper derives its findings from observations and fieldwork conducted in the month of May in 2013 during a pilgrimage to one of the most popular pilgrimage centre in Chandigarh, the sacred Mansa Devi Temple. understand with various challenges faced by the tourists while visiting a pilgrimage site. Study found that the various services like Prasad, shading arrangement etc. are appreciated and some are like the queue system is not appreciated by the tourists

Keywords: Religious Tourism, Tourist Perception, Mansa Temple

Introduction

The word tourism derives from the verb tour meaning "travel." Travelers, whether alone or in a group, date back to ancient times- the sign, perhaps, of an innate need in man. In ancient Greece, for example, people would travel to attend the Olympic Games or to worship the gods in particularly important temples.

Tourism is travel for recreational, leisure, or business purposes. The World Tourism Organization defines tourists as people "travelling to and staying in places outside their usual environment for not more than one consecutive year for leisure, business and other purposes". International tourist arrivals (overnight visitors) grew by 4% in 2012, topping the 1 billion mark globally for the ?rst time in history. Despite continued economic volatility around the globe, demand for international tourism held up well throughout 2012. With an additional 40 million tourists (+4%), international arrivals reached 1,035 million, up from 995 million in 2011. In order to celebrate the historic 1 billion milestone UNWTO launched the campaign One Billion Tourists: One Billion Opportunities, calling on tourists to make their actions count.

Tourism in India

Tourism in India is a large industry. India offers myriad flavours mingling in the steam of a country coming of age. Teeming with over a 1.27 billion people who voice over a million concerns in fifteen hundred different languages, India is where people live with variety, thrive on diversity and are too familiar with largeness to let it boggle them. The number of Foreign Tourist Arrivals (FTAs) in India during 2012 increased to 6.58 million from 6.31 million in 2011. The growth rate in FTAs during 2012 over 2011 was 4.3% as compared to 9.2% during 2011 over 2010. The growth rate of 4.3% in 2012 for India was better than the growth rate of 4% for the International Tourist Arrivals in 2012. The share of India in international tourist arrivals in 2012 was 0.64%, India's rank in international tourist arrivals declined to 41st in 2012, from 38th in 2011. India accounted for 2.82% of tourist arrivals in Asia and the Pacific Region in 2012, with the rank of 11.

Tourism continues to play an important role as the foreign exchange earner for the country. In 2012, foreign exchange earnings (FEE) from tourism were US$ 17.74 billion as compared to US$ 16.56 billion in 2011, registering a growth of 7.1%.

Number of domestic tourist visits in India during 2012 was 1036.3 million (Provisional) as compared to 864.53 million in 2011, with a growth rate of 19.9 %. Number of Indian national departures from India during 2012 was 14.92 million as compared to 13.99 million in 2011, registering a growth rate of 6.7%.

The FTAs in India continued to grow from 1.28 million in 1981, to 1.68 million in 1991, 2.54 million in 2001, to reach 6.58 million in 2012. During the year 2012, India registered a positive growth of 4.3 % over 2011. The compound annual growth rate (CAGR) in FTAs in India during 2001 to 2012 was 9.0 %.

The Ministry of Tourism designs national policies for the development and promotion of all forms of tourism. In the process, the Ministry consults and collaborates with other stakeholders in the sector including various Central Ministries/agencies, state governments, Union Territories and the representatives of the private sector. Concerted efforts are being made to promote new forms of tourism such as rural, cruise, medical and eco-tourism. The Ministry also maintains the Incredible India campaign. India's rich history and its cultural and geographical diversity make its international tourism appeal large and diverse. It presents heritage, religious and cultural tourism along with medical, business and sports tourism.

Emergence of Religious Tourism in the World

In pre-Christian times, the oracle at Delphi played an especially important role in ancient Greece. The panhellenic religious feasts held at Olympia every four years and at Delphi led to the two sites becoming famous outside Greece. The oracle at Delphi, in particular, exercised a strong attraction, drawing a large number of pilgrims.

Latin literature in its turn often mentions the otia, the periods of free time that the upper classes devoted to activities other than work. The horae subsicivae of the Romans, for example, were given over to leisure activities as a well-earned rest after work. During their otia, the Romans used to visit cities with particular climatic conditions, such as Pompeii.

The Middle Ages are marked by journeys and pilgrimages to holy places. This is the period in which "religious tourism" became popular with its interdependent means of transport, accommodation for pilgrims, and stops along the route at which peddlers would sell "relics." The most common destinations of the period were Santiago de Compostela, Czestochowa, and Rome. In the Middle Ages, pilgrimages were a collective phenomenon that was an integral part of the Christian world. Pilgrims were considered to be extremely spiritual and were held in high regard by society. Pilgrims were "the initiated" who sought to free themselves from the structures surrounding them and to ascend to a new level of existence. To go on a pilgrimage meant leaving behind the worldly aspects of life so as to concentrate on the purity of one's faith. When they returned home, pilgrims were greeted with admiration and were aware of having taken a further step toward spirituality.

In Medieval times, the ecclesiastically legitimated pilgrimage represented elements of a very precise nature: the "movement" of the journey, the religious "motivation," and the "destination," which had to be a place that was considered holy. In general, pilgrimages arose from the search for salvation and, sometimes, the need to be physically healed. Medieval travelers undertook their journeys for a purpose-to increase their spirituality-and in this sense pilgrims in the Middle Ages were clearly different from those who traveled to satisfy their curiosity.

As time passed, "tourism" came to mean the opportunities available to the increasing mass of individuals who felt attracted by these offers of excursions for pleasure. The growing demand led to the birth of travel agencies; the first was founded in Leicester in 1841 by Thomas Cook. He went on to become famous because, in

1866, he organized the first tour of the United States and, in 1872, the first round-the-world tour.

At the beginning of this century, tourism was turning into a business, although it slackened in the first half of the century, owing to the two world wars. After these difficulties, tourism came to signify the personal transfer from one place to another of income for the purposes of consumerism as the result of economic well-being and technological progress.

Tourism has led to the creation of new habits and different behavior and life models as well as a different conception of time. It has generated a movement of culture that encourages travelers to see and understand social, cultural, and environmental differences: The *homo turisticus* has become the symbol of an evolved society.

Today, the old pilgrimage sites have begun again to attract masses of pilgrims, the difference now being that the pilgrims also come across tourists on holiday. What does this mass movement signify? A search for salvation or a return to the roots of the past as a form of resistance against the rationality of modern times? Without a doubt, the tourist industry and the media are offering pilgrimages as consumerism. Given that tourists share the same attitudes as pilgrims-in other words, the search for authenticity at different levels of depth and involvement-it could be said that pilgrims are partly tourists and that tourists are partly pilgrims. Thus they complement one another; the promotion of "religious" tourism today, seen as both devotional and cultural, is proof of the existence of this common "search."

The rediscovery of pilgrimages also shows that religious values, doctrines, and institutions have lost nothing of their status in, and their influence over, everyday behavior. This means that the modern individual is seeking transcendental values to overcome the fragments, the discontinuity, of modern society and that he or she is the "pilgrim tourist" of modern times.

Review of Literature

Religious tourism, also commonly referred to as faith tourism, is a form of tourism, where people travel individually or in groups for pilgrimage, missionary, or leisure (fellowship) purposes. The world's largest form of mass religious tourism takes place at the annual Hajj pilgrimage in Mecca,Saudi Arabia. North American religious tourists comprise an estimated $10 billion of the industry.

Modern religious tourists are more able to visit holy cities and holy sites around the world. The most famous holy cities are Jerusalem, Mecca and Varanasi. The most famous holy sites are the Church of the Nativity, The Western Wall, Brahma Temple at Pushkar and the Kaaba. Religious tourism has existed since antiquity. A study in 2011 found that pilgrims visited Jerusalem for a few reasons to understand and appreciate their religion through a tangible experience, to feel secure about their religious beliefs, and to connect personally to the holy city.

According to Rinschede, Religious Tourism is a term widely used in theory and practice to refer to contemporary travel patterns to pilgrimage sites. Religious tourism is considered to be a 'specific type of tourism whose participants are motivated either in part or exclusively for religious reasons' (Rinschede, 1992, p. 52) in such a way that it is 'closely or loosely connected with holiday-making'. The destination for religious tourism is generally a sacred site, a pilgrimage site or a religious heritage site. It combines two opposite ends of the binary - sacred and profane - as reflected in the pilgrimage-tourism dichotomy (Nolan and Nolan, 1992; Smith, 1992). Often, the key aspects of pilgrimage - the motivation for the trip, form of the journey and a sacred destination - are used to explain religious tourism where leisure and holiday activities occur as supplementary opportunities within the need for religious travel (Tyrakowski, 1994).

In India since the 1970s, there has been 'a period of religious creativity' marked by the expansion of Indian religious movements to the west and the 'emergence of Hindu religious movements that revolve around solving the stresses and strains of contemporary life' for middle and upper-class Indians (Madan, 2004, p. 265). The new climate of uncertainty and alienation, search for self-identity, sense of fulfilment and 'spiritual striving' by the welloff urban middle-class is reflected in the rise of religious renewal and the growing numbers of charismatic gurus who provide a 'religion of choice' for satisfying the spiritual needs of this class (Warrier, 2004, p. 14). New technologies of mass communication have also fuelled the new religiosity of the Hindu middle classes and the business of religious devotion. Television, print media and the Internet have helped revive some traditional practices and transformed others, including virtual temples, virtual pilgrimage rituals and virtual blessings (Rinehart, 2004).These new trends in religiosity have played a significant role in transforming the nature of pilgrimage travel and the emergence of religious tourism in India. The Domestic Tourism Survey, conducted in 2002-2003 by the Indian government's Ministry of Tourism, indicates that travel for religious purpose and pilgrimage formed the most significant component in domestic tourism, with more than 100 million people travelling to various religious events, temples and pilgrimage sites.1 According to the survey, short-term trips by middle- and upper-income groups now contribute a substantial share of travel to sacred sites; nearly 50% of package tours and almost 20% of one-day trips are for religious and pilgrimage purposes (NCAER, 2003, p. 33). The increased volume of religious travel has been accompanied by qualitative changes in terms of visitors and the organisation of the tourism industry (Kaur, 1985). The foray of Thomas Cook, the international tour company, into the domestic pilgrim travel market of India with the promise of three-star comforts for its clients, offering of insurance policies for pilgrims, coming of hotel chains in holy cities, indicate new developments in the pilgrimage industry and reflect a higher degree of consumerism and hedonistic behaviour that is typical of tourists (Shinde, 2008a). Hundreds of tour operators, through numerous websites, offer comfortable and often luxurious package deals for pilgrimage tours to some of the most popular pilgrimage circuits in India, with catchlines such as 'deluxe moksha [salvation]' and 'instant nirvana'. The new patterns of travel by upscale clientele, including young professionals, rich non-resident Indians and foreigners reflect the increasing use of hotels and resorts and services offered by tourism enterprises. With new demands, new suppliers have also surfaced. Following Nolan and Nolan (1992), at least three different yet related submarket segments can be identified in religious tourism: cultural tourism, spiritual tourism and religious travel. Using psychological and organisational parameters (Tomasi, 2002) can explain the differences and similarities between these (Reader, 2007), but one aspect that clearly distinguishes them is entrepreneurship. Cultural tourism revolves around the cultural experience that people want to derive from visiting a religious site, festivals or religious performances. Many government tourism agencies and private tour operators engage in the packaging of tours around pilgrimage circuits and the promotion of festivals and special events as cultural products. The study focuses the challenges and problems encountered during the visit to particular pilgrimage destination.

Perspective of Religious Tourism in India

Religious Tourism can be defined as travel with the core motive of experiencing religious forms, or the products they induce, like art, culture, traditions and architecture. Being one of the most ancient civilizations of the world, India has been in contact with almost all the major religions of the world, and despite being dominated by Hinduism in the present context, religions like Islam, Buddhism and Christianity have also influenced a sizeable portion of the population, apart from niche religions like Sikhism, Jainism, Vaishnavism, Jewism that grew as an offshoot to the major religious schools of thought.

There are two distinct aspects to Religious Tourism in India; one, the faith of the domestic tourist, who has a spiritual attachment to the deity destination in line with their religious beliefs; the other is the 'foreign' tourist, someone belonging to a different religion, region or country, for whom the destination and the religious practices have the dimension of 'novelty', a spiritual experience different from their own, despite the ethical values being delivered remaining the same. From the domestic market's perspective, there is a fine line dividing business and belief. Many temples, mosques, churches, gurudwaras and other major religious centres, in today's socio-economic structures, are tangible assets in terms of infrastructure and the workforce they employ, thereby implying that the institution has to monetize itself in order to be able to meet its everyday survival in societal environments. Based upon the nature of the product, intensity and region of travel, Religious Tourism is divided into the following major categories:

- Pilgrimages
- Missionary travel
- Leisure (fellowship) vacations
- Faith-based cruising
- Crusades, conventions and rallies
- Retreats
- Monastery visits and guest-stays
- Faith-based camps
- Religious tourist attractions

Mata Mansa Devi Temple

Mata Mansa Devi is a Hindu temple dedicated to goddess Mansa Devi, a form of Shakti, in the Panchkula district of Haryana state in India. The temple complex is spread of 100 acres (0.40 km2) of the Shivalik foothills in village Bilaspur, near Mani Majra, and Panchkula, 10 km from Chandi Mandir, another noted Devi shrine in the region, both just outside Chandigarh. It is one of the prominent Shakti temples of North India. Thousands of devotees visit the shrine from various parts of the country, and especially during the Navratra mela, this number rises to lakhs everyday for the nine auspicious days.

History of the Mata Mansa Devi Temple

Maharaja Gopal Singh of Mani Majra constructed the present main temple of Shri Mansa Devi, which is situated on the Shivalik foothills in village Bilaspur, Tehsil and District Panchkula, during the period 1811-1815. At a distance of 200 meters from the main temple is the Patiala temple which was constructed by Karam Singh, a Sikh, the then Maharaja Patiala in the year 1840. This temple had the patronage of Manimajra State. After the merger of princely states into PEPSU the Patronage of State Govt. ended and the temples remained neglected. The raja of Manimajra then appointed pujari as 'khidmatuzar' of this temple whose duty was to worship the deity of the temple. After the merger of princely State into Pepsu these pujaris became independent on the matter of controlling and managing the affairs of the temple and the land attached to the temple. They could neither maintain this temple nor provide necessary facilities to the visiting devotees and thus the condition of the temple deteriorated day by day. So much so that there were no proper arrangements for pilgrims visiting the temple during Navaratra melas. The complex was in awfully neglected condition till the establishment of the Board.

About The Study

This paper aims to investigate challenges in religious tourism, what problems occur and difficulties are faced by a tourist on any particular pilgrimage site. The paper derives its findings from observations and fieldwork conducted in the month of May in 2013 during a pilgrimage to one of the most popular pilgrimage centre in Chandigarh, the sacred Mansa Devi Temple. The methods included in-depth interviews and surveys, the observance of public behaviour, and data collection through filling questionnaires from the tourists. 50 questionnaires were filled in order to understand challenges in religious tourism. The common themes covered in the questionnaire included views on pilgrimage, visitors, rituals, services and challenges. These included 10 local residents of tri-city & 40 from native states to understand the travel patterns of visitors.

Data Analysis and Interpretation

Data analysis is considered to be important step and heart of the research in research work. After collection of data with the help of relevant tools and techniques, the next logical step, is to analyze and interpret data with a view to arriving at empirical solution to the problem. The data analysis for the present research was done quantitatively with the help of both descriptive statistics and inferential statistics. The descriptive statistical techniques like mean, standard deviation and t-test are applied for the inferential statistics.

From the table 1 it is evident that there are approximately equal number of males and females, majority were under 30 years of age and second majority people were between 30-45 years which included almost equal number of married and singles. In education 38% possess majority in graduation and 32% were post-graduates. Population was a mix from all working areas i.e. public, private and business with majority working in private sector and maximum income of the population was 20,000 & above according to the survey. Further it can also be inference that highest number of participants (32 %) are working in private organisations, whereas the second highest number of visitors are the students with 26 %. So it can be said that for the marketing purpose these two segments of tourists are the viable options to target.

Table 2 indicates about the willingness of the tourists to come back to Chandigarh again which is very impressive as the result comes out to be 88%. Which further can be restated that the majority of the tourist visiting the site are satisfied with their experience and will be the repeated tourists in future?

After analysing the results in Table 3 it was found that; Guides at Mansa Devi temple are available & fully qualified, Transport infrastructure to reach Mansa Devi is appropriate, Ample parking facility is available, Local transportation easily available for Mansa Devi temple, Proper safety and security measures are available, Mansa Devi is a clean religious spot and no problem of pocket pickers at the temple.

It was also found that tourists faced the problem of over-crowding during the visit to Mansa Devi, they are annoyed by beggars outside Mansa Devi temple, signage and instruction boards are up to expectation level and food near the temple complex is satisfactory.

Findings of the Study

After the data collection and analysis of the data we are here with the results of the study. We have taken the data from tourists at Mansa Devi temple from various age groups possessing different occupation and we came to results that the services provided at Mansa Devi which are satisfactory and significant are appropriate transport infrastructure, ample parking available, easily available local transportation, proper safety and security measures available, Mansa Devi a clean spot and no problem of pocket-pickers & non-satisfactory and non-significant service is annoying by beggars. It can further be concluded that Mansa Devi as a religious tourist destination provides almost satisfactory results from the tourist opinions with few more options to develop.

Recommendations

After the extensive study on the religious tourism and problems faced by the tourist recommendations can be suggested such as under;

- The government should take steps like special marketing strategy, developing tourism circuits and scrutinizing religious trusts to boost religious tourism in the country.
- Laying out a roadmap for the development of all religious centers in the country and there is a need to develop integrated infrastructure for religious tourism development and improving connectivity to specific religious tourism circuits.
- "The huge potential for religious tourism in India can be realized if problems associated with the carrying capacity on the region, waste management, air pollution, and monetization of religion and lack of scrutiny of religious trusts are dealt with in earnest. As India has abundance of religious centers across the country, there is need to create nodes near religious centers, where there is already a basic infrastructure present and plan day trips from there.
- A separate board should be set up to prepare and implement plans to provide necessary facilities to the devotees and also ensure conservation of cultural atmosphere consistent with sentiments of visiting devotees.
- Especially for Mansa Devi, Chandigarh there should be trained instructors and guides who could help the tourist to know about the history and the importance of the temple. Problem of beggars should be solved by the government and cleanliness of toilets and area outside the temple should be in check regularly. There should be more signage which could help the tourists in a better way and hygienic food must be available for the tourists nearby.

For future it is recommend that study should be done in whole North-India so that broader view and scope of religious tourism can be known.

Discussions

Issues being faced in the development of Religious Tourism in the Country

Tourism acts as a crucial enabler in facilitating development of basic infrastructural facilities, generates income for the local community as well as the government, balances regional development strategies through 'umbrella' effect, and fosters peace and socio-cultural harmony. However, tourism development in any region needs to be regulated to prevent the negative impacts.

Most religious centres in the country, major or minor, suffer from short but intense seasons that alter the dynamics of the region for the rest of the year. In part a derivative of the problem of carrying capacity, the waste management problem has aggravated as science and technology grew to usher us into the 'era of plastic'.

In the race for developing as many niches as possible, there is often the issue of religion being 'monetized', as the host community gets increasingly driven by the 'profit motive'. The sheer volume of travel in this niche makes the figures mind boggling. While trains still manage to absorb a majority of the travel volume, quite a substantial number of major religious tourism sites in India are still only accessible by road or foot, or a combination of the two (take the case of hilly regions).

There is a need to put forward regulations which governs the financial status and regulation of religious trusts as it looks to allay global concerns about money laundering and terrorist financing activities. Such a law will also pave the way to make public names of organizations that claim tax exemption to ensure greater Transparency. This is especially crucial in a scenario when some of India's religious trusts are among the richest in the world.

Government Interventions to stimulate the development of Religious Tourism in India

The Government is very much aware of the importance of religious tourism not only as an economic enabler, but also a tool to ensure communal harmony. Some recent notable initiatives are as follows:

1. IRCTC has given much needed boost to the Buddhist Circuit, providing a holistic product that addresses transport, sightseeing and accommodation requirements. Apart from this, airports have also been made operational in Bodh Gaya, thereby facilitating direct movement of tourists from South East Asian countries, a major part of the clientele.
2. Seven new tourist circuits will be developed across the country to facilitate travel to and stay at religious places. Work has already begun to prepare detailed project reports for Sufi, Buddhist & Jain, Christian, Sikh, Hinduism and Sarva Dharma circuits.The Sufi circuit will include Delhi, Agra, Fatehpur Sikri, Bijapur, Shirdi, Aurangabad, and the Awadh region,besides the dargahs in J&K, Punjab, Haryana and Uttarkahnad. The Christian circuit will have the churches of Goa, Kerala and Tamil Nadu. The Sarv Dharma Circuit, to promote national integration, will be aligned along Tirupathi-Chennai-Velankanni-Nagoor and Vaishnodevi - Golden Temple-Sacred Heart Church (Delhi)-Nizamuddin.

Conclusion

The study makes us understand with various challenges faced by the tourists while visiting a pilgrimage site. Study found that the various services like Prasad, shading arrangement etc. are appreciated and some are like the queue system is not appreciated by the tourists and this led to a conclusion that the services such as cleanliness, availability of guides are instructors, hygiene food and problem of beggars must be taken care by the government or shrine board.

Table 1: Profiling Respondents

		Frequency	Percentage
Gender	Male	23	46
	Female	27	54

Age (years)	Under 30	30	60
	30 - 45	16	32
	45 - 60	3	6
	More than 60	1	2
Marital Status	Married	26	52
	Single	24	48
Education Level	Below Matriculation	3	6
	Matriculate	11	22
	Graduate	19	38
	Post Graduate	16	32
	Above Post Graduate	1	2
Occupation	Public Sector Employee	9	18
	Private Sector Employee	16	32
	Businessman	10	20
	Student	13	26
	Any Other	2	4

Table 2: Willingness to come to Chandigarh again

	Frequency	Percentage
Yes	44	88
No	2	4
Can't Say	4	8

Table 3: T-test values

	Mean	Std. Dev	t-value	Sig.
Did you face the problem of over-crowding during visit to Mansa Devi	2.74	1.367	-1.345	.185
Annoyed by beggars outside Mansa Devi temple	3.16	1.390	.814	.420
Infrastructure for visitors at this religious centre is sufficient	3.24	1.255	1.353	.182
Instructors and guides at Mansa Devi temple are available and fully qualified	2.42	1.126	-3.641	.001
Transport infrastructure to reach Mansa Devi is appropriate	3.82	1.101	5.267	.000
Ample parking facility is available	3.56	1.280	3.093	.003

Local transportation easily available for Mansa Devi temple	3.74	.828	6.317	.000
Proper safety and security measures are available	3.60	1.178	3.601	.001
Toilets are clean and easily available	2.88	.824	-1.030	.308
Accomodation is easily available	3.24	.938	1.809	.077
Mansa Devi is a clean religious spot	3.58	1.090	3.764	.000
No problem of pocket pickers at the temple	3.52	1.199	3.066	.004
Garbage collection and disposal systems at religious activity sites are working properly	3.34	1.206	1.994	.052
Religious activities experience is up to expectation level	3.44	1.215	2.561	.014
Signage and instruction boards are up to expectation level	2.88	1.256	-.676	.502
Food near the temple complex is satisfactory	2.94	.913	-.465	.644

References

"Pilgrimage and Modernity," Social Compass 2(1989):138-245

http://en.wikipedia.org/wiki/Mata_Mansa_Devi_Mandir

http://sdt.unwto.org/sites/all/files/pdf/conclusions_en.pdf

http://www.ficci.com/spdocument/20207/Diverse-Beliefs-Tourism-of-Faith.pdf <accessed on 17.01/2014>.

Kaur J. 1985. Himalayan Pilgrimages and New Tourism. Himalayan Books: New Delhi.

Madan T. 2004. India's Religions: Perspectives from Sociology and History. Oxford University Press: New Delhi.

Nolan M, Nolan S. 1992. Religious sites as tourism attractions in Europe. Annals of Tourism Research 19 (1): 68-78.

Reader I. 2007. Pilgrimage growth in the modern world: meanings and implications. Religion 37: 210-229.

Rinehart R. 2004. Contemporary Hinduism: Ritual, Culture, and Practice. ABC-CLIO: California.

Rinschede G. 1992. Forms of religious tourism. Annals of Tourism Research 19 (1): 51-67.

Shinde K. 2008a. Religious tourism: exploring a new form of sacred journey in North India.

Smith V. 1992. The quest in guest. Annals of Tourism Research 19: 1-17.

Timothy D, Olsen D (eds). 2006. Tourism, Religion and Religious Journeys. Routledge: London. Timothy D, Wall G. 1997. Selling to tourists: Indonesian street vendors. Annals of Tourism Research 24 (2): 322-340.

Tomasi L. 2002. Homo Viator: from pilgrimage to religious tourism via the journey. In From Medi-eval Pilgrimage To Religious Tourism: The Social and Cultural Economics of Piety, Swatos J, Tomasi L(eds). Praeger: Westport; 1-24.

Tyrakowski K. 1994. Pilgrims to the Mexican Highlands. In Pilgrimage in the Old and New World, Bhardwaj S, Rinschede G, Sievers A (eds).Dietrich Reimer Verlag: Berlin; 193-246.

http://tourism.gov.in/writereaddata/CMSPagePicture/file/marketresearch/publications/India%20Tourism%20Statics(2012)%20new.pdf <accessed on 11/01/2014>.

NCAER. 2003. Domestic Tourism Survey: 2002-03. National Council of Applied Economic Research and Ministry of Tourism and Culture, Government of India: New Delhi.

http://articles.economictimes.indiatimes.com/2012-04-16/news/31349699_1_religious-tourism-tourism-circuits-religious-trusts

BARRIERS IN SUSTAINABILITY: A TOURISM PERSPECTIVE

Arun Sharma

Research Scholar Tourism Management, School of Tourism Travel and Hospitality Management Central University of Himachal Pradesh Dharmshala TAB - Shahpur sharma.arun84@gmail.com

Abstract: The worldwide competition for economic growth has brought the situation for every tourist destination to improve its overall infrastructure and utilize the available resources (natural, cultural, economical, political, social etc) for the purpose of improving destination image. In this critical situation the word, sustainable tourism development is far away from the reality because the rapid consumption and modification of resources by the human being for the personal use has lead them to die unnatural death.

This research article highlights the barriers in the sustainable tourism development in the selected area under study by examining various factors and using qualitative research techniques to generalize the results. The article concludes with suggestive measures for sustainable development.

Keywords: Resources, Destination Image, Sustainable Development.

Introduction

Tourism is a unique industry in terms of the range and diversity of products. Indeed very few industries involve so many activities to create a product. Furthermore tourism has this specificity that it is consumed directly on site inside the boundaries of the destination. Another fundamental characteristic is that the tourist is a direct and integral element of the production process. So the tourism product is influenced on the one hand by the industry, which provides basics constituent part of the product and on the other hand by the needs, motivations and expectations of tourists. Numerous problems are due to the nature of the tourism activity itself. The literature identifies a huge amount of weaknesses, but some of them are more related to sustainability than others. In this paper, the major weaknesses will be discussed on a sustainable stand-point. The WTO (2004) offers the following definition of sustainable development:

"Sustainable tourism development guidelines and management practices are applicable to all forms of tourism in all types of destinations, including mass tourism and the various niche tourism segments. Sustainability principles refer to the environmental, economic and socio-cultural aspects of tourism development, and a suitable balance must be established between these three dimensions to guarantee its long-term sustainability."

As an example, Hunter (1997) has defined the principles that sustainable tourism development should be based on:

- Meeting the needs and wants of the local community in terms of quality of life improvement;
- Fulfilment of the tourism demand and of the tourism industry and continue to attract people to be able to meet the first aim;
- The preservation of cultural resources (tangibles and intangibles), the natural environment and all the other local resources on which tourism is based in order to achieve the two preceding aims.

Ritchie and Brent (2005) argue that from a destination stand-point, the issue is not only to bring development under control but also to encourage appropriate forms of tourism. Indeed, they want to underline that to increase the economic prosperity, it is not enough to enhance the cultural, social and environmental well-being of a destination. Indeed those authors think that sustainability is made by four pillars which are : the ecological, the economic, the socio-cultural and the political ones (governance). They also said that these four pillars are interdependent which introduce the notion of system. Indeed, the sustainable tourism paradigm is also built on the theory of a systemic functioning. For example, if a tourist activity needs some ecological resources, it is necessary to control it and to limit the economic benefit in order to not destroy the resource. The case of a small hill town Dharmshala Mcleodganj has been highlighted in this study with a special focus on sustainability.

Literature Review

Mountains are often used as a metaphor for stability and strength, but their ecosystem is inherently weak and has limited tolerance for human activity and above all for aggressive tourism. The higher and more remote they are the more fragile they can be. The ecology of tourism is a sad narrative of negatives, losses of flora and fauna, degradation of mountain slopes, trails polluted with garbage, overburdened landscapes and unseemly urbanization (Singh 1999). The implementation of sustainable practices in tourism related companies is an object of discussions by many academics. There are various researches made about incentives and obstacles while switching towards sustainable business model (Le & Hollenhorst, 2005; La Lopa & Day, 2011). The definition of sustainability in tourism is rather wide and not strictly defined. Higgins-Desbiolles (2009) defines sustainable tourism as an answer to negative impacts that the industry creates. However, most of the literature reflects to three main aspects of sustainability in business: economic, social and environmental (Figge & Hahn, 2006). Economic aspect is defined as a way of saving companies costs, while social factor reefers to benefiting local community (creating the employment). Environmental sustainability is related to preservation of natural resources. Tourism industry, as any other, is profit driven and is based on co-modification of culture and environment, as well as exploitation of people (Higgins-Desbiolles, 2009). It emerged together with the ideology of consumerism; therefore the whole idea of sustainability is not more than sustaining the profit (Higgins-Desbiolles, 2009). Sustainability goes against capitalism, because it means limitation of growth. However, the whole industry is based on natural recourses (nature and culture) therefore tourism businesses have to switch their interest to sustain them, otherwise the sector will suffer in longer term (Vukonovic). The majority of leading tour operators already realized that the dramatic changes to their external operating environment calls for a need to reshape their working attitudes (Dunbar, 2009). Therefore, it is essential to understand barriers that discourages and incentives which stimulate companies to move towards sustainability.

Firstly, the decision to adopt sustainable practices presents many challenges for tourism related enterprises. Although the benefits to communities and individual companies are evident and the recourses are available the motivation to change is far from universal (La Lopa & Day, 2011). Business managers knows that introduction of innovations usually takes a lot of time, effort and often causes destruction in organizational climate (La Lopa & Day, 2011). Each organization has its corporate culture, composed of values, beliefs, attitudes (Graci, 2010). Since environmental issues are usually isolated from a corporate values, the attempts to implement them doesn't function (Graci, 2010). The successful accommodation of sustainability practices is largely related to personal believes. Graci (2010) states that unsupportive management can be a great limitation towards the development of sustainability. If people do not see the necessity for a change, they refuse it and they don't stand for it, any attempt to introduce the novelty is most likely to fail (La Lopa & Day, 2011). According to Le and Hollenhorst (2005), before making any decisions managers evaluate the resistance of employees. The attempts towards a changes tend to work faster, if it is easy for employees to understand the benefits (Le and Hollenhorst, 2005). The particularity with tourism products is that in most cases the quality can not be tested before the consumption. Therefore, if employees do not understand the necessity for adopting innovations, they won't be able to perceive this sustainable tourism image to their costumers (Le & Hollenhorst, 2005).

The other barrier towards sustainability is a lack of knowledge (Graci, 2010; La Lopa & Day, 2010). Graci (2010) emphasizes, that environmental awareness of managers is rather low and it leads to a slow uptake for future initiatives. However, most of the managers, in this case in hotels, knows about the existence of solar power, waste battery collection as a means to save costs, but the knowledge how to dispose them is inadequate (Graci, 2010). Implementation of sustainability requires long term thinking. In contrary, capitalistic environment of tourism businesses leads to short term goals. The main problem noted by Graci (2010) is that without increase in general environmental awareness there is no incentive for tourism enterprises to implement sustainable ideas, except the ones who bring fast economic gain.

One more limiting factor for innovations, is that sustainable practices are considered to be expensive. La Lopa and Day (2011) suggest that businesses should be educated about the purchasing costs being lower, than benefits of being sustainable. Companies do not realize that once they invest, the economic gains in a long term will be bigger. Therefore, financial recourses is defined as an another limitation for implementing sustainable business approach. Rojo (2009) notes that natural recourses are considered to be public goods, therefore, investing in their preservation does not bring direct economic benefits to the company. The recent economic downturn made companies to revise their expenditures. Hence, increase of sales at any costs becomes a primary goal, while any socially or environmentally friendly activity is considered to be less important. Since in the times of economic crisis dropping sales is one of the major concerns, the companies could try to sustain their income while adopting yield management schemes. Such type of management focuses on profit made per customer and not on growth of clients. Yield management principles are mostly used by airline companies, large hotel chains and lately by destination management organizations (Macbeth & Northcote, 2005) but it could be also adopted by a smaller scale businesses, like tour operators.

The idea of high expenses while implementing sustainability partly arises because of governmental policies. Usually, The National Tourist Authorities (NTA) and Tourism Destination Organizations (TDO) are responsible for encouraging tourism companies to impede sustainability (La Lopa & Day, 2011). Quite often such organization establishes guidelines for nature and culture friendly approach and certifies the companies who follow the rules (La Lopa & Day, 2011).

However, acquiring such certificate leads to many hours of bureaucratic work and requires solid financial resources to fulfill the imposed obligations (Jarvis, Simcock, Weeden, 2010). Therefore small and medium sized companies quite often fail in adopting sustainable tourism practices (Jarvis, Simcock, Weeden, 2010). According to Lee and Hollenhorst (2005) firms perceive uncertainty in government policies as a risk, and does not invest in innovations. This barrier could be removed, if governments would agree on more friendly policies towards sustainability implementation. For instance, providing subsidies for necessary technology. Figge and Hahn (2006) states that companies contribute to sustainability only if the expenses are lower than the perceived benefits. However, most of the scholars relate sustainability with the positive image of the company (Le &Hollenhorst, 2005; Jarvis, Simcock & Weeden, 2010). Therefore, marketing is recognized to be the biggest driving force towards sustainability. For instance, quite often companies strive to get "green label", because they believe that this creates a good image and distinguish them from the competitors. Le and Hollenhorst (2005), states that "becoming green" by implementing environmental innovations is a great strategy towards differentiation in the hyper competitive environment. However, do these companies represent the acquired positive image in the right way? Jarvis, Simcock and Weeden (2005) states that after obtaining the certificate, enterprises use it as a tool to charge higher prices for their services. By implementing environmentally friendly approach companies save costs on energy, water and waste bills (Jarvis, Simcock & Weeden, 2010), but they are not willing to share the saved costs with their clients by offering lower prices. That's why Jarvis, Simcock and Weeden (2010) concludes, that companies overestimate the numbers of clients who are willing to pay more for sustainable holiday. Another problem is that "sustainable campaigns" in travel business are being used as a marketing tool. Higgins-Desbiolles (2009), notes that large tour operators are only paying lip service to sustainable tourism and fails moving towards sustainability taking into account their relationships with tourism destinations. Mass tourism consumers have money to spend, therefore big companies created a new, "green" product, to make people to pay even more. Therefore, if the companies will claim that they are implementing responsible travelling when in reality just abusing the popularity of sustainable ideas, it will have negative effects and customers will get disappointed. Their unfulfilled visions about contribution to something good will become an obstacle for honest companies to make an effort towards sustainable practices and address them successfully.

Problem Statement

The ever-increasing flow of tourists to Dharmshala (Winter Capital of Himachal Pradesh in India), Mecklodganj, the Mini capital of Tibetan often called "Mini Lhasa" has severely strained this town's limited resources. Earlier, only the rich and the affluent came here. For most of the Indians this place remained a distant dream. The time has now changed, per capita income has increased and purchasing power of the average Indian has soared. The place has became the hot seat of honourable Dalai lama All this has resulted in a vast number of middle class tourists flocking here. As a consequence, the locals have started feeling the burden of numerous hardships. Plans so far promoted by the Government at State and Central level have ranged from callous negligence of the fragile environment conditions to disregard of native people and their cultural sensitivities. Dharamshala town now resembles a more urban centre than the beautiful resort it had once been therefore the need for sustainable tourism has been emphasized in this study.

Objectives of the study

1. To identify and analyse the main problems in sustainable tourism development in the hills.
2. To examine Tourism policies and its implications on tourism and environment in Dharamshala region (Dhauladhar range).

Methodology

The methodology included a literature review, including secondary data both published and unpublished and the extensive experience of the author through personal observation over more than ten years. The published data includes information from various publications of Central and State Governments, books, journals, internet and newspapers. The unpublished data has been collected from Dharmshala Municipal Corporation, Directorate of Transport, Himachal Pradesh State Pollution Control Board, Department of Tourism and Civil Aviation and other non-government agencies. Carefully selected content has been analysed for making suggestions.

Destination Profile

Dharamshala, known as **"Scotland of India"** is situated in the **"Dhouladhar"** range of the Himalayas, which is in Kangra district of Himachal Pradesh in India. This town is divided into two parts (the upper Dharamshala, which is called Macliodganj, is the chief centre of Labhapanchi Bodh religion in India and the main town is the lower Dharamshala). Since 1959, Macliodganj has been the chief centre of spiritual and political activities of the 14th Dalailama. This is also the capital of Tibet's government in exile. Its prime minister is 'Samdhong Renepo'. This is also called mini Lhasa. Saint John churches of Dharamshala is famous for its coloured patchful glasses. The British Vice-Roy and Governor general Lord Elgin was buried at this place. Dharamshala covered by Pine, Lok and Devdar trees is also famous for snow skating and mountaineering. Gaddi, the famous veterinary occupant peoples of Himachal Pradesh are basically the residents of this region. The first Gorkha rifle regiment of Indian Army was formed here in the second half of 19th century, which is today famous for its bravery and courage. It had won many medals by setting example of extreme brave in the north-west frontier war, the First World War and the Second World War. Captain Ramsingh of Khanyara village near Dharamshala was in 'Azad Hind Fauj'of Subash Chandra Bose. The famous patriotic song 'kadam-kadam badhaye ja' was written by him, which is very popular, even today among soldiers. Dharamshala is a year round magnet for tourists and hot seat of honourable sh. Dalai Lama. Tourists come to hang out in the villages around the town, adventure tourists come for trekking, paragliding; and Indian honeymoon couples or families come for the cool mountain air and their first taste of snow on a day trip to Mcleodganj and nearby places. Centre for Tibetan art and culture, 5000 Meter peaks, 14 Passes, and the home of the Gaddis, an indigenous tribe of Himachal Pradesh makes the Dharamshala region in Kangra, a unique destination. This is a hill station lying on the spur of the Dhauladhar range about 17 kms north- east of Kangra town. The snowline is perhaps more easily accessible at Dharamshala than at any other hill resort and it is possible to make a day's trek to a snow-point after an early morning's start. Hindi, Punjabi, English and Pahari are understood and spoken by the people engaged in tourism trade. Hill town is located between 1250 m to 1550 m (Dharamshala) have temperature of Max. 38 C in June; Min. 0 C in Jan. The annual rainfall varies between 290 cm to 380 cm second highest rainfall in the country. The best season to visit this place is between January to June and September to December. July-August is rainy season.

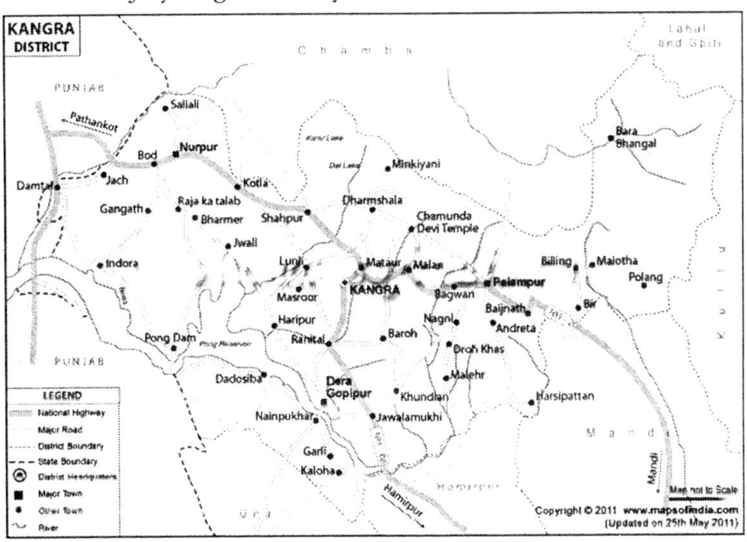

Source: www.mapsofindia.com

Accessibility: The nearest airport at Gaggal is 14 km away after which it is accessible by road. Pathankot is the nearest broad gauge railway terminal to Dharamshala. From Pathankot there is a narrow gauge railway line up to Kangra (94 km) and from here Dharamshala is 17 km by road. Direct and regular bus service from

Delhi (520 km), Chandigarh (250 km), Jammu (210 km), Shimla (238 km), Chamba (185 km) and Manali (240 km).

Mythological Beliefs and History: Due to natural beauty and spiritual environment of this region (Kangra valley), there were activities not only of Hindus but also associated with Bodh and Jaina religions from ancient times. In 9th ce.a.d, at Mashrur, 15 monolithic temples associated with Hindu religion were constructed on the basis of Ellora's Kailashnath temple, where statues of Ram, Sita and Laxman were established. Shiva gumpha temple was made at Trilokpur during this period. In 15th ce.a.d, 18 Jaina temples (colonies) were constructed at a place Muda Vidri, which is famous as 'Jaina Kashi'. The most famous among these is 'Kavandvaste' (thousand pillars) .There is monolithic pillars and metallic statues of Jaina Trithankars, which is a fine piece of sculpture. The fort of Dhameri was constructed in this natural surroundings in 15th ce.ad .It was named 'Nurpur' by Mughal emperor Jahangir being impressed by its natural beauty and the structure of the fort. The British had occupied Dharamshala in 1848 .In 1852, a sub-centre of British cantonment was established here and it was made the administrative headquarter of Kangra district. In 1860, the chief centre of Gorkha Rifles Regiment was established and due to this reason, Dharamshala was developed as a town in the post-period. Due to destructive earthquake of 1905, most temples and buildings of Dharamshala were converted into ruins. But very soon the town regained its glory by reconstruction. In 1959, Dharamshala was suddenly publicized on the world map, when the 14thDalailama Tenjing Jilatsu along with thousands of Tibetans, migrated and came to Dharamshala after the Chinese attack on Tibet. A Government-in-exile was formed after getting permission from the Indian government. In 1960, Dalailama established the 'Namgyal matha'. The chief centre of Tibetans was formed in Macloidganj, upper Dharamshala, where several mathas, vihars, educational institutes and social service centre were established later. The famous Tibetan library was established by Dalailama in 1960. There are approximately 80,000 manuscripts of Tibetan history, politics and culture which are compiled in to books. This is supposed to be the world famous institutes to know about Tibet. Dharamshala was rapidly developed as a commercial and tourist place between the decades of 1980 and1990 .There were so many places related to snow skating ,mountaineering ,picnic etc. constructed and developed here. Its natural surroundings are similar to just like heaven for nature lovers.

Major Places Tourist places:

1	**Namgyal matha**	This matha in Dharamshala was established by Dalailama in 1959.At present, there are Boudh Bhikshus who live here. Tantrik activities like-Kalchakra, Yamentak, Vrajkalia is practiced here. The proper Namgyal matha was established by the 3rd Dalailama Sonam Gyatso in 1575 at Lhasa.
2	**Bhagsunag temple**	This temple of Lord Shiva is situated at a distance of 2 km. from Macliodganj market. He is the chief worship able God of Gorkhas. There is a beautiful waterfall on the hill near the temple. The temple was established by the local king Dharamchandra.
3	**Saint John Church**	This church was established in 1852 .This church made up of brown stones has been decorated with coloured glasses. This is 7 km away from Dharamshala .In 1863, Vice-roy Lord Elgin was buried here.
4	**Kunalpathri**	This is known as a Shaktipithas where Bhagwati Sati's head was chopped down. The placed goddess is called Kalpeshwari.
5	**Dal lake**	At a height of 15000 ft and surrounded by deodar trees, the natural scenery of this lake is very attractive also have old kali temple. This lake is 2 km away from Macliodganj. It is the belief that there was a ashram of saint Durwasha.

6	**Norbulinka institute**	This is formed to protect and develop the Tibetan art and culture by the religion and culture ministry. There is a great Japanese impact on this cultural centre. It is 4 km away from Dharamshala.
7	**Chinmaya Tapovan**	This was established by Swami Chinmaiyanand, a famous Krishna follower and saint. There is an established centre of meditation and yoga in the natural environment. The Raghunath temple and huge Hanuman statue attracts at the very first eye-sight.
8	**Chamunda Devi temple**	There is a famous Chamunda Devi temple at a distance of 15 km from Dharamshala. It is the belief that Aadishakti killed Chund and Mund demons at this place. There is a chief God Aadikeshwar. There is ancient temple of Aadi Himani Chamunda forwarding up 16 km from here.
9	**Masrur Monolithic Temple**	15 km south from kangra, there is a group of 15 monolithic temples in which there are statues of Ram, Laxman, Sita etc. These temples are supposed to be of 8th ce.a.d.
10	**Dharamkota**	Dharamkota is a chief picnic spot at a distance of 10 km from Dharamshala .From here, one can see the incredible scene of Kangra valley and Himachal. Here you can meet the traditional Gaddi community.
11	**Kangra fort**	This historical kangra fort, constructed in rock art, is situated at a distance of 18 km

from Dharamshala. According to the structure and natural formation of the fort, this looks to be imtranspermeable

Major Festivals: Beside celebrating all the major festivals of India, Dharamshala is well known for the special events as: Saka Dava (chief festival of Dharamshala's Tibetan Boudh, which is celebrated on the 15th day of 4th moon month according to Tibetan calendar. The three great events of Lord Buddha's life -birth, achievement of knowledge and Mahaparinirvan is remembered on this occasion), Losar (Tibetan New Year. On this occasion people wear traditional Tibetan dresses and so the whole Macliodganj looks like the second Lhasa), The birthday of 14th Dalailama is celebrated on 6th July every year. The Gaddi dance organized on this occasion attracts tourist and followers.

Major Issues of Sustainability: The present structure of Dharmshala town was originally designed by the British Administration for town was basically planned for the military purpose which later on became the chief centre of spiritual and political activities of the 14th Dalailama. Britishers shortlisted this place as a health resort with a secondary function as the summer capital of British India before deciding about Shimla. Now the situation and function of this city has changed without changing the city structure to suit its functional requirements. During recent decades nothing tangible could be done to guide its growth pattern on scientific lines. Thus unplanned and haphazard growth has resulted in a number of environmental problems.

1. **Policy and Institutional development:** Planning for tourism in the area is done in an effort to attract foreign tourists because of the need for foreign exchange rather than a concerted effort to make areas of tourist significance and the communities therein sustainable. The desire for short-term gain is part of human nature. This is particularly evident in Macliodganj, where a growing demand is almost automatically met by increased supply in the shape of construction of roads, hotels, resorts, and motivated by the fear of losing out in the competition for profits. The demand

induced growth pattern has not resulted in a sustainable basis for mountain tourism. As a result, the natural landscape of Dharamshala has been subjected to environmental stress, exploitation and degradation. It has started losing its attractiveness for tourism.

2. **Lack of retention of benefits from Tourism:** Urban outsiders provide the goods and services demanded by the tourists, particularly from Delhi and capitals. Accommodation and Catering tends to be dominated by the formal sector, ranging from luxury class hotels to guesthouses. The tours and expeditions are often organized by private travel Agencies, which have mushroomed here, having head offices or tie ups outside Dharamshala. Often local people undertake the least remunerative occupations.
3. **Seasonality:** The summer tourists often place such high demands on resources at specific periods every year, that is, peak summer months from April to June when there are summer holidays in neighbouring hot plains, Durga Puga holidays, occasional snowfall in winters, Christmas holidays in December and New Year Eve celebrations (Batra 2001), that this hill resort is paralyzed for a short time after these periods.
4. **Exploitation of Natural Resources:** In Himachal Pradesh, sightseeing and peaceful natural environment is the main reason for tourist influx. The root of the crisis is the degradation of the resource base. There is a total decay of most urban pockets, particularly those reroute to major destinations. A large proportion of the congestion is a direct consequence of tourist traffic and infrastructure built for tourists. Overcrowding can result in an increased risk of damage to a site and heavier wear and tear.
5. **Haphazard development:** Unplanned urbanization has put the hill ecology under tremendous strain. Unplanned and haphazard growth of towns is causing deforestation and environmental problems. Pine trees, which once dominated the skyline, have given way to large concrete structures. The built infrastructure facilities like roads, electricity, water supply, and rapid urban expansion has taken place at the expense of natural beauty and environment.

A big stretch of Dadi and Kotwali Bazar started sinking a few years' ago. Many buildings in this area have developed cracks. Now the entire highway is dotted with industrial estates, hotels and houses. Clusters of Dhabas (food shops on the road) and big signboards on the highway have taken their toll and the splendid view and natural ambience of thick forests have been at the receiving end.

6. **Travel ethics among Tourists:** How many of the tourists visiting have Eco-sense and appreciation of the town? A tourist need not have the same emotions and sentiments about the destination, which a native has. A tourist wants quick value for his money. Dharmshala is going to face problems of pollution due to large-scale commercialization. At the sightseeing places, one can find abandoned food packets, pan-masala wrappers, empty beer bottles, polythene bags littered here and there on the hills. Near church area, visitors, just to write their names or graffiti in an attempt to immortalize them by scratching trunks of the trees! The impulse of the majority of mass tourists is driven by their need to escape the heat, and not by considerations of taking in the sights of the natural and cultural splendours of the state.
7. **Carrying Capacity:** In order to derive maximum benefits from tourism resources and to allow tourism product diversification, baseline information on ecology, and social and cultural systems is required. It is on this basis that tolerable limits of acceptable change, or environmental., economics and social carrying capacity considerations can be brought to bear in the planning and management of tourism.

Suggestions:

1. Tourism planners should act responsibly. It is essential to have a clear vision of what is desired from tourism. It should be the endeavour of the government to prevent mushrooming of the hotel industry, which has already crossed the desired limits in many key tourist places. Simply stating that growth in this industry is desired is meaningless if there are no clear strategies to achieve it. They should go for sustainable management of resources available.

Balanced consideration should be given to the needs of natives and interests of tourists.

2. The need of the hour is to develop the concepts of 'fair trade' in tourism, whereby locals should gain a fair share of the benefits of tourism. This implies a more direct role for residents and government in dealing with tourists directly rather than using intermediaries, especially outside tour operators. Authorities should identify and assess the role of environmental resources for community development and this can be linked with tourism development. Government should encourage the behaviour that conserves resources, links local community- based activities with tourism.
3. Adequate space for parking of vehicles should be provided at McLeodGanj. The visitors can be encouraged to leave their cars parked at specific points and trek to nearby places or use public transport.
4. In the publicity brochures, tourism promoters should not promote a site or locality, which is seen to be over-visited. Such sites or locations should be promoted only when the season is over. Steps should be taken to decongest the city by shifting offices to nearby places.
5. Here the approach is to accept that some wear and tear is inevitable, even with normal usage. The importance of sensitive design needs to be stressed. The scale of new development and the materials used must be in harmony with the surrounding environment. The construction of buildings should be such that they blend well with the local architecture. People should be persuaded to construct only eco-friendly buildings, which do not destroy the scenic beauty. Buildings should not be allowed to be constructed on the highways as they obstruct the flow of traffic.
6. There should be restrictions on the use of sites that can- not control the crowd and also channels the impact of the visitors. The presence of guards can keep watch over natural wealth, supervise and stop unruly behaviour deliberately.

7. The tourists visiting destination at the entry points should be given information material prescribing "Do's" and Don'ts". Educating the visitor about the place and importance of a sensitive environment at a hill station is equally important. Last, emphasis must be laid on tourism-related help in the planning and management of tourism at a hill station.

Conclusion

Travel industry is focused on natural resources and the negative impacts caused by tourism provokes attention to change management strategies of tourism businesses. The sustainability "movement" put the tourism enterprises into the spotlight, therefore we can claim that the industry has the moral obligations to spread good examples of sustainability. Managers are afraid that the costs to persuade their staff towards environmentally friendly activities will cost more than the gained benefits. Sustainable approach is understood as costly investment. Local government should reduce the level of bureaucracy exercised on environmentally and socially responsible companies. Through joining various "green" movements companies hope to increase the advertising possibilities. Unfortunately, usually it only stays the advertising tool and in reality little is done to sustain natural recourses. Thus, this advantage can turn into obstacle for businesses with honest intentions due to mistrust of costumers, willing to contribute to responsible travel. Major initiative required for sustainable mountain tourism is the formulation of a long-term policy clearly delineating the role of tourism is expected to play in the overall development of the hill region. The policy should be developed on the basis of comprehensive appreciation of the value of environmental, cultural and heritage resources in the hills. One of the essential facts in planning and development of mountain regions is the fact that mountains are inherently weak and fragile, having meagre tolerance for human intervention, particularly for the resource consuming activities that interfere with their cybernetics and inbuilt anti-repair system. It should be recognized that Dharamshala like many hill stations built by the British in India, is a precious national heritage. It is high time that the municipal corporation and the state government attach utmost priority to ensure appreciation of the value of environmental resources. Only planned development based on research and well conceived sustainable tourism policy, respecting limits of growth and involvement of local people can promise desired results in the realms of ecology and economy. Finally, the achievement of sustainability depends on moral responsibility of each individual.

References and selected bibliography:

Ali, A. (1994). Environmental protection of the Himalayas- A mountaineer's View. New Delhi: Indus Publishing Company.

Batra, A. (2001). Ecotourism in Shimla Region. Doctoral Thesis, India: Kurukshetra University.

Centre for Mountain Tourism and Hospitality Studies(1999). Research Projects, Journal of Tourism, vol.4, H.N.B. Garhwal, University, Srinagar Garhwal, pp.: 76-82,93-94.

Denniston, D.(1996). Mountains: vital for human survival. People & the Planet, On-line Library Document. E-mail: wwpub@igc.apc.org

Dunbar, M. (2009). Brits leads way on sustainability. Canadian Travel Press, 42(5): 8. Retrieved 16 November, 2011, from EBSCO database.

Desbiolles-Higgins, F. (2009). The elusiveness of sustainability in tourism: the culture-ideology of consumerism and its implications. Tourism and Hospitality Research, 10(2): 116-129. Retrieved November 16, 2011 from EBSCO database.

Figge, F., Hahn, T. (2004). Sustainable value - added measuring corporate contributions to sustainability beyond eco-efficiency. Ecological economics, 48: 173-187. Retrieved November 15, 2011 from Science Direct database.

Gupta, V. and Shah, k. (1999). Tourism in the Himalayas: Seizing the Opportunity, Mtn-Forum On-line Library Document.

Graci, S. (2010). Examining the factors that impede sustainability in China's tourism accommodation industry: a case study of Sanya, Hainan, China. Journal of Hospitality Marketing and Management, 19: 38-55. Retrieved November 16, 2011 from EBSCO database.

Inskeep, E. (1992). Achieving Sustainable Tourism Development, Travel Trends, New Delhi, p: 6.

Inskeep, E. (1996). Tourism Planning: All Integrated and Slistainable Development Approach. New York: Van Nostrand Reinhold.

Jarvis, N., Simcock, N., Weeden, C. (2010). The benefits and challenges of sustainable tourism certification: A case study of the Green Tourism Business Scheme in the West of England. Journal of Hospitality and Tourism Management, 17, 83-93. Retrieved November 17, 2011 from EBSCO database.

Khan, A.R. (1996). Man Environmellt and Developmellt ill Himachalt'radesh. New Delhi: Indus Publishing Company.

La Lopa, M., J., Day, J. (2011). Pilot study to assess the readiness of the tourism industry in Waled to change to sustainable tourism business practices. Journal of Hospitality and Tourism Management, 18: 130-139. Retrieved November 17, 2011 from EBSCO database.

Le, Y., Hollenhorst, S. (2005). Perceptions of vietnamese tours companies toward adopting sustainable tourism practices. An International Journal of Tourism and Hospitality Research, 16(1): 79-99. Retrieved November 17, 2011 from EBSCO database.

Macbeth, J., Northcote, J. (2005). Conceptualizing yield sustainable tourism management. Annals of Tourism Research, 33(1): 199-220. Retrieved November 16, 2011 from Science Direct database.

Rai, H.C. (1998). Hill Tourism Planning and Development. New Delhi: Kanishka Publication Distribution.

Roberts, Sh., Tribe, J. (2008). Sustainability indicators for small tourism enterprises - an exploratory perspective. Journal of Sustainable Tourism, 16 (5): 575-594. Retrieved November 17, 2011 from EBSCO database.

Rojo, M. (2009). Economic development versus environmental sustainability: the case of tourist marinas in Andalusia. European Journal of Tourism Research, 2(2): 162-177. Retrieved November 15, 2011, from EBSCO database.

Sharma, P. (1997). Toward Sustainable Mountain Tourism', International Center for Integrated Mountain Development (rCIMOD), Newsletter, no. 28, Kathmandu, Nepal, pp.: 12-14.
Singh, S.c. (1989). Impact of TOllrism on MOllntaill Enviromncllt. Meerut: Research India Publications.

Singh, T.V. (1989). The Kullu Valley-Impact of Tourism Development In Mountain Areas. New Delhi: Himalayan Books.

Singh, T.V. (1999). Keep the Sharks out of the Mountains. Our Planet On-line Library Document.

Sreedhar, R. (1995). Mountain Tourism in Himachal Pradesh and the Hill districts of Uttar Pradesh. ICIMOD Discussion Paper, Series No.MEI 95/6,Kathmandu, Nepal.

Swarbrooke, J. (1999).Sustainable Tourism Management. Wallingford: CAB! Publishing, Wallingford, UK. and pp.: 183-192.

Urban Environmental Maps- SHIMLA (1997). By the Academy for Mountain Environics. India: Dehradoon

Vukonovic, B. (n.d.). Can sustainability be questioned? Retrieved November 16, 2011, from EBSCO database.

Web resources:

http://web.ebscohost.com/

http://www.palaeoresearchsociety.com/

http://www.endruralpoverty.org/what-we-do/community-based-tourism

http://woodlandventures.co.in (accessed on 23rd June 2013)

http://www.assocham.org/

http://www.himsatta.com/

http://www.himachaltourism.gov.in?

http://yatra2yatra.com

ECOTOURISM: A VIABLE SOLUTION TO DEVELOP GREEN PRACTICES AT TRIKUTA HILLS IN JAMMU & KASHMIR, INDIA

Bharat B. Sharma

Research Scholar, Centre for Mountain Tourism and Hospitality Studies, Hemwati Nandan Bahuguna Garhwal University Srinagar, Garhwal.

bharat4sai@gmail.com

Sonia Sharma

Assistant Professor, School of Tourism and Hospitality Services Management, Indira Gandhi National Open University, New Delhi.

soniasharma@ignou.ac.in

Abstract: Ecotourism has manifested itself as a tool for conservation where timely introduction and execution of ecotourism policies has helped many tourist destinations to revive and even saved them from extinction. The present study was carried out to evaluate the environmental degradation & ecological effects of over crowding due to mass tourism on Trikuta hills, also known as Mata Vaishno Devi Hills of Jammu Shiwaliks in India, and assessing the possible opportunities of openings for sustainable development through ecotourism within the area. This paper has largely relied on interactions with people from different backgrounds for their views on possible ecotourism promotion. Structured questionnaire was carried out to obtain first hand information. To get to analysis of data arithmetic mean, standard deviation and percentage methods were used. The results revealed that developing ecotourism is imperative for sustainable development of the area. With 86.7% of locals having knowledge about flora, fauna and culture of the region; majority of travel agents welcoming the sustainable development and tourists having shown highest mean value of 4.19 towards being close to nature justifies that ecotourism development is extremely viable thereby promoting green practices at Trikuta Hills.

Keywords: ecotourism, environment, tourist, local, employment, awareness

Ecotourism can act as a core of sustainability if its principles are applied in an appropriate manner. It includes a responsible travel to natural areas that conserves the environment and improves the well being of local people (TIES, 1990). Ecotourism Australia defines it as "ecologically sustainable tourism with a primary focus on experiencing natural areas that foster environmental and cultural understanding, appreciation and conservation." Though tourism industry emerged as a smog free industry and major source of revenue generation but with the petition of time, competitions and demand from contemporary tourism it has accelerated its direction towards attenuation of natural resources. Trikuta hills were always blessed with tourist movement due to religious tourism ever since but with the institution of Shrine Board in 1988 the tourist numbers increased many folds giving opportunity for construction of many hotels and other allied services to accommodate ever increasing demand of visitors. Tourism being one of the most important forces shaping our world (Cohen & Kennedy, 2000) grew with mass movement of people from long time which in the wake of tourism has resulted in drastic, non reversible harsh environmental issues even leading to loss of many beautiful destinations forever and needs to be addressed immediately. Due to large number of tourists visiting the shrine there has been tremendous reduction in the forest cover as local vegetation of the area was removed to build hotels and various other facilities to accommodate increased tourist traffic. Where as forests are one among many popular ecotourism destinations due to their values for tourists interested in nature, locals and culture. There were many negative impacts due to unplanned growth which included illegal construction of hotels & shops, plastic dumping or disposal at Banganga stream of water, Sewerage waste dumping leading to dirty streets and roads; congestion of traffic. Along with this there is a distrust and frustration among locals for getting only low paid jobs and mainly are involved as labourers and/or pony owners whereas higher positions are rarely given to them. As much of profit moves out of destination and locals don't get much opportunity to get involved in business there must be a strategy to involve locals in decision making and projects that bring long term relationship with environment where by providing a viable solution to sustainable development. Here, ecotourism can act as a saviour to the issues of locals and environment as it includes nature based form of tourism whose ideal type is characterised opposite to unsustainable mass tourism involving products and destinations of small scale, rural rather than urban and locally controlled (Weaver 1993). These statements got strong support in literature by (Johnson 1990; Fennel and Smale 1992; Prosser 1994; Sindiga 1999 and Muller 2000). It is estimated that mountains account for roughly 15-20% of the global tourism market, generating between 70 and 90 billion US dollars per year (FAQ, 2005). Studies have shown that tourism is one of the more alternative livelihood options for the people in the Himalayan region (Sharma, 2000; East et al., 1998). Even (Cawley & Gillmor, 2008, Oliver & Jenkins, 2003; Saxena, Clark, Oliver, & Ilbery; 2007) dictate on the rhetoric involvement & participation of locals in sustainable tourism development. Tourism should contribute to economic diversification of a region through establishment of a range of ecologically sustainable tourist and recreational areas and activities based on the regions natural and man made attractions' (WADPUD, 1994) and ecotourism can manage Himalayan tourism in the best ways and provide immediate solution to many problems of unsustainably and unequal distribution of physical and economic growth of the destination.

Study Area Map

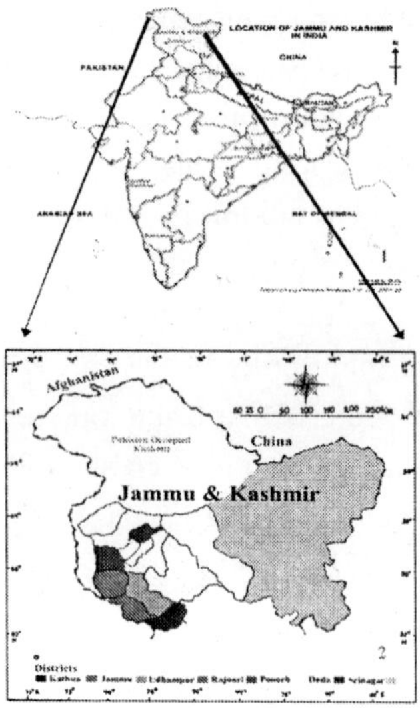

Fig-1: Showing the location of study area

Study Area

Present research was carried out in the Trikuta Hills located in Jammu district of Jammu and Kashmir state of India which lies between Latitude: 32°59'N and Longitude: 74°57'E falls under jurisdiction of tehsil Reasi of Jammu province. It is well connected by national highway 1A at a distance of 42 kilometres from Jammu.

Jammu is also called as city of temples with large number of religious destinations in and around Jammu. There is high turnover of tourists due to Mata Vaishno Devi shrine which involves many nearby villagers into workforce at various levels. There is good network of roads and railways is starting services soon. The population of Jammu & Kashmir in 2011 census was 12,548,926. Its geographical area is 222,236 sq. km2 and accounts for 6.76 percent of the country's size. With the improvement in education slowly but gradually locals of the Katra and its surrounding have improved literacy rate in recent years and village Panthal has highest literacy rate. The main occupation of these locals is tourism and around one third of population is still under agriculture and local labour. The jobs involving tourism other than shopkeepers and hotel owners are mainly workers in hotels, restaurants, pony/ horse operators, goods transportation, cleaners and many such jobs which provide them just enough income to run their livelihood. Nearby villages are having tremendous natural beauty which could be retained by proper planning for future development of Ecotourism for sustainable development rather than unplanned growth of hotels around the area. Seeing the volume of tourists visiting Katra town, the locals still need more benefits to share.

Review of Literature

The aim of this paper is to represent ecotourism as a form of sustainable tourism that contributes towards sustainability of Trikuta hills and its environs along with local population. The current scenario at Trikuta hills calls for immediate action plan in terms of following green practices and implementation of ecotourism policies which would strive to improve the living standards of local communities along with environmental sustainability. Forest areas which are considered important places for the protection of ecological systems and natural resources as well as for the recreational and tourism opportunities for the people (Boyd, 2006) are to be safeguarded from the current illegitimate practices and to be provided with strong support of stringent laws. Ecotourism initiatives that have participation and support of locals are more likely to become socially, economically and ecologically sustainable and contribute to the development of local communities and regions (Scheveys, 1999; Gurung and Seeland 2008). Similarly sustainable tourism as a form can maintain its viability in an area for an indefinite period of time (Butler, 1993). Whereas four fundamental pillars that needed to be followed for a more responsible form of tourism include: (1) minimum environmental impact; (2) minimum impact on and maximum respect for host cultures; (3) maximum economic benefits to the host country's grassroots; and (4) maximum 'recreational' satisfaction to participating tourists (Hetzer, 1965). Thus, when arguing for an ecotourism initiative, it is essential that questions about who, how and even why, in relation to participation, are answered (Gonale Guerrero, 2009) as these answers would provide a clear roadmap for developing ecotourism. It is well noted that tourists rarely travel to satisfy one motive rather have multiple motivations (Crompton, 1979; Mansfield, 1992; Mayo and Jarvis, 1981; Uysal and Hagan, 1993) which increases the viability of developing ecotourism in Trikuta hills along with gratification of religious motives. In the context of Himalayas (Bagri and Gupta 2001) explained its importance and benefits to local people. As ecotourism has potential for economic transition, regional development, community empowerment and the creation of employment opportunities for peripheral areas (Hall and Byod, 2003) and indigenous communities (Butler and Hinch, 1996) these practices must be induced and exercised in best ways at Trikuta hills and its environs to reap maximum benefits to local communities. Following these practices and principles it is not too far when these hills and its surroundings would be seen as a model for Ecotourism destination.

Research Methodology

The study used both primary (self administered questionnaire) and secondary sources of data (relevant books, research journals, newspapers, magazines and internet websites). Extensive study of secondary data along with physical visitation to Trikuta hills and surrounding villages was carried out to evaluate the environmental degradation and socio-cultural effects on local population due to mass tourism. As a method of collecting respondents' data, four (4) questionnaires were developed to get information from J&K Tourism Department; 30 Travel agents or Tour operators; 140 Locals; and 550 tourists related to various impacts of mass tourism. To analyse data the methodology used was through Descriptive statistics (Mean, Standard Deviation, and Percentage) to obtain results from the questionnaires taking all the respondents as a group. Study undertook the objectives to study the motivational factors, examine the source of Information and to identify the activities of the tourists visiting J&K towards ecotourism. Paper also works to find the perspective of tourists, locals, and government & private operators of tourism towards a viable solution to the environmental issues caused due to mass tourism. Tourists were categorized on the basis of demographic characteristics like gender, age, education, occupation, income, region and group composition and their responses on various parameters were analyzed to find out the differences, if any, amongst the sub-groups.

Findings:

Opinion of Private Operators

Tour operators & Travel agents play a vital role in promotion, marketing and subsequently development of a particular destination. As widely known fact that tourists decision, in majority, are dependent upon advice and guidance of their agents hence this becomes imperative to understand the point of view of tour operators and travel agents while deciding upon ecotourism development at Trikuta hills. First questionnaire with nine closed end questions in relation to the promotion of ecotourism was used to find opinion of travel agents / tour operators. Upon analysis of data of private operators for empirical study and making contemplated comparisons by applying various statistical tools it was clear that there is positive response from tour and travel agents in favour of ecotourism development with around (77%) of travel agents and tour operators having knowledge about ecotourism; a large percentage (66.67%) knew about the awareness programmes organized by NGOs for conservation of environment; and majority of the travel agents informed that they followed the guidelines framed by the government for conservation of environment which were necessary steps towards conservation of local environment.

Perception of locals

Second questionnaire was administered on a group of 140 locals of villages across the study areas. They were asked nineteen closed end questions in relation to the development of ecotourism in their region. During analysis of the questionnaire dealing with perception and involvement of locals towards ecotourism revealed that locals play a vital role in the development of ecotourism and it is imperative that they must understand the concept at first place. By doing so they are more involved and proactive in ecotourism development activities. Concept of ecotourism though very familiar and widely discussed by academia and policy makers, was not so common with locals. The locals were explained about the concept & its benefits and subsequently asked 19 questions which revealed that very few (16.67%) locals had knowledge or heard about ecotourism. The vital product "flora and fauna", which is quite abundant in J&K state was known by majority of (86.67%) locals. Any ecotourism activity involves innate locations and depends largely upon flora and fauna. Having knowledge about flora and fauna adds to the viability of ecotourism. Similar was the case with knowledge of folk tales and culture related to the region. It was interesting to notice a positive outlook from locals towards setting up of own ventures. 90% of locals were enthusiastic and ready to start own set ups only if they were provided loan and infrastructural. (86.67%) of locals welcomed and were interested to encourage tourist movement into their locality along with 90% of locals who consider that ecotourism could contribute in opening new job opportunity for them. Hence it is very clear that ecotourism initiatives that have the support and participation of the local people are more likely to be socially, economically and ecologically sustainable and contribute to the development of local communities and regions (Scheveys,1999; Gurung and Seeland 2008). With positive and encouraging grounds on setting up of own ventures, (60%) locals needed rigorous training to start these ventures. As Morrison (2002) argues that the lack of management skills and training among small tourism business contribute to their endangerment rather than their sustainability. Hence, it is imperative that locals are provided with immense training before setting up ecotourism ventures. Although with many positive factors of support and knowledge of ecotourism among locals it is also understood that as deforestation has always lead to negative effects on ecology and environment. 73.3% of locals contest that natural calamities like land slides and forest fire have been caused due to mass deforestation. During the year 1992 to 1999 an alternative track from Katra to the Vaishno Devi shrine was built where a foot track of 18 feet wide and 5.5 Km long was constructed. To make the track, the mountains were detonated with the help of explosives which weekend the rocks in place and also lost the thick forest cover forever which has lead to increased landslide in the area. Along with forest, it affected the wild life and other fauna which were displaced and scattered away.

As there is immense pressure on Katra with more than 10 million people visiting annually, it is important that there are some alternative destinations which can be utilised in reducing burden of overcrowding at Katra in a way to scatter them to nearby Ecotourists destinations which can also reap the benefits of its beauty and natural resources. Around (30%) of locals reported that there are many destinations in the vicinity of Katra which have high ecotourism potential but not popular among visitors such as Baba Dhansar, Baba Jito, Nav pindi etc, which could be developed in a planned way. Hence it is imperative that such destinations must be developed according to ecotourism policies and follow green practices to restore sustainability along with bringing these destinations into the tourism map of Jammu.

Motivation of tourists for Ecotourism

Trikuta hills and its environs are blessed with paramount natural beauty, flora and fauna which are core in development of ecotourism destination. Motivation has been referred to as psychological or biological needs and wants, including integral forces that arouse direct and integrate a person's behaviour and activity (Dann, 1981, Pearce, 1992; Uysal and Hagan, 1993). Where as Pearce, Morrison and Rutledge, 1998 defined tourist motivation as "the global integrating network of biological and cultural forces which give value and direction to travel choices, behaviour and experience." To understand the motivation of tourists, third questionnaire was administered on sampled (550) tourist population for visiting ecotourism destination. Motivation factors affecting tourists to visit ecotourism destination were understood through structured questionnaire from the visitors at Katra. Table-1 below depicts fourteen factors with mean their values out of which; being close to nature, opportunity to be with friends and relatives, being physically active and experiencing peace and tranquillity of natural environment were having highest mean values which are quite favourable factors towards development of ecotourism and to add on the support from local population deems it fit to promote ecotourism with all these credentials.

Table 1: Motivations Statements for Tourists

Motivational Variables	No. of Respondents	Mean	S.D
Experiencing peace & tranquility of the natural environment	550	4.10	1.369
Being close to nature	550	4.19	1.265
Seeing wildlife in its natural habitat	550	3.86	1.388
Escaping the urban environment	550	3.86	1.323
Absence of crowds	550	3.90	1.387
Being physically active	550	4.12	1.267
Positive previous experience	550	4.00	1.393
Rest and relaxation	550	4.09	1.321
Reputation of the site	550	4.16	1.298
Having exciting and adventurou experiences	550	3.94	1.360
Availability at a reasonable price	550	3.81	1.417
Visiting as many ecotourism destinations as possible	550	3.98	1.356
Opportunity to be with friends and/ or relatives	550	4.17	1.276
Being able to tell my friends about my experiences	550	4.17	1.277

Source of Information

Next section of the questionnaire was to know the source of information used by the tourists about ecotourism destinations. For development of any tourism product, it is essential to understand tourist's knowledge about destination along with their interest level to take appropriate steps in supporting green practices at ecotourism destinations. Altogether 12 source of information were presented before the tourists in the present study. The tourists were asked to reply on a 3 point scale: 'never', 'sometimes' and 'frequently use'. The mean and standard deviations of the tourists' responses were calculated and depicted in Table-2. Television (mean 2.56) and word of mouth (mean 2.54) were two most important sources reported by the tourists. The tourists also gave importance to travel agents, newspapers, internet and information brochure as important sources of information. With the inclusion of technology in tourism it is evident that marketing such destinations becomes very easy affair and people would appreciate and try to learn about the importance of such destinations if proper explanations and information is provided.

Table 2: Source of Information

Source of Information	No. of respondents	Mean	S.D
Word of Mouth	550	2.54	0.68
Travel guide/ books	550	1.63	0.65
Brochure	550	1.75	0.67
Visitor Information Centre	550	1.64	0.63
Magazines	550	1.56	0.61
Environmental clubs/ organizations	550	1.61	0.69
News Papers	550	2.09	0.85
Television	550	2.56	0.66
Travel agents	550	2.09	0.70
Internet	550	2.05	0.85
Radio	550	1.53	0.63
Auto clubs	550	1.35	0.59

Activities Help in Promoting Ecotourism

Another important aspect in the development of tourism product along with knowledge of motivation factors and sources of information was to find out what all activities enhance ecotourism in the perspective of tourists. To understand activities that help in promoting ecotourism, tourists' were asked questions through structured questionnaire with eighteen questions. The mean and standard deviations of the responses obtained from the tourists depicted in Table-3 shows that the tourists were of the opinion that people should come forward voluntarily to establish NGOs for the promotion of ecotourism in the state. Tourists were interested to tell their friends and relatives about ecotourism concepts and practices at the destination. With regard to behaviour of the local people towards tourists, the respondents stated that the behaviour should be warm and friendly. The tourists in the study have expressed their interest to purchase local handicrafts as a gift to relatives, friends and well wisher. They also suggested that more concrete roads and jeep-able roads may be built in the eco-fragile environment for the easy access.

Table 3: Activities Help in Promoting Ecotourism

Activities promoting Ecotourism	No. of Respondents	Mean	S.D
Voluntarily establish NGOs for promotion of ecotourism.	550	4.02	1.35
Tell friends and relatives about ecotourism concepts and practices at the destination.	550	4.06	1.29
The behavior of local people towards tourists should be warm and friendly.	550	4.02	1.24
Purchase local handicrafts as a gift to relatives, friends and well wisher.	550	4.00	1.30
Preferred locations for accommodation of the ecotourists in the forest	550	4.11	1.28
Concrete roads and jeep able roads are suggested in the eco-fragile environment.	550	4.04	1.39

Discussion

It is evident from the survey that increasing number of pilgrims to the Vaishno Devi Shrine, Katra create problem of overcrowding, noise pollution, water pollution and air pollution. On eastern side of the town, railway track and railway station are constructed. On western side there is little scope of expansion as there is steep fall and a nalla towards Reasi. Development is taking place in the southern side of the town and on both sides of the Domel-Katra highway where most of the land has been sold to the hoteliers who are trying to encroach the adjoining forests. Due to absence of sewage treatment plant in the Katra town and proper garbage management system, the town faces lots of difficulties and creates health problems. The large amount of solid waste produced everyday is dumped in the hill slopes around one km away from the town. The Trikuta hills area is geologically and ecologically fragile. The hills are prone to erosion and landslides. It is estimated around 11.06 sq. km of forest area has been destroyed due to alternate track to Bhawan. Though it is always dangerous to construct multi-storied buildings along the fragile mountain slopes, it is sad to see that shrine board has constructed three-storied staff quarter building and the three-storied Manokamana Bhawan along the new foot track. Many more proposals for multi-storied may come up. The authority should take care of these proposals from environmental point of view. Due to helicopter service from Katra to Sanjichat there is constant noise pollution and disturbance to the native animals which needs immediate attention. Continuous movement of vehicles, use of speakers with high intensity by the shopkeepers, and shouting of thousands of visitors here and there, the town experiences noise pollution. Visitors come from all parts of the country and abroad and their behaviour and culture leaves impacts on the local people specially the youngsters are affected more by the behaviour and fashion. Alcoholism, smoking and gambling and also loss of ethics are serious concerns. Besides change of tradition and customs, change in norms, values, duping the visitors etc have arisen. There is an increase in crime rate also. Providing a solution in progress and development of ecotourism in the area will certainly reap the benefits to locals and to the environment in many folds.

Here are few solutions which could bring in some changes in the ways things are done which would lead towards following green practices:

- Home stays should be introduced which would reduce the increasing pressure to construct more hotels.
- Adjoining villages should be involved in tourism activities as they would also be able to distribute the pressure of overcrowding

and help locals to earn money as this would run almost round the year.

- Ecotourism in the adjoining villages could be helpful in creating opportunities in the following ways:
  a) Organic farms could employ locals and could supply fresh vegetables and dairy in market instead of getting from other states.
  b) Poultry farms supplying local breed of fouls and chicken could be helpful.
  c) Horse and pony operators could be trained for eco-tourism tracks and could help in employment.
  d) Local artists manufacturing handicraft and souvenirs could get more exposure and importance.
  e) Musicians and folk dancers platforms to be set up which could get employment and lead to revival of culture.

Jammu and Kashmir has been attracting tourist for nature tourism but it is of utmost importance to save these treasures and enforce Ecotourism for the safeguard of destination itself and for future generations.

Conclusion

This paper identified problems due to overcrowding & unplanned growth at Katra and also provides viable solutions for sustainable development as a long term resolution for local environment and that implementation of above said solutions can make Katra as "Ecotourism destination" which promotes sustainable development and application of green practices more effectively. This would also ensure participation of locals and provide more power in decision making and as is case of Maori communities in Australia where local people were trained to provide ecotourism services which in turn contribute to revive respect for traditions and enhance local livelihoods (Scheyvens, 1999: 246). Providing employment opportunities through ecotourism that endow with a sustainable solution to current job market along with resolving the issues of unemployment as more options are open to tourist in exploring of local areas during the visitation to Mata Vaishno Devi shrine. By following the above options the tourists will get first hand exposure to local culture, environment and help reducing pressure of overcrowding at one particular spot. Also this approach towards sustainability would change the image of Katra town and more and more tourists would support environment which in long run would ultimately coin Katra as an ecotourism destination. To further enhance development of ecotourism there should be special centres called as "Ecotourism Training Centres" to be set up. These centres would undertake duty of training villagers in promoting their profession & enterprise in collaboration of department of tourism, forestry and rural development. "Eco-trainees" should be sent to the states of Sikkim, Andaman and Kerala to understand how ecotourism is developed and is successful. These all solutions would bring a sustainable development where environment will act as its own saviour with the help of locals in the wake of ecotourism.

References

Bagri S.C. and Gupta S.K. (2001) "Tourism and Pilgrimage in Garhwal Himalaya: Planning and Development Issues" in Kandari O.P. and et. al. (edited) Garhwal Himalaya: Nature, Culture and Society, pp. 385-412, Transmedia Media House, Srinagar, Garhwal, India.

Butler, R. (1993). Tourism, an Evolutionary Perspective. In : J.G.Butler, R and Wall, G., Editors, 1993.

Boyd, S.W., 2006. The TALC model and its application to national parks. In: The Tourism Area Life Cycle: Applications and modifications, R.W. Butler (Eds.). Channel View Publications, Clevedon. pp: 119-138.

Butler, R. and Hinch, T. (eds) (1996). Tourism and Indigenous People. International Thomson Business Press, London.

Cohen, R. & Kennedy, P. (2000). Global Sociology. Houndsmills, Basing Stoke, UK: Macmillan Press

Crawley, M., & Gillmor, D. A. (2008). Integrated rural tourism: Concepts and Practice. Annals of Tourism Research, 35(2), 316-337.

Crompton, J.L. (1979). Motivations for pleasure vacations. Annals of tourism research. 6, 408-424.

Conceptualising Integral rural Tourism- Tourism geographies: An International journal of Tourism space, places & environment vol 9 no.4, pp. 347-370.

Dann, G.M.S. (1981). Tourism Motivation: An appraisal. Annals of Tourism Research. 8 (2), 187-219.

East, P.,Lugee, K., and Inmann, K. (eds.) (1998). Sustainability in Mountain Tourism: Perspectives for the Himalayan Countries. Innsbruck-Vienna: Book Faith India and studien Verlag Austria.

FAO (2005) Mountain Tourism: Making It Work for the Poor. Rome: PAIA-MTNS/FAO

Fennel, D. and Smale, B. (1992). Ecotourism and Natural Resource Protection: Implications of an Alternative Form of Tourism for Host Nations. Tourism Recreation Research 17(1): 21-32.

Gonale Guerrero, G. (2009). Community organisation for tourism: A Mexican case study. University of East Anglia, Norwich.

Gurung, D. B. and K. Seeland (2008). "Ecotourism in Bhutan: Extending its benefits to Rural Communities." Annals of Tourism Research, 35(2): 489-508.

Hall C.M. and Boyd, S. (2003) Ecotourism in Peripheral Areas, Channel View Publication, Clevedon, UK.

Hetzer, N.D. (1965) 'Environment, Tourism, Culture', Links (July), reprinted in Ecosphere (1970) 1(2): 1-3.

Johnston, B. (1990). Introduction: Breaking Out of the Tourist Trap. Cultural Survival Quarterly 14(1): 2-5.

Mansfeld, Y. (1992). From Motivation to actual travel. Annals of Tourism Research. 19, 399-419.

Mayo, E.J., & Jarvis, L.P., (1981). The psychology of Leisure Travel: Effective Marketing and Selling of Travel Services. Boston: CBI

Muller, F. (2000). Ecotourism: An Economic Concept for Ecological Sustainable Tourism. International Journal of Environmental Studies 57: 241-251.

Oliver, T., & Jenkins, T. (2003). Sustaining rural landscapes: he role of integrated tourism. Landscape Research, 28(3), 293-307.

Pearce, P., Morrison, A.M., & Routledge, J.L. (1998). Tourism: Bridges across Continents. Sydney: McGraw-Hill.

Pearce, P.L. (1992). Fundamentals of Tourist Motivation. In D.Pearce and R. Butler (Eds.), Tourism Research: Critiques and Challenges. (pp. 113-134). London: Routledge.

Prosser, R. (1994). Societal Change and Growth in Alternative Tourism. In Cater, E. and Lowman, G. (eds.) Ecotourism: A Sustainable Option? Chichester, UK. Wiley: 19-37.

Saxena, G., Clarck, G., Oliver, ., & Illbery, B. (2007). Conceptualising integrated rural tourism. Tourism Geographies, 9(4), 3347-370.

Scheyvens, R. (1999). Ecotourism and the empowerment of local communities. Tourism management, 20(2), 245-249.

Sharma, P. (ed.) (2000). Tourism as Development: Case Studies from the Himalaya. Innsbruck: Himal Books and studien Verlag.

Sindig, I. (1999). Alternative Tourism and Sustainable Development in Kenya. Journal of Sustainable Tourism 7: 108-127.

Uysal, M., & Hagan, L.A.R. (1993). Motivation of Pleasure Travel and Tourism. In M.Kahan, M., Olsen, & var (Eds.). Encyclopedia of Hospitality and Tourism. (pp. 798-810). (New York: Van Nostrand Reinhold).

WADPUD, 1994. Central Coast regional strategy: A Strategy to Guide Land Use in the Next Decade: Prepared for the Central Coast Planning Study Steering Committee as Part of the Strategic Planning Program of the State Planning Commission. 1st Edn., The Department, Perth, W.A., p p: 113.

Weaver, (1993). Ecotourism in the small island carribean, journal, 3,(4), 457-465.

https://www.ecotourism.org/what-is-ecotourism cited on 25.12.2013.

GUEST SATISFACTION IN THE HOSPITALITY SECTOR: A STUDY OF HOTELS IN PUNJAB

Bharat Kapoor

Assistant Professor, School of Hotel Management and Tourism, Lovely Professional University, Jalandhar, bharatkapoor22@gmail.com.

Amrik Singh

Assistant Professer, School of Hotel Management and Tourism, Lovely Professional University, Jalandhar, amrikmhm@gmail.com.

Abstract: One of the biggest contemporary challenges of management in service industries is providing and maintaining guest satisfaction. In order to be successful in the market it is not sufficient to attract new customers managers must concentrate on retaining existing customers implementing effective policies of customer satisfaction and loyalty. In hotel industry customer satisfaction is largely hooked upon quality of service. An organizational approach focused on customer satisfaction can improve customer loyalty, thus increasing the positive image of the touristic destination. Hence, exploring the importance for customers of hotel attributes in hotel selection is indispensable. Research on the topic of guest satisfaction, which translates into the consideration of whether or not customers will return to a hotel or advice it to other tourists, is pivotal to the success of the hospitality business. Neglecting to pay attention to those hotel attributes considered most important by guests, may lead to negative evaluation of the hotel, thus restricting the chance of repeat patronage. We perform a qualitative analysis of a large hotel in Punjab. Through the analysis of this case we evaluate the overall customer satisfaction level for the hotel and for each service supplied. We conclude discussing the result and proposing improvement in customer satisfaction management of the hotel.

Keywords: Customer satisfaction, Hotel industry, Service marketing

Introduction

In a bid to promote Punjab as a major tourist destination, the state is inviting investments from private players in the hotél sector .Guest satisfaction is a business philosophy which tends to the creation of value for customers, anticipating and managing their expectations, and demonstrating ability and responsibility to satisfy their needs. Qualities of service and customer satisfaction are critical factors for success of any business (Gronoos, 1990; Parasuraman et al., 1988). As Valdani (2009) points out: enterprises exist because they have a customer to serve.

The key to achieve sustainable advantage lies in delivering high quality service that results in satisfied customers (Shemwell et al, 1998). Service quality and customer satisfaction are key factors in the battle to obtain competitive advantage and customer retention. Customer satisfaction is the outcome of customer's perception of the value received in a transaction or relationship, where value equals perceived service quality, compared to the value expected from transactions or relationships with competing vendors (Blanchard & Galloway, 1994; Heskett et al., 1990; Zeithaml et al., 1990). In order to achieve customer satisfaction, it is important to recognize and to anticipate customers' needs and to be able to satisfy them. Enterprises which are able to rapidly understand and satisfy customers' needs, make greater profits than those which fail to understand and satisfy them (Barsky & Nash, 2003). Since the cost of attracting new customers is higher than the cost of retaining the existing ones, in order to be successful managers must concentrate on retaining existing customers implementing effective policies of customer satisfaction and loyalty. This is especially true in the hotel industry.

These days one of the biggest challenges for managers in the hotel industry is to provide and sustain customer satisfaction. Customer requirements for quality products and service in the tourism industry has become increasingly evident to professionals (Lam & Zhang, 1999; Yen & Su, 2004). Guest relationships are a strategic asset of the organization (Gruen et al., 2000) and customer satisfaction is the starting point to define business objectives. In this context, positive relationships can create customer's higher commitment and increase their return rate. Hotels are increasing their investments to improve service quality and the perceived value for guests so as to achieve better customer satisfaction and loyalty, thus resulting in better relationships with each customer (Jones et al., 2007). Relationship quality has a remarkable positive effect on hotel guests' behavior: it creates positive word of mouth (WOM) and increments repeated guest rates (Kim et al., 2001).

In this paper, after a review of the main literature on customer satisfaction and retention in the hotel industry, we confront a real case (Hotel Sporting Club of Doaba region, Punjab) and analyze, using a qualitative methodology, whether there is a positive correlation between the customer oriented business philosophy, adopted by the management of Sporting Club, and the achievements obtained in terms of customer satisfaction. We study the case of Sporting Club Hotel using the critical incident approach (Hayes, 2008) with semi-structured and unstructured interviews (Lindlof & Taylor, 2002), that we performed to both management and customers. Our empirical study gathers information by the combined use of different interview methodologies in order to evaluate the influence of customer oriented business philosophy on customer satisfaction. We analyze the results to highlight eventual gaps among managers' expectation and results and to evaluate the overall customer satisfaction level for the hotel and the specific one for each service supplied. We conclude discussing the results and proposing improvements in customer satisfaction management for the hotel.

Literature overview

In the past, tourism has been often considered as the natural outcome of environmental and cultural resources of a specific territory. In this view, the role of hospitality enterprises cannot influence demand levels and is merely limited to the supply of services to tourists. Le Blanc & Nguyen (1996) suggest that marketing efforts should be directed to highlight the environmental characteristics of the location in order to attract new customers. The constant increase of demand of touristic services, and the request for higher standards by the guests, has enforced the competition among hospitality suppliers and highlighted how the attractivity of the touristic destination is influenced by the standards of the services provided by the local hotels.

In this scenario, providing high quality services and improving customer satisfaction are widely recognized as fundamental factors boosting the performances of companies in the hotel and tourism industry (Barsky & Labagh, 1992; Le Blanc, 1992,; Le Blanc et al., 1996; Stevens et al., 1995, Opermann, 1998). Hotels with good service quality will ultimately improve their profitability (Oh & Parks, 1997). In a competitive hospitality industry which offers homogeneous services, individual hoteliers must be able to satisfy costumers better than their counterparts (Choi & Chou, 2001).

To obtain loyalty and to outweigh other competitors, hotel providers must be able to obtain high levels of customer satisfaction for the service supplied. There are several studies that analyze the needs and the desires of tourists. A research by Wuest et al. (1996) defined the perception of hotel attributes as the degree to which guests may find various services and facilities critical for their stay in a hotel. Hotel's attributes such as cleanliness, price, location, security, personal service, physical attractiveness, opportunities for relaxation, standard of services, appealing image, and reputation are recognized as decisive by travelers to assess the quality of the hotel (Atkinsons, 1988; Ananth et al., 1992; Barsky & Labagh, 1992; Cadotte & Turgeon, 1988; Knutson, 1988; McCleary et al., 1993; Rivers et al., 1991; Wilensky & Buttle, 1988).

According to a survey carried out by Barsky & Nash in 2006, regarding the main hotel chains worldwide, between 2002 and 2005, the importance of loyalty programs for guest's decision on where to stay increased from 32% to 34%.Although the search for new locations is certainly the most important factor for many tourists, several studies highlighted that there is a good portion of customers that chose to repeat their holidays' destination, showing a certain degree of loyalty (Oppermann, 1998; Fyall et al., 2003). These studies on tourists' loyalty indicate five main factors which affect the repetition of the trip to the same tourist place: the desire to reduce the risk of making a mistake when choosing an alternative destination; the chance to meet the same people again the emotional affection to a specific place; the possibility to explore the place better ; the desire to show the place to other people. Hoteliers need to fully acknowledge which service attributes are most likely to influence customers' choice intentions (Richard & Sundaram, 1993).

A satisfied guest promotes positive WOM at no cost for the enterprise and with effect and credibility that are superior to those of conventional advertising (Lee et al., 2006, Tarn, 2005, Villanueva et al., 2008). WOM effect is also amplified by the World Wide Web (Dominici, 2009; Trusov et al. 2009).

Customer satisfaction is the starting point to build customer loyalty, therefore a long-term relationship. This creates a loyalty's stock in the enterprise which improves corporate image. The consolidation of relations with guests leads to repeated patronage. On the other hand, an unsatisfied customer may represent a danger for the enterprise. A research, conducted by Cherubini (1997), shows that only 4% of unsatisfied customers complains to the business explaining the reason of their unsatisfaction, and each client who doesn't officially complain generates a negative WOM which can involve also 1000 people.

Hence, both exploring the importance for customers of single attributes in hotel selection and to systematically survey their level of satisfaction are indispensable. Research on the topic of guest satisfaction, which translates into the consideration of whether or not customers will return to a hotel or advise it to other tourists, is pivotal to the success of the hospitality business. Neglecting to pay attention to those hotel attributes considered most important by guests leads to negative evaluations of the hotel, thus restricting the chance of repeat patronage.

Methodology

Measuring guest satisfaction in the hotel industry is important in order to know guests' opinions. Each guest has different expectations about hospitality services, thus it is important to know their impressions not only by aggregated statistics but also singularly; determine the expectations, the needs and the requests of customers; overcome the gaps between customers' expectation and services offered supervise the operations of the enterprise as a system.

Guests' loyalty represents a homogeneous cluster which can be measured using behavioral and attitudinal variables. In our analysis we focus on various hotels in Doaba region, Punjab. We performed the survey during the summer of 2008. In our survey we used both field and desk research methodology.

We started with a "desk" analysis and then we administered a survey to hotel managers and guests then we cross checked the information obtained. In chronological order we proceeded to: analyze the corporate web-page and visit the location in order to verify the truthfulness of the information supplied to customers interview the management of the hotel to verify the existence of a customer oriented philosophy administer a questionnaire to the director of the village to confirm the results of the interview administer questionnaires to 100 guests (on 122 we attempted to interview) of the hotel using the Critical Incident Approach (Hayes, 2008). The Critical Incident Approach focuses on obtaining information from customers about the services and goods they encountered in the past. This approach can be used both for customers and staff. For our analysis we submitted semi-structured interviews to guests. We prepared an interview guide based on the desk research regards the company web-page and their promotional material.

A semi-structured interview is a flexible interview methodology, allowing new questions to be brought up during the interview as a result of what the interviewee says. The flexibility given to answers by this interview methodology gave us the possibility to shed light on particular needs of customers which may not have been perceived by the management. The incidents are then employed to create classes of satisfaction items based on shared common words, used in the incident statement. These satisfaction items are then applied to detect crucial customer quality requirements.

Using the Critical Incident Approach, we interviewed 100 customers with semi-structured interviews, asking each of them to describe 5 positive and 5 negative aspects of the overall service offered by the hotel. The 5 positive aspects are: organization; kids' club; number of services provided; family atmosphere; good entertainment.

We then used semi-structured interviews for the questionnaires about the quality of each service and we administered it to the same target. We classified 52 verbal expressions used by guests to describe specific services supplied. Using the information gathered administering the interviews; we determined the level of customer satisfaction for each service supplied.

To verify the existence of a real customer oriented approach on behalf of the management, we compared, for each service supplied by the hotel, the results regards the perceptions of the quality of services of the management with those of the guests.

Analysis and results

From the unstructured interviews administered to the management, it emerged that Sporting Club Hotel's target are families. Families are considered by the hotel's management the ideal target because they are more sensitive to customer loyalty policies. The hotel has a good repeated patronage rate with 20% of guests that have already spent their holidays in the hotel in the past. The hotel works especially during summer and national holidays and gives several possibilities of trips to visit the main touristic attractions in Doaba region. In 2008 it had about 35.000 guests. Desk analysis shows that the corporate vision refers specifically to customer satisfaction.

Desk analysis and unstructured interviews to management show that customer loyalty programs are promoted and managed by the management and in particular by the head of the marketing office.

The main promotion channels are distribution of promotional material through travel agencies experience trips, where local tour operators, press, opinion leaders are invited to visit the hotel Web-page TV programs to describe the hotel participation to fairs public relations.

Respondents were asked to describe 5 positive and 5 negative aspects about the overall service perception, and could answer with minimum 1 to maximum 2 phrases for each question for the specific services. Verbal expressions obtained have been first grouped by service questioned and expression and then classified according to the judgment of the expression when the interviewee was asked about the service. Appendix shows the results of the semi-structured interviews regarding the attributes and expressions used by interviewees.

What emerges from the semi-structured interviews is an overall positive customer satisfaction level. The main strengths of the hotel are: the restaurant, the entertainment program and the organization; the weaknesses are the beach and the rooms. We compare the results about the managers' perceptions of quality of the hotel's services of the management with those of guests, using the Customer Satisfaction Convergence Matrix (Cuomo, 2000).

Conclusions

Our qualitative analysis of the Sporting Hotel of Doaba region in Punjab shows that the level of customer satisfaction is good both considering the overall evaluation and the single services (6 out of 8 of the single aspects examined). Human resource management in particular results to be especially effective in entertainment and restaurant service.

By interviewing the hotel's management about the results, it emerged that they didn't have the perception of the gaps we found in beach and room services. Though the latter service heavily depends on the quality of the hotel's structure, a certain degree of improvement maybe obtain through a concrete effort towards their customization.

In general, the main factor which limits the Sporting Club Hotel's ability to achieve higher customer satisfaction levels is the standardization of services that reduces the possibility to customize the offer for specific guest needs. Indeed, from the unstructured interviews to the hotel's management it became apparent that the organizations adopts a "push" marketing approach. The offer of touristic services is decided by the management and not in collaboration with customers nor considering their specific needs. Moreover customer satisfaction is not used to differentiate the services supplied.

Another weakness of the customer satisfaction management system of the hotel is that a structured CRM (Customer Relationship Management) system has not yet been implemented. Even if a customer database exists, the data collection is not even planned, and the data gathered can't be easily found and used by management for marketing decisions. Any benchmarking information about customer satisfaction levels is missing, so the management doesn't have a clue about what competitors are doing.

The Sporting Club hotel has a good potential to satisfy customers and compete, but to improve its customer satisfaction standards the management needs to adopt new and more advanced CRM procedures. The decision process about the key issues regarding customer satisfaction should not be based only on accounting and cost data, but also on a customer database created ad hoc.

Even if the case we studied has been chosen because it is representative of other similar businesses in the area, the main limit of this research is that it is circumscribed to only one hotel. We plan in the near future to make other qualitative analysis on other hotels in the same area and compare the results in order to obtain a wider view about customer satisfaction in Punjab hotels.

References

Atkinson, A. (1988). Answering the eternal question: what does the customer want? The Cornell Hotel and Restaurant Administration Quarterly, 29(2): 12-14.

Ananth M., DeMicco F.J., Moreo P.J., & Howey R.M. (1992). Marketplace lodging needs of mature travelers. The Cornell Hotel and Restaurant Administration Quarterly, 33 (4): 12-24.

Atkinson A. (1988). Answering the eternal question: what does the customer want?. The Cornell Hotel and Restaurant Administration Quarterly, 29 (2): 12-14.

Barsky J., & Labagh R. (1992). A strategy for customer satisfaction. The Cornell Hotel and Restaurant Administration Quarterly 35 (3): 32-40.

Barsky J., & Nash L. (2003). Customer satisfaction: Applying concepts to industry- wide measures. The Cornell Hotel and Restaurant Administration Quarterly, 44 (4): 173-183.

Barsky, J., & Nash L. (2006). Companies update loyalty programs, increase effectiveness. Hotel & Motel Management, 22(11): 28-29.

Berkman H.W., & Gilson C. (1986). Consumer Behavior: Concepts and Strategies, 3rd ed., Kent, Boston.

Blanchard R.F., & Galloway R.L. (1994). Quality in retail banking. International Journal of Service Industry Management, 5 (4): 5-23.

Cadotte E.R., & Turgeon N. (1988). Key factors in guest satisfaction. The Cornell Hotel and Restaurant Administration Quarterly, 45-51.

Choi T. Y., & Chu R. (2001). Determinants of hotel guests' satisfaction and repeat patronage in Hong Kong hotel industry. International Journal of Hospitality Management, 20: 277-297.

Cuomo M. T. (2000). La Customer Satisfaction, vantaggio competitivo e creazione di valore. Cedam, Padua.

Dominici G. (2009). E-Marketing. Analisi dei cambiamenti dai modelli di business al mix operativo, FrancoAngeli, Milan.

Fornell C. (1992). A national customer satisfaction barometer: the Swedish experience. Journal of Marketing, 56: 6-21.

Fyall A., Callod C., & Edwrds B. (2003). Relationship Marketing: The Challenge for Destinations. Annals of Tourism, 30 (3): 644-659.

Gronoos, C. (1990). Service management and marketing: managing the moments of truth in service competition. Lexington Books, USA.

Gruen T. W., Summers J. O., & Acito, F. (2000). Relationship marketing activities, commitment, and membership behaviors in professional associations. Journal of Marketing, 64 (3): 34-49.

Halstead D., & Page Jr. T.J. (1992). The effects of satisfaction and complaining behavior on consumers repurchase behavior. Journal of Satisfaction, Dissatisfaction and Complaining Behavior, 5: 1-11.

Hayes B. E. (2008). Measuring Customer Satisfaction and Loyalty, 3rd edition, ASQ Quality Press, Milwaukee, USA.

Heskett J.L., Sasser W.E., & Hart C.W.L. (1990). Breakthrough Service. The Free Press, New York.

Jones D. L., Mak B., & Sim J. (2007). A New Look at the Antecedents and Consequences of Relationship Quality in the Hotel Service Environment. Services Marketing Quarterly, 28(3): 15-31.

Kandampully J., & Suhartanto D. (2000). Customer loyalty in the hotel industry: the role of customer satisfaction and image. International Journal of Contemporary Hospitality Management, 12 (6): 346-351.

Kim W. G., Han J. S., & Lee E. (2001). Effects of relationship marketing on repeat purchase and word of mouth.

Journal of Hospitality & Tourism Research, 25 (3): 272-288.

Knutson B. (1988). Frequent travelers: making them happy and bringing them back. The Cornell Hotel and Restaurant Administration Quarterly, 29 (1): 83-87.

Kotler P., Bowen J.T., & Makens J.C. (2010). Marketing for Hospitality and Tourism 5th edition, Pearson.

Lam T., & Zhang H. (1999). Service quality of travel agents: the case of travel agents in Hong Kong. Tourism Management, 20: 341-349.

LeBlanc G. (1992). Factors affecting customer evaluation of service quality travel agencies: an investigation of customer perceptions. Journal of Travel Research 30 (4): 10-16.

LeBlanc G., & Nguyen N. (1996). An examination of the factors that signal hotel image to travelers. Journal of Vacation Marketing 3 (1): 32-42.

Lee J., Lee J., & Feick L. (2006). Incorporating word-of-mouth effects in estimating customer lifetime value.

Journal of Database Marketing & Customer Strategy Management; 14 (1): 29-39.

Lindlof T. R., & Taylor B. C. (2002). Qualitative communication research methods 2nd edition. SAGE Publications.

McCleary K.W., Weaver P.A., & Hutchinson J.C. (1993). Hotel selection factors as they relate to business travel situations. Journal of Travel Research, 32 (2): 42-48.

Parasuraman A., Zeithaml V., & Berry L. (1988). SERVQUAL: a multiple-item scale for measuring consumer perceptions of service quality. Journal of Retailing, 64 (1): 12-40.

Oh H., & Parks, S.C. (1997). Customer satisfaction and service quality: a critical review of the literature and research implications for the hospitality industry. Hospitality Research Journal, 20 (3): 35-64.

Oppermann M. (1998). Destination Threshold Potential and the Law of Repeat Visitation, Journal of Travel Research, 37 (2): 131-137.

Pizam A. (1994). Monitoring customer satisfaction, in: Davis, B., Lockwood, A. (eds.), Food and Beverage Management: A Selection of Readings, Butterworth-Heinemann, London.

Richard M.D., & Sundaram D.S. (1993). Lodging choice intentions: a causal modeling approach. Journal of Hospitality and Leisure Marketing, 1 (4): 81-98.

Rivers M.J., Toh R.S., & Alaoui M. (1991). Frequent-stayer programs: the demographic, behavioral, and attitudinal characteristics of hotel steady sleepers. Journal of Travel Research, 30 (2): 41-45.

Shemwell, D.J., Yavas, U., & Bilgin, Z. (1998). Customer-service provider relationship: An empirical test of a model of service quality, satisfaction and relationship-oriented outcome. International Journal of Service Industry Management, 9: 155-168.

Tarn D. (2005). Marketing-based tangibilisation for services. Service Industries Journal; 25 (6): 747-772.

Trusov M, Bucklin R., & Pauwells K. (2009). Effects of Word-of-Mouth Versus Traditional Marketing: Findings from an Internet Social Networking Site. Journal of Marketing, 73 (5): 90-102.

Valdani E. (2009). Cliente & Service Management, Egea, Milan.

Villanueva J., Yoo S., & Hanssens D. (2008). The Impact of Marketing-Induced Versus Word-of-Mouth Customer Acquisition on Customer Equity Growth. Journal of Marketing Research (JMR),45 (1): 48-59.

Vijayadurai, J. (2008). Service Quality, Customer Satisfaction and Behavioural Intention in Hotel Industry.

Journal of Marketing & Communication, 3(3): 14-26.

Wilensky L., & Buttle F. (1988). A multivariate analysis of hotel benefit bundles and choice trade-offs.

International Journal of Hospitality Management, 7 (1): 29-41.

Wuest B.E.S., Tas R.F., & Emenheiser D.A. (1996). What do mature travelers perceive as important hotel/ motel customer service?, Hospitality Research Journal, 20 (2): 77-93.

Yen A., & Su L. (2004). Customer satisfaction measurement practice in Taiwan hotels. Hospitality Management, 23: 397-408.

Zeithaml V., Parasuraman A., & Berry L.L. (1990). Delivering Quality Service. The Free Press, New York.

ENVIRONMENT FRIENDLY PRACTICES ADOPTED BY THE HOTEL TO PROMOTE SUSTAINABLE TOURISM: A CASE STUDY OF THE HOTEL CABBANA, PHAGWARA, PUNJAB

Divoy Chhabra

Lecturer, School of Hotel Management and Tourism Lovely Professional University Phagwara, Punjab, Pin - 144401.divoychhabra@gmail.com

Sanjeev Sharma

Assistant Professor, School of Hotel Management and Tourism Lecturer, School of Hotel Management and Tourism Lovely Professional University Phagwara, Punjab, Pin - 144401.

Abstract: The Hotel sector is regarded as an industry of which activities constitute a greater impact on the environment both positively as well as negatively. But it can be said that negative impacts on the environment are more if it has not adopted any environmental friendly measures. Hotels consume vast amount of energy, water and non-durable goods, and discharge a huge amount of raw and solid waste in different quantities to the natural areas like water bodies. As this is a very common problem for the tourist destinations calling for greater hotel's participation in sustainable tourism practices by committing to environmental management system (EMS). This paper tries to find out sustainable tourism practices most commonly can be adopted by hotels as well as the practices which are being followed by the Hotel Cabbana which is also known as Ecotel Hotel as a case study. The main findings are mainly the environmental friendly practices such as energy saving measures, as well as the use of energy-efficient equipment and products. Adopting these practices the hotels of this region can gain benefit from improved image to the guests and the local communities as well as the enhancement of a safe and healthy environment for hotel guests and employees.

Keywords: Sustainability, Environmental friendly practices, Hotels, Environmental management

Introduction

The tourism economy represents 5 per cent of world GDP, while it contributes to 6-7 per cent of total employment. International tourism ranks fourth (after fuels, chemicals and automotive products) in global exports, with an industry value of US$1trillion a year, accounting for 30 per cent of the world's exports of commercial services or 6 per cent of total exports; 935 million international tourists were recorded in 2010 and 4 billion domestic arrivals in 2008. In over 150 countries, tourism is one of five top export earners, and in 60 it is the number one export. It is the main source of foreign exchange for one-third of developing countries and one-half of Least-developed countries.

The rapid growth in both international and domestic travel, the trends to travel farther and over shorter periods of time, and the preference given to energy-intensive transportation are increasing the non-renewable energy dependency of tourism, resulting in the sector's contribution of 5 per cent to global Green House Gas emissions. Other challenges include excessive water consumption compared with residential water use, discharge of untreated water, the generation of waste, the damage to local terrestrial and marine biodiversity, and the threats to the survival of local cultures, built heritage and traditions.

Ecotourism is a form of tourism involving visiting fragile, pristine, and relatively undisturbed natural areas, intended as a low-impact and often small scale alternative to standard commercial (mass) tourism. Its purpose may be to educate the traveler, to provide funds for ecological conservation, to directly benefit the economic development and political empowerment of local communities, or to foster respect for different cultures and for human rights. Since the 1980s ecotourism has been considered a critical endeavor by environmentalists, so that future generations may experience destinations relatively untouched by human intervention.

Ecotourism focuses on socially responsible travel, personal growth, and environmental sustainability. Ecotourism typically involves travel to destinations where flora, fauna, and cultural heritage are the primary attractions. Ecotourism is intended to offer tourists insight into the impact of human beings on the environment, and to foster a greater appreciation of our natural habitats.

Eco-tourism activities should follow the following principles:

- Minimize impact
- Build environmental and cultural awareness and respect
- Provide positive experiences for both visitors and hosts
- Provide direct financial benefits for conservation
- Provide financial benefits and empowerment for local people
- Raise sensitivity to host countries' political, environmental, and social climate
- Support international human rights and labour agreements

Overview of Hospitality Industry

The hospitality industry is an umbrella term for a broad variety of service industries, including, but not limited to, hotels, restaurants, casinos, catering enterprises, resorts, and clubs. The industry is very diverse and global, and is greatly impacted by fluctuations within the economy as also by various happenings across the world. As per the Wikipedia: "Hospitality is the act or practice of being hospitable, that is, the reception and entertainment of guests, visitors, or strangers, with liberality and goodwill. Hospitality frequently refers to the hospitality industry jobs for hotels, restaurants, casinos, catering, resorts, clubs and any other service position that deals with tourists."

Hospitality Industry comprising a hotel & catering Industries is one of the fastest growing industries in the world. In the global contest to the sector has witnessed booming growth in the past decades or two especially after the opening of the economy. Besides India with its reach historical past & varied geographical locations like hill stations & beaches has always been a very attractive tourist destination. Efforts by the Govt. to promote India as a prime tourist destination in the world as paying dividends & there has been a definite increase in the volume of the international tourists visiting the country. More encouraging has been the steady growth in the number of Indians traveling within the country both for the pleasure & business as fall out of the increasing levels of income & education. All these have augured well for the hotel industry which has grown tremendously both in terms of capacity & service.

Impact of the operations of tourism Industry on the Environment

The tourism industry faces a multitude of significant sustainability-related challenges. These challenges include:

1. Energy and GHG emissions;
2. Water consumption;
3. Waste management;
4. Loss of biological diversity; etc.

There are a number of key areas within a hospitality establishment that need to be considered when reducing negative environmental impacts. Like:

1. **Energy Management:** The hospitality sector is a huge consumer of energy. Methods for managing energy in hospitality establishments can include:
   - Reduction in energy consumption, i.e. switching off air-conditioning units when not in use, blocking sun with window tinting and/or blinds, installing solar hot water heaters
   - Replacement of old equipment, i.e. Purchasing of high energy efficient equipment
   - Regular maintenance of equipment, i.e. enforcing a fixed maintenance schedule to keep equipment running appropriately.
   - Replacement of fossil energy sources with renewable ones available locally, such as wind or sun (solar power)

- Phase out of CFCs (chlorofluorocarbon) in refrigeration products and replacement with internationally accepted agents

Resource Management:

- Reduction in use of paper products and increased use of recycled paper (e.g. 20 cases of recycled paper substituted for non-recycled paper save 17 trees, 1476 liters of oil, 264986 liters of water, and 4100 kWh of energy)
- Reduction in use of plastic/products and increased use of recycled plastic/other packaging material
- Recycling all waste material - To facilitate disposal and recycling, waste should be separated into the following areas and disposed to establishment standards:

Paper:	Cardboard, paper, containers, packaging
Plastic:	Packaging, bags, bottles wrappers
Glass:	Bottles, broken glass, containers, jars
Food Waste:	Unusable waste scraps, trimmings, old oils, etc. (used oils and fats should never be poured down drains, they should be poured into drums and collected by a contractor)
Metal:	Aluminium cans - an aluminium can saves energy to run a television set for three hours

Chemical Waste—should be handled according to the manufacturer's instructions and in compliance with local government and environmental regulations. Toxic chemical waste should not be poured down sinks, and used bottles or containers will require special disposal procedures. Refer to the procedures in place at your workplace in relation to the safe disposal of these products

Composting yard and kitchen waste that can then be used as alternative source for gas

Water Management:

- Water-efficient technology, i.e. low-flow showerheads and taps fitted with flow restrictors, which reduce water wastage, check for leaking tap

- Rainwater harvesting, i.e. utilising rainwater from the roofs to supply water for toilets, laundry and gardening, minimising wastage of rainwater
- Grey water system, i.e. treating water with low pollutants from sources like the laundry room, sinks and showers and then diverts it for other uses like watering of garden.

Need for Eco-Friendly Practices:

Travel and tourism are human-resource intensive, employing directly and indirectly 8 per cent of the global workforce. It is estimated that one job in the core tourism industry creates about one and a half additional or indirect jobs in the tourism-related economy. The greening of tourism, which involves efficiency improvements in energy, water, and waste systems.

Introduction to Hotel Club Cabbana and its Eco Friendly Practices

Hotel Cabbana is a 5 star hotel in Jalandhar with a lavish property sprawling across 17 acres of lush greenery. Aiming to be the best luxury hotel in Punjab, the property has incorporated every possible amenity and provides a dedicated service to make the experience here one of a lifetime.

The hotel offers 47 excellently appointed rooms and 4 lavish suites. All guest rooms come with the most luxurious fittings and best of facilities. Hotel Cabbana also offers a unique spa experience with the right fusion of age-old therapies and modern spa technologies. State-of-the-art Gymnasium, therapy rooms, sauna facilities and Jacuzzis are also available to guests here.

A good number of restaurants and bars have also been created here, catering to diverse needs. From casual drinking to fine dining Hotel Cabbana has it all. While 'Fusion' lets you dine on mouth-watering sizzlers and house smoke grills, '888' serves you the most exotic drinks and mocktails. Club Cabbana provides all modern facilities to enhance stay experience and make holidays memorable.

Eco Friendly Practices followed at Hotel Club Cabbana

a) Club Cabbana follows an Environment Policy which follows the following principles:

- Optimizing the usage of Resources such as Energy, Water and Paper.
- Striving to go beyond the applicable Environmental Laws and Ecotel requirements.
- Continue pollution prevention practices.
- Implementing Environmental Awareness in our Suppliers, Team members, Guests and the Local Community.

b) 3 R Theory

- Reduce
- Recycle
- Reuse

c) Environment 5 Globes

- Solid Waste Management
- Energy Efficiency
- Water Conservation & Preservation
- Environmental Commitments
- Employee Environmental Education & Community Involvement

d) Four Garbage Bin Theory

- Red bin ------ for non-recycle material (oily papers, painting material, oily waste product)
- Green bin ------ for recycle material (wood, paper, card boards)
- White bin ------ for dry garbage (empty bottles, plastic bags, glass, empty cans)
- Black bin ------ for wet garbage (waste food)

e) Solid Waste Management

- Old discarded Bed Sheets, Towels and Napkins issued by housekeeping dept. are used for cleaning purpose.
- Most of fabrication works and festival decorations are carried

out departmentally with scrap material.

- Used and replaced nut bolts and other hardware items are reused by cleaning, greasing and de rusting them.
- The empty tins of paints are used for storing of spares and hardware items.
- Discarded bamboo, choir rope, bricks are used for festival decorations.
- Water level controllers are efficiently used for water boilers, steamers and bain-marie to prevent burning out of heating elements (coils) due to lack of water in the heating pan.
- Imported equipments are normally repaired / modified by either repairing the parts or by locally available ones.
- Papers are reused on both sides, and envelopes are reused for mailing of letters.
- Rechargeable batteries are used for U.P.S; Emergency lighting system.
- Black boards are used for displaying messages and daily consumption. (Messages to dept. staff regarding pending jobs. Daily consumption for knowledge of all)
- Photocopies on both sides of paper.
- Print on both the sides of the paper.
- Printed computer stationary used for as rough pads.
- Reusing envelopes by writing the guest name & room number by pencil,
- News papers are offered on request as per their choice.
- Common newspaper rack made of rubber wood placed in the lobby.
- Brochures/tariff cards are distributed only on request. Every year we change our published tariff & on the balance brochure we reprint the new tariff instead of printing new ones.

f) Energy Conservation Practices

- 20W and 40W Tube lights with energy saving chokes

- All lights are CFL Lamps.
- Electronics Master Control panel in guest rooms controls lights and A/C unit has a unique feature of a green button, pressing which the thermostat of the A/C unit steps up by two degrees thereby saving energy. All lights are also put off when the key card is removed.
- All the tube lights in public area are having energy saving ballasts that reduce the power consumption by 25%.

g) Air Conditioning Plant

- The refrigerant used in A/C plant is eco-friendly alternative i.e. R22 instead of CFC refrigerant. The Mono Screw Chillers, which have the least no. of moving parts, operate on 25% to 100% loading steps. (Demand Base Control)
- All other refrigeration units including walk-in coolers, deep freezer etc. uses 134 A & 404 A gases that are environmentally friendly.
- The hot discharged gas of the compressor is utilized for heating the water at 50 degree C. before it enters the condensers. This process eliminates the requirement of Boilers. (hot water production)
- Screw chiller 70 tons and 56 tons.

h) Energy Saving Button

- By pressing Button from 26 deg C to 28 deg C = Saving is 2 deg C
- Water flow per FCU per hour 3.6 GPM x 3.75 ltr x 60 minutes x 2 deg C = 1620 liters (kcal/h)
- 1620 liter converting to watts (Power consumption)
- 1 liter or 1kg of water heating or cooling power requirement 1.163 watts
- 1620 × 1.163 = 1884 watts x PF 0.85 = 1601 watts
- 1620 watts / 1000 watts = 1.60 kw

  Since the power saving is 1.60 kw saving in Rs.1.6kw × Rs. 7.0 per units = Rs. 11.20 per hour

If the guest press for 6 hours = 1.6kwh × 6 = 9.6Kwh

Example: - Average 30 % Guest press the Eco - button and average 70 % occupancy in 36 Room's.

= 25 room's × 1.6 Kwh x 6 Hrs. × Rs.7 per unit = 1680Rs. / Day

i) Water Conservation and Preservation

- Aerators are used in all the taps to reduce consumption. (Increase of pressure and decrease of volume)
- Sensors are fitted to wash basin taps, urinals in public areas.
- Guest Room Showers are specially designed for discharging of 10 liters. Of water per minute.
- Guest Room W.C. is attached with Cistern flushing System which flushes 6 liters of water per flush instead of 15 - 20 liters.
- Back wash water of water filtration plant is collected back in flush tank which reduces the intake water supply.
- Water level controllers are fitted with all water tanks to avoid overflowing of water and to stop the pumps.
- Periodic back wash of sand and carbon filters and regeneration of resin filter is carried out to maintain good quality of water.
- Sign board is displayed on every tap as "Save Water" for educating the users.
- Regular checking of tap leakages and attending to it. (Replacing of worn out washers and spindles).
- Use of bottles for drinking water in the department, (for total consumption, and no wastage).

j) Employee Education and Community Involvement

- Regular refresher classes are taken on ECOTEL Practices.
- Interaction with visiting students from various schools and colleges and briefing them about ECOTEL practices followed in the kitchen. Case in point-Veermata Jijabai Technological Institute on 18-10-2008,Ramniranjan Jhunjhunwala College

- Team members are encouraged to take part in various competitions and events organized by the CABBANA Green Team. Photos of kitchen team
- Pest control classes taken by Mr. Rudy of Victor Pest Control.

Summary and Conclusion

This paper outlined and studied the eco-friendly practices by the hotels in implementing environmental practices within their organizations. Many owners and managers are concerned with short term profitability and the need to meet budgets and deadlines. The implementation of an environmental strategy requires time and an investment outlay in order to achieve long term sustainability. There are a number of hotel managers who believe the introduction of environmental practices and policies can often be a deterrent for guests as they associated environmentally friendly hotels as lacking in luxury products and services. It is clear that the price sensitive guest does not want to pay for green initiatives and guests searching for a luxury break do not want to sacrifice their levels of comfort for the sake of the environment.

There is a resistance by managers to undertake formal environmental management programmes. This is due to lack of knowledge and training and also the investment in time, money and resources that is required in order to comply with standards and procedures leading to additional barriers to implementation. Hotel club Cabana is a good initiative in the environmental sustain practices as well as the contribution in the development of the society by contributing in various ways. This hotel can be used as a role model in further development of the development of sustainable tourism in this region.

References

Carter, E. (1994). Eco Tourism: A Sustainable Option? John Wiley & Sons, Brisbane, 3-18.

Edward J. J. (2007). Incorporating Sustainability into Community Development. Retrieved February 5, 2007, from http://www.planetizen.com/node/22756.

Fleischer and Pizam, A. (1997). Rural tourism in Israel, Tourism management, 18(6) Elsevier Science Ltd, 367-372

Gangte, M. (2011). The Paradise Unexplored In India. Retrieved June 1.2011, from http://www.morungexpress.com/analysis/66403.html

Hall, C. M. & Boyd, S. (Eds.) (2005). Nature-based Tourism in Peripheral Areas: Development and Disaster? Channel View Publications, Clevedon. ISBN: 1-84541-000-9 (Pbk) ISBN: 1-8541-001-7 (Hbk).

Hall, D. (2000). Tourism and Sustainable Community Development; Sustainable Development Tourism, London, Routledge. 48, 15.

PROMOTING CULTURE: A STUDY OF HOSPITALITY MANAGEMENT INSTITUTES OF UTTARAKHAND VIS-À-VIS BY REGIONAL CUISINE AND ITS DEVELOPMENT

Gaurav Garg

Associate Professor Amrapali Institute of Hotel Management, Shiksha Nagar, Haldwani gary281178@gmail.com

Vikash Prasad

Assistant Lecturer Dr. Ambedkar Institute of Hotel Management Chandigarh vikash.ihmghy07@gmail.com

Abstract: Uttrakhand, long called adobe of the gods has a culturally colorful society. The religious, social and cultural urges of the people finds an expression in various fairs & festivals. The region has a rich and ancient culture & shows a distinctive pattern with the elements from each of the ethnic groups and sub - group that reside in this place. It can be said that the cultures of Uttrakhand is a juncture where different cultures of the Kumauni - Garhwali meet. Uttrakhand socially houses seven different cultures.

Uttrakhand belongs to some of the holiest Hindu shrines and for more than a thousand years, pilgrims have been visiting this region in the hope of salvation and purification of sin. Being such an old pilgrimage destination the cuisine of this northern state has never received much attention. No region can be considered to possess a robust cooking cultural heritage if the cuisine is not up to mark. The culture of Uttrakhand has maintained a good standard of culinary system. The Pahari Cuisine has a tremendous capacity to heal and nurture the human life in the most purified form. The food has been cultivated in a more original way of ages which helps the locals to live a very healthy life in such tough conditions.

Being a tourism state Uttrakhand has become a hub of hotel management institutes. These institutes can play a vital role in the promotion of regional cuisine. It can be used as a platform, where regional cuisine can be researched on and hidden treasures can be explored to provide a new dimension to the tourism sector. They are required to practice the art of nurturing the region so as it would turn itself into a tourist attraction.

Keywords: Regional Cuisine, Garhwali Cuisine, Kumauni Cuisine, Hotel Management Institutes, Cultures.

Introduction

Uttaranchal is a culturally colorful society. The religious, social and cultural urges of the people of Uttaranchal find an expression in various fairs and festivals, which are in turn closely linked to the social and economic activities of the region. Uttarakhand State was carved out of the state of Uttar Pradesh on November 9, 2000. It is divided into two broad regions--Garhwal and Kumaon. The state is comprised of 13 districts, namely, Chamoli, Pauri, Tehri, Uttarkashi, Dehradun, Haridwar and Rudraprayag in the Garhwal region and Nainital, Almora, Pithoragarh, Udham Singh Nagar, Champawat and Bageshwar in the Kumaon region. Of these 13 districts, four districts (Nainital, Haridwar, Dehradun and Udham Singh Nagar) have large areas in the plains, whereas the other nine districts comprise the hill region of the state. Uttarakhand, in spite of being a small state, has certain key features that make it distinct from other states of the country and highlights its potential for development. However, development has predominantly been in the plains and the hill districts have been left behind.

All the hill districts have subsistence farming as their main economic activity. Due to subsistence livelihood, migration and a remittance economy operate in the hill districts. They are land-locked with huge distances between the markets and resources. Because of these constraints, traditional agriculture cannot be the lead sector for development. Thus the state faces the challenge of promoting livelihoods to minimize migration through local employment and income generation, and to enhance the quality of life of people living in villages. The positive features of these hill districts are that they have enormous potential for tourism, a suitable climate for high-value agriculture, and a pleasant environment due to 60 percent forest cover. These have to be harnessed for a development strategy. The development strategy for Uttarakhand hills should be based on developing brand equity under the name of Organic Green State and an **Uttarakhand Brand Equity Fund** should be set up. This can be achieved by working towards this common goal through infrastructure development, tourism promotion, agriculture diversification, poultry- and wool-based livelihoods, and SMEs based on the above that capture linkages with industry and tourism. At the same time, the hill districts of Uttarakhand have tremendous potential. The vast natural resources add to the state's attractiveness as an investment destination, especially for tourism and agriculture- and forest-based industries. Uttarakhand is the first state in the country to have created a Tourism Development Board by legislation. Also, it is the first one to be called an organic state.

The tourism industry is a major contributor to the economy of Uttaranchal, with the Raj era hill-stations at Mussorie, Almora, Ranikhet and Nainital being some of the most frequented destinations. To this region also belong some of the holiest Hindu shrines, and for almost 2000 years now pilgrims have been visiting the temples at Haridwar, Rishikesh, Badrinath and Kedarnath in the hope of salvation and purification from sin. Recent developments in the region include initiatives by the state government to capitalize on the burgeoning visitor trade. The state also plays host to some of the worst conceived big dam projects in India such as the monstrously large Tehri dam on the Bhagirathi-Bhilangana Rivers.

Tourist: A Boon to the Region

The Tourism Sector has a tremendous flow of tourist be it Inbound or Outbound & same for the Foreign Tourist. The stats show a considerable growth of travelers in India (Table No.1) for the foreign Tourist. The marginal reduction in the growth rates can be categorized due to various reasons especially decrease in the world economic growth rate.

Table No. 1

Year	FTAs in India	Annual Growth (%)
2000	2649378	6.7
2001	2537282	-4.2
2002	2384364	-6.0
2003	2726214	14.3
2004	3457477	26.8
2005	3918610	13.3
2006	4447167	13.5
2007	5081504	14.3
2008	5282603	4.0
2009	5167699	-2.2
2010	5775692	11.8
2011	6309222	9.2
2012	6577745	4.3

Source: Bureau of Immigration, India

It is apparent in Graph 1 that numbers of foreign tourist visits to States/ UTs during last 10 years have been consistently registering an increasing trend, except for marginal decline in foreign tourist visits in the years 2001, 2002 and 2009. The domestic tourism has also grown by leaps and bounds in India.

Graph No. 1

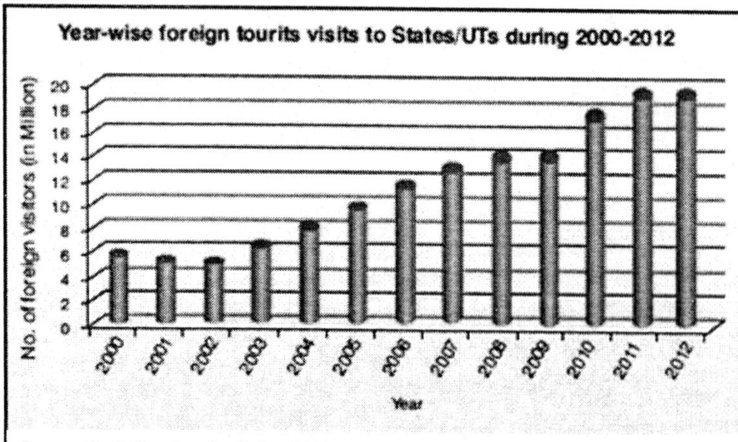

Source: IndiaTourism Statistics-2012

The Table No. 2 shows the exact position of the domestic traveler. Graph 2 clearly represents the details discussed above. It is apparent that numbers of domestic tourist visits to States/UTs during last 10 years have been consistently registering an increasing trend.

Table No. 2

Year	Tourist Visits		Annual Growth Rate	
	Domestic	Foreign	Domestic	Foreign
2002	269598028	5157518	14.0%	-5.1%
2003	309038335	6708479	14.6%	30.1%
2004	366267522	8360278	18.5%	24.6%
2005	392014270	9947524	7.0%	19.0%
2006	462321054	11738892	17.9%	18.0%
2007	526564478	13256637	13.9%	12.9%
2008	563034107	14380633	6.9%	8.5%
2009	668800482	14372300	18.8%	-0.1%
2010	747703380	17910178	11.8%	24.6%
2011	864532718	19497126	15.6%	8.86%
2012	1036346657	20731496	19.87%	6.33%

Source: Indian Tourism Statistics-2012

Domestic and Foreign Tourist visit to Sates /UTs 2002-2012

Graph No. 2

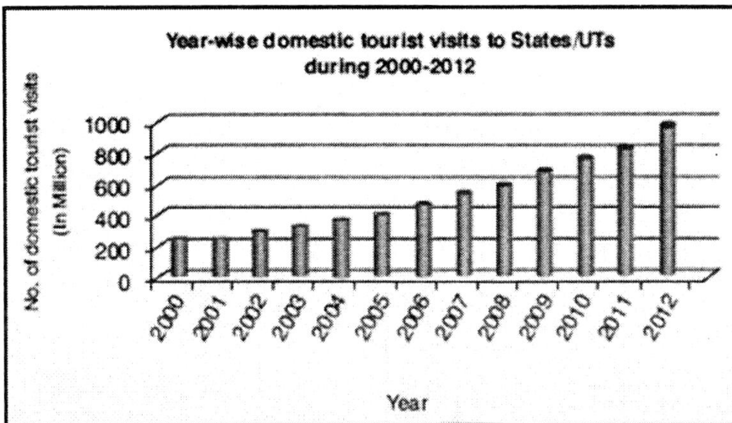

Source: Indian Tourism Statistics - 2012

In many words Tourism has been a main attraction for Uttarakhand Especially Domestic. This can be clearly proved by the statistics provided by MOT thru Indian Tourism Statistics -2012.

Domestic tourism has increased in Uttarakhand by 3.1% which is evident in Table No.3. Yes, there has been a decline in the Foreign Tourism by -0.8%.

Table No. 3

State/ UT	2011		2012		% Growth (2012/11)	
	Domestic	Foreign	Domestic	Foreign	Domestic	Foreign
Haryana	5968062	130435	6799242	233002	13.55	78.63
Himachal Pradesh	14604888	484518	15646048	500284	7.13	3.25
Jammu & Kashmir	13071531	71593	12427122	78802	-4.93	10.07
Jharkhand	10796286	72467	20421016	31909	89.15	-55.97
Karnataka	84107390	574005	94052729	595359	11.82	3.72
Kerala	9381455	732985	10076854	793696	7.41	8.28
Lakshadweep	9424	567	4417	580	-53.13	2.29
Madhya Pradesh	44119820	269559	53197209	275930	20.57	2.36
Maharashtra*	55333467	4815421	66330229	5120287	19.87	6.33
Manipur	134505	578	134541	749	0.03	29.58
Meghalaya	667504	4803	680254	5313	1.91	10.62
Mizoram	62174	658	64249	744	3.34	13.07
Nagaland	25391	2080	35915	2489	41.45	19.66
Odisha	8271257	60722	9052871	64719	9.45	6.58
Puducherry	897896	52298	981714	52931	9.33	1.21
Punjab	16416638	150958	19056143	143805	16.08	-4.74
Rajasthan	27137323	1351974	28611831	1451370	5.43	7.35
Sikkim	552453	23602	558538	26489	1.1	12.23
Tamil Nadu	137512991	3373870	184136840	3561740	33.91	5.57
Tripura	359515	6046	361786	7840	0.63	29.67
Uttar Pradesh	155430364	1887095	168381276	1994495	8.33	5.69
Uttarakhand	25946254	124653	26827329	124555	3.4	-0.08
West Bengal	22256968	1213270	22730205	1219610	2.13	0.52

Source: Indian Tourism Statistics-2012

Graph 3 clearly shows the percentage of the top 10 states in context to the domestic tourism and Uttarakhand still has a comparatively fair share if kept in mind its inception and foundation. Foreign Tourist has marginally rejected Uttarakhand and that is where the State Ministry needs to concentrate and develop to make it a positive affair.

Graph No 3

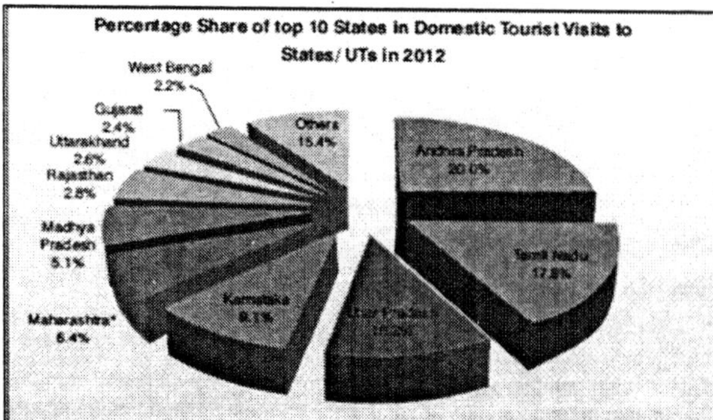

Source: Indian Tourism Statistics-2012

Table No. 4 reflects Uttarakhand at 8th position in the overall Domestic Tourist Sector while the foreign picture is a bit grim as it slides down to 17th position. There is a requirement of an aggressive policy to develop the tourism culture in the state to improve the position.

Table No 4

State/ UT	Tourist Visits (Numbers)		Percentage Share		Rank in 2012	
	Domestic	Foreign	Domestic	Foreign	Domestic	Foreign
Punjab	19056143	143805	1.84	0.69	13	16
Rajasthan	28611831	1451370	2.76	7	7	5
Sikkim	558538	26489	0.05	0.13	27	23
Tamil Nadu	184136840	3561740	17.77	17.18	2	2
Tripura	361786	7840	0.03	0.04	29	26
Uttar Pradesh	168381276	1994495	16.25	9.62	3	4
Uttarakhand	26827329	124555	2.59	0.6	8	17
West Bengal	22730205	1219610	2.19	5.88	10	6

Source: Indian Tourism Statistics-2012

Tourist arrivals in Uttarakhand can be studied as consistent till 2012. The below Table No. 5 uploaded on the official website shows the steady flow of tourist has gradually increased in the state.

Table No. 5

Tourist Statistics of Uttarakhand Year 2000 to 2012

(in Lakh)

Sl	Year	Dom.	For.	Total
1–	2000	110.79	0.57	111.36
2–	2001	105.49	0.55	106.04
3–	2002	116.52	0.56	117.08
4–	2003	129.30	0.64	129.94
5–	2004	138.30	0.75	139.05
6–	2005	162.81	0.93	163.74
7–	2006	193.58	0.96	194.54
8–	2007	221.54	1.06	222.60
9–	2008	230.64	1.12	231.76
10–	2009	231.54	1.18	232.72
11	2010	309.72	1.36	311.08
12	2011	266.66	1.43	268.09
13	2012	282.92	1.41	284.33

Source. www.uttarakhandtourism.gov.in/tourist statistics of year 2000-2012.pdf

Culture: Relation with the Regional Cuisine

The region of Uttarakhand can be broadly divided into two regions when we have to discuss about the cuisine. The Pahari cuisine as it is popularly known has Garhwali cuisine and Kumauni Cuisine. Both these cuisines have a different regional influence on their food and still are considered as same. The cuisine has influence of the geographic location, invasions, foreign settlers in the region and even the developmental activities that have undergone in the past decade of its existence.

Food is one of the major concerns when traveling in any distant land. So fret not because the cuisine of Uttaranchal has diverse flavors, colors and ingredients. The Himalayan state of Uttarakhand has an uncomplicated yet mouth-watering cuisine. The food is tremendously wholesome to suit the high-energy necessities of the mountainous and wintry region. Natives of Uttaranchal mostly eat a vegetarian meal though mutton and chicken are also savored. Rice is the indispensable food for the people of Uttaranchal. In Uttarakhand, Hash seeds, locally known as 'Bhang' are used as an essential spice.

Though the basic ingredients of both Garhwali and Kumauni cuisine are the same, there are some basic differences that tell apart the two. The distinctive trait of the Kumauni cuisine is the tightfisted use of especially milk and milk-based products as cows from hilly areas do not yield high-quality or amount of milk. The similarity between both of them is the liberal use of Ghee (clarified butter) and charcoal cooking. Both Garhwali and Kumauni are fond of lentil or pulses and 'Bhatt' or rice. To combat the extreme winters and possible exhausting of food, they also use Badi (sun-dried Urad Dal balls) and Mangodi (sun-dried Moong Dal balls) as substitute for vegetables at times.

Kumaun is one of the two regions and administrative divisions of Uttarakhand, a mountainous state of northern India, the other being Garhwal. It includes the districts of Almora, Bageshwar, Champawat, Nainital, Pithoragarh, and Udham Singh Nagar. It is bounded on the north by Tibet, on the east by Nepal, on the south by the state of Uttar Pradesh, and on the west by the Garhwal region.

Important towns of Kumaon are Haldwani, Nainital, Almora, Pithoragarh, Rudrapur, Kashipur, Pantnagar, Mukteshwar and Ranikhet. Nainital is the administrative centre of Kumaon Division and this is where the Uttarakhand high court is located.

Kumaon has its own distinct and impressive traditions, festivals and fairs. Its people are brave, hard-working and honest and its cuisine is high on taste and nutrition. The food habits of Kumauni's change according to the seasons. So if in winters, Manira, Til Laddus or Madua Rotis are preferred, in summers, Dubukas with Cholia Rotis are savored. To actually enjoy a calm, cool and enchanting trip to Kumaon, tourists should not miss the exquisite cuisine and enchanting culture of the region. The cuisine is also influenced by the settlers from the other states especially Punjab and Uttarpradesh. The use of spices in the cuisine favors the Punjab region while the use of whole wheat flour pre-nodes the neighboring state. The famous food of Kumaun includes Baante (A special dish made with Radish and Yoghurt), Karaal(An Urad dal Preparation considered to be very healthy), Moong dal Dubka(A kind of Lentil Soup served with Bhatt and especially savored in Winters), Aloo ke Gutke(Local Fried potatoes cooked with cumin and other spices to perfection even with bhang seeds), Palyoo(A curry made from sour yoghurt and pakoras similar to the Punjabi Kadhi), Churkhani(A Kumauni version of a Black Bean Soup with the correct amount of garam Masala), Kappa(A dish made with spinach having a course texture of vegetable and similar to the Saag), Rus(a dal made out of combination of various lentils and served with steamed rice and a good amount of ghee before serving) etc. The food completely supports the lifestyle of the locals and the less use of milk is completely visible in the cuisine. Although the infusion of milk and milk products have changed the cooking styles of the locals however the deep rooted use of ingredients still remain the same for the locals and especially the hill settlers.

Garhwal is the north-western region and administrative division of the northern Indian state of Uttarakhand which is home to the Garhwali people. Lying in the Himalayas, It is bounded on the north by Tibet, on the east by Kumaon region, on the south by Uttar

Pradesh state, and on the north-west by Himachal Pradesh state. It includes the districts of Chamoli, Dehradun, Haridwar, Pauri Garhwal, Rudraprayag, Tehri Garhwal, and Uttarkashi. The people of Garhwal are known as Garhwali and speak the Garhwali language. The administrative center for Garhwal division is the town of Pauri.

The Cuisine has a very distinct flavor and cannot be termed under one head. However the food is considered to be healthy and full of nutrients and is constituted with the ingredients of hot and cold characteristics. Some of the main dishes served in the Garhwal Region are Chainsoo (A Roasted Black Gram Dal Preparation which has a high percentage of protein content), Kafuli (A spinach leaves preparation like a thick gravy), Jholi (A gravy made out of tubers and root vegetables and bodied with curd), Phaanu (A lentil preparation made out of different lentils, similar to Chainsoo but with overnight soaked lentils), Thechwani (crushed into pieces of raddish or potatoes and made into a curry), Baadi (Made from mandua Flour and best accompanied with Gahat ki Dal), Roat and Arsa are some of the brads used here. Apart from this Gahat dal, Madhua ki Roti, Jhangore ki Kheer, Saani Mooli aur Nimbu and the famous Baal Mithai are common dishes found in both the regions.

The cuisines of both the regions are similar yet different and they combine together to make the Uttarakhand cuisine. The food has a huge variety of dishes and preparations and especially a huge bank of herbs and spices and rare herbs that is used in the cooking with the traditional food, which helps in the survival of the locals in such an arid climate and yet it provides a soothing effect to the taste buds.

Methodology

The data was collected from a sample of 300 tourists visiting various sites in Uttarakhand and a feedback with the help of a detailed Questionnaire was taken regarding various aspects of regional cuisine. The Tourists who responded were 184 males and 116 females. 102 tourists were in the age group of 20-25 years, 84 were in the age group of 25-30 years, 76 were in the age group of 30-35 years, 21 were 35-40 years and 17 were above this age group. 60% were there on vacation and leisure purpose, 24% were for Business purpose and the rest were for religious reasons. The result has been discussed under the following heads and a brief conclusion was derived from it after analyzing the answers given by the tourist.

- The tourists visiting the region were asked about the regional cuisine. The derived response from the questionnaire is as follows along with its graphical representation.

Barely aware	197
Little knowledge	58
Aware	20
Good Knowledge	15
Excellent knowledge	10

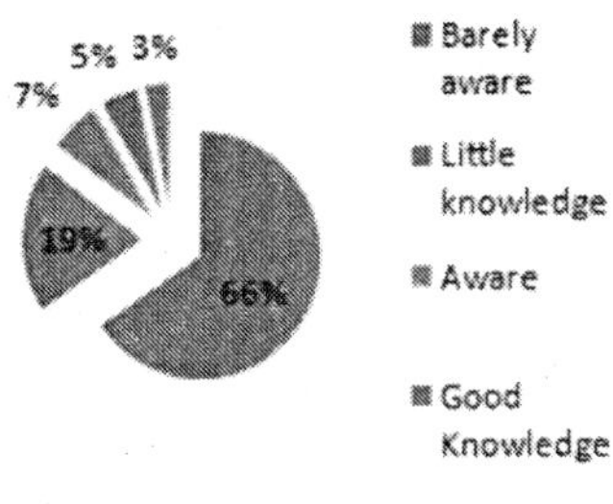

Awareness of the tourist towards Pahari Cuisine

Perceived Result:

The result clearly shows a vast percentage of the tourist having bare minimum or in-fact no knowledge about the regional cuisine which clearly indicates the popularity of the regional cuisine compared to the other cuisines like Punjabi, Gujarati or even South Indian for instance.

- The tourist were asked about the promotional activities they found on the various sources regarding the region or its cuisine

Internet	115
Magazines	42
Friends	56
Newspapers	27
Others	35

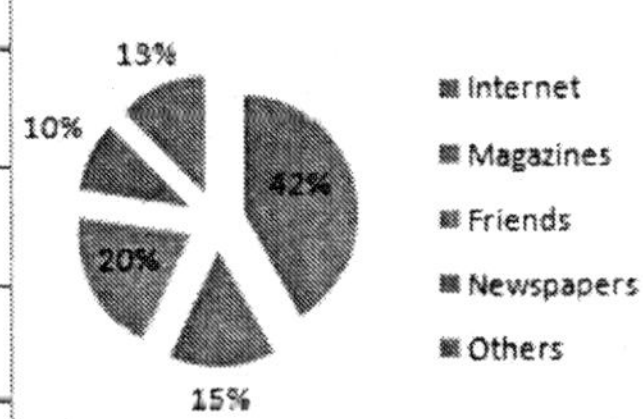

Promotional activities in the region/cuisine

Perceived Result:

This shows the tourist got the awareness about the culture, places and other information from the various sources and predominantly from the web services. The tourist visiting the region is not only educated but also net savvy and likes to use the internet for finding the information

- The tourist were requested to provide the details of the information regarding the food of Uttarakhand on these sources of information

Poor	186
Satisfactory	15
Informative	15
Educating	10
Exciting and interesting	5

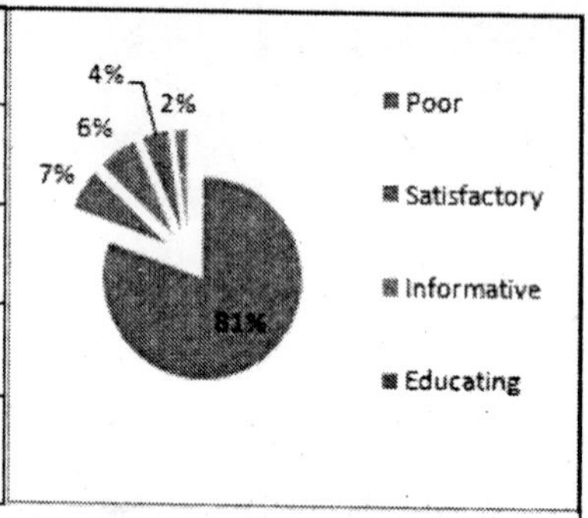

Information regaring Cuisine on various sources

Perceived Result:

The results from not all of the respondents, gives us a clear indication about the promotion of food on these sources of information and makes the food in this region on a back foot and a least priority commodity used for marketing and promotional purpose.

- The Tourist were asked if the restaurants they used the services of provided them with any regional cuisine, dishes if any

Never	215
Once	10
Not frequently	3
Frequently	1
Regularly	0

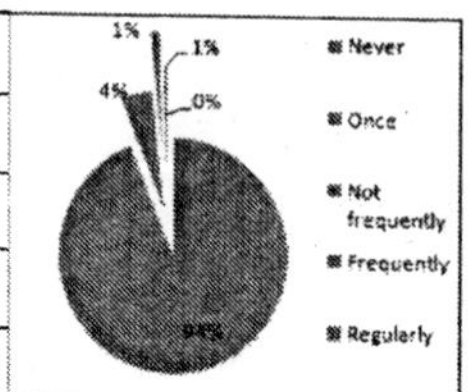

Regional Cuisine served at place of accomodation or visit

Perceived Result:

The result indicate over a serious problem of the locals not taking interest of promoting their regional food and barely someone might find some dishes of the regional cuisine in a eatery or probably by roadside in a shack especially cooking meat. There were no restaurants serving authentic regional food in the region.

These are some of the indicators of the situation or one would say the position of our own regional cuisine in the region of Uttarakhand. This denotes the interest we as natives are taking to promote a cuisine which if explored can be of a great help not only from the culinary aspect but from the view of promoting the tourism of the region by discovering various avenues useful in the field of medicinal food, rustic cuisine, or even an indicator to represent the culture of the region. The promotion of the cuisine can be a great help to even nurture the cultural cuisine which has been a hidden or an undercover secret for centuries which will definitely help the economic growth of the region. This can be developed in an industry which can have the support of various pillars like the excellent soil culture, the freshness of the policy making, the infrastructural development happening in the region and educating the benefits of the promotion to the locals and making them a part of the promotional campaign so as they could also benefit along with the regional economy.

When we discuss about the various aspects of the development happening in the region one must have in the mind that the promotion can be tapped at a very early stage by the tourism sector as they have the biggest workforce suitable for this job. The work force is none other than the budding hoteliers and the hospitality graduates passing out every year from the hotel management colleges from the region.

Uttarakhand from its existence from the year 2000 has seen the development of various hotel management colleges in the region. Today the total number of colleges affiliate to various universities, either state or from outside, count up to 150 in numbers and an average of 6000 students are getting into the industry every year.

All these students study the hotel management curriculum as prescribed by the affiliated universities. The students have various topics regarding the managerial or the management of the hotels. We ask a question to the authorities as to why don't we have a subject to promote the entrepreneurship in students at this very stage. The students have topics like Hotel Law, then why not a subject where the student can learn how to become a future entrepreneur. Students should be given a detailed insight as to how to set up a small restaurant and what are the pre requisites for setting up of the business.

The Authorities should have a look at the curriculum which has not been reviewed since its inclusion and if it has been then why has none of the learned men thought about the position of our regional cuisine in the curriculum. The curriculum as attached Appendix 1 clearly shows the weight-age given to the regional cuisine in the theory and practical aspects.

The student is aware of their regional cuisine as they have been savoring the food since birth. They can be the best judge and the best critics for the regional food. It is the responsibility of the university, which is also a governmental body, to help the Hospitality management institutes to nurture these students so as to make them efficient enough to become the Brand Ambassador for the region. They, even if settled outside the region, should be in a continuous process to promote their regional cuisine. They should promote the regional food at the hotel level whenever they get a chance. Organizing of regional food festivals, Themes can be one aspect and even introducing some dishes in their menus can be a step toward promotion.

Today the region require a lot of promotion and especially the culture as the new breed is getting away from their roots and getting influenced by the westerners. The role of Hospitality Management Institutes becomes that much more important when we talk about the research work done in the field of regional cuisine in the region. The Institutes are required to encourage the good deed. However only the Institute cannot be responsible for the research work, but the University and even the government should have an insight into promoting the research work so as to benefit from it during promotion of the culture in the region.

Suggestions

The detailed study of the regional cuisine, its position in the region, various avenues for promoting the tourism and culture of the region and the role of hospitality management institutes in the development of the region has led to various suggestions that can be categorized as below

- The Government should promote the regional cuisine as it is one of the most easily and effective factor for increasing the awareness of the culture of the region.
- The Universities should have a rain check being done about the editing of the curriculum that is required so as to promote tourism by making a stronger student as a brand Ambassador.
- The Hospitality Management Institutes should be inclined towards promoting the students to conduct more and more research work for the promotion of tourism.
- The Authorities should set up a fund which would facilitate the researchers to conduct various researches in the field of regional cuisine which will promote the tourism and cultural heritage.
- The authorities should make necessary amendments in the curriculum to have future prospects of students converting into entrepreneurs in the region and help in promoting the regional cuisine.
- The Government should help and support these entrepreneurs by providing them various subsidies for setting up of restaurants and food outlets which will have the authentic regional food served. This will also create awareness about the regional cuisine along with the promotion of the culture.
- The government should organize in collaboration with the Hospitality Management Institutes various food festivals to create awareness in the people about the regional cuisine
- There should be an effort made towards discovering more medicinal food items which can be used to promote a different

kind of tourism as in case of Kerala (Ayurvedic oils, Massages, etc). We can utilize the natural herbs for the promotion of the cuisine by creating a new line of dishes in collaboration with the Institutes.

- The Institutes can help in making the authentic dishes more presentable to the tourist which in their original form might not look such appealing.

References:

Department of Food, Ministry of Agriculture, Archive 1962

Indian Tourism Statistics Report for year 2000-2012, Market Research Division, Ministry of Tourism, Government of India.

Uttarakhand Tourist Statistics Report for Year 2000-2012

Quinn, J. and Purcell, K., "Exploring the education - employment equation in hospitality management: a comparison of graduates and HNDs", Proceedings of the Third Annual CHME Research Conference, Napier University, Edinburgh, April 1994.

Barron, P. and Maxwell. G., "Students' perceptions of the hospitality Industry - reality or chimera?", Proceedings of the Second Annual CHME Research Conference, Manchester Metropolitan University, Manchester, April 1993.

Collins, A.B. (2002). Gateway to the real world, Industrial Training: dilemmas & problems. Tourism Management, Vol. 23, 1 Feb. pp93-96

Barrows & Bosselman; Hospitality Management Education,

LeBurto, S, & Murray, K. (1994) The Educational value of captive hotels. The Cornell HRA Quaterly, 35, (4), 72-79

Tas, R. (1988) Teaching Future Managers. The Cornell HRA quarterly, 29(2), 41-43

Walo, M. (1999) The Latest win win strategy in recruiting hotel staff; Hotel Management, 12(7), 32-33

Kumaon University Archive

Uttarakhand Technical University Archives

Uttarakhand Open University Archive

Uttarakhand Technical Board of Education Archives

Industrial Training Manual, AIHM, 2012

ITDC Industrial Training Manual

Ministry of HRD, Govt. of India official website

Teaching material available in A.I.H.M Haldwani, Nainital, Library

A REVIEW PAPER ON MANAGING AND DEVELOPING ORGANISATIONAL CULTURE IN HOSPITALITY INDUSTRY

Himanshu Malik

School of Hotel Management & Tourism,

Lovely Professional University himanshu.18051@lpu.co.in

Abstract: The traditional approaches to strategy that are adopted by managers do not recognise the importance and power of culture as an integrating and unifying "driver" of action within organisations. Organisational culture affects organizations (both positively and negatively). Corporations that have been successful in establishing and fostering strong culture perform better. The author finds that an effective culture must be aligned with employee values and should be consistent with the environment in which the organization operates. While it is best to establish a strong culture during an organization's infancy, it is also possible to change an existing culture. Such change is best accomplished by modelling desired behaviour at all levels of management and by planning events that foster frequent interaction among cross-functional employees.

Keywords: Organisational culture, Hospitality, Managing, Developing.

Introduction

To write a review paper about the concept of organizational culture is very exciting as it is a very interesting phenomenon that deals with values and beliefs of members with in an organisation and can bring a distinct advantage to the organisation once managed and developed in an appropriate manner. Though initially it is difficult to understand and differentiate it from culture in anthropology on the grounds of what the concept does and should mean and how it should be used in our efforts to help organizations. This paper is an attempt to find out answer to these questions.

According to the Webster's dictionary, culture is the ideas, customs, skills, arts, etc. of a given people in a given period. Astute managers have realized that any organisation also has its own corporate culture. Kumar 2006, in his research states that the concept of culture is taken from the field of Anthropology. The term culture is widely used by sociologists, anthropologists and behavioural scientists. Culture means symbols and value; which is strong widely shared core values; and is also looked upon as the moral spiritual and intellectual attainment of man. Culture provides a harmonious and balanced development of all the senses in man, intellect, emotion, intuition, and perception. Culture is the most important and basic element; it is inside in every human being and is what we are. Culture plays the role of a mentor, which makes human being substantiate to accepted ways of life. It is the flesh as well as the spirit. It releases as well as enslaves him. It defines the norms of behaviour and provides the mechanism, which secure an individual his personal and social survival.

Luthans (2011), identifies organizational culture as a pattern of basic assumptions-invented, discovered, or developed by a given group (organisation) as it learns to cope with its problems of external adaptation and internal integration-that has worked well enough to be considered valuable and, therefore, to be taught to new members as the correct way to perceive, think, and feel in relation to those problems. The concept of organizational culture is different from sociological concept of culture. Social culture is the mean to an end, the end being the holistic development of one's own personality and one's own society. Although, the concept of organisational culture is generally derived from its Anthropological equivalent into, the context of an organisation is very different from that of the societies with which Anthropologists and Social theorists are typically concerned. Organisations are bounded, purposive and intentionally structured in ways that societies are not, and where as societies embrace their member's lives, organisations like other institutions are directly concerned with only part of those lives.

Organisational culture is seen as a component by Jarad (2010) that determines the appropriateness of a firm's activities that can contribute to its performance. In fact, organizational culture is not just an important factor of an organisation; it is the central driver of superior business performance. He also states that a strong market culture drives organisational performance and success.

The present research focuses on to studying organisational culture, in reference to hospitality industry, through various researches conducted in the last decade. Further the research will suggest how organisational culture can be managed and developed in an organisation with the help of same.

Objectives

Following are the objectives of this research:

1. To study organisational culture as a concept through review.
2. To suggest measures for managing and developing organisational culture.

Research design

The research is designed to be conducted by using the existing research done in the context of organisational culture with hospitality industry. The process will consist of identifying the studies done in the last decade on the topics of organisational culture and its understanding in hospitality industry. The next step will be to review all the identified study and understand the concept of organisational culture in hospitality industry, and study its effect on organisation and then to give suggestions for managing and developing organisational culture in the hospitality industry.

Literature review

Organisational culture can be described as a system of meanings which are commonly adopted by the members of an organisation which differentiates one organisation from the other. Further the core of an organisation's culture can be identified by certain traits like innovation and risk taking, attention to detail, outcome orientation, people orientation, team orientation, aggressiveness and stability. (Robbins et al, 2012).

Culture is described as an invisible power of any organization by Kondalkar (2007). He further states when working and thoughts of employees are institutionalized, an organizational culture is formed, organisational culture guides the employees, organizational culture is not in the organisation from the beginning it is framed over a period of time, it has to be invented and later developed over a period of time, It enables employees to perform within the framework of the organization's culture. Thus organisational culture is farmed over a period of time and it is referred as organisation of values and beliefs of members in an organisation.

The concept of organizational culture has been defined in a number of ways. Lau and Ngo (1996) explain that organizational culture is a combination of things and understanding that are commonly shared among organizational members. Philosophies, ideologies, values, assumptions, expectations, perceptions, norms, sayings, behaviour, heroes, and traditions are some of these common things, there maybe more. In their study Lau and Ngo identified four components of organisational culture namely general cultural characteristics, leadership style, institutional bonding and strategic emphases. These four components are considered to represent four types of culture. First is group culture which is primarily concerned with human relations and focuses on flexibility and the internal organization. Second, developmental culture also focuses on flexibility and change but this is concerned with the external environment in relation to growth, resource acquisition, creativity, and adaptation. The third rational culture has a stress on productivity, performance, goal fulfilment, and achievement. While the fourth, Hierarchical culture deals with internal stability, uniformity, coordination, and efficiency within organisation.

MacIntosh and Doherty (2010) state that employee's insight of the nature and strength of organisational culture is an important component for human resource management, change management, leadership, work related behaviour and attitudes that can influence performance. Author also said that values and beliefs that inspire organisational culture reflect the organisational leader's priority and main reason for existence of organisation. Profitability is the main purpose of existence of any organisation and one of the critical components to increase performance is to study organisational performance, Abu-Jarad et al. (2010). The authors further state that there is an optimistic relationship linking organisational culture and organisational performance. Strong culture establishes the suitability of the activities that add to the performance of the organisation as organisational culture is the essential driver for outstanding business performance. Organisational culture as described by Robert et al (2012) is the precise compilation of values and norms that are mutual to the people and groups in an organisation and that organize the mode they cooperate with each other and with the stakeholders external to the organisation. In the impressive amount of literature Wang G.L. (2012) mentioned that some studies concerning organizational culture highlights the four concepts of "consensual culture", "developmental culture", "rational culture" and "hierarchical culture", a fact that exactly matches the model of organizational-culture dimensions proposed by Quinn & McGrath (1985). Organisational culture is the basic pattern of shared assumptions, values, and beliefs considered to be the correct way of thinking about and acting on problems and opportunities facing the organization. It defines what is important and unimportant in the company. One might think of it as the organisation's DNA-invisible to the naked eye, yet a powerful template that shapes what happens in the workplace. The person known for notable association with study of organisational culture Edgar (2004) states in his book that it is a concept and the forces that are shaped in social and organisational situations, drawn from culture, are powerful. If one does not recognize the function of these forces, he becomes victim to them. Therefore, organizational culture, which is the philosophies, ideologies, values, assumptions, beliefs, expectation, attitudes and norms that are shared by its employee and help the organization in keeping it intact.

The findings of the various studies have led the researcher to conclude that if the organisational culture is effective and efficient in the organisation, it helps to increase the performance among the employees ultimately resulting high performance organisational culture. Organisational culture still does not have a unique definition, however defined as: The dominant values espoused by organisation, the philosophy that guides policies towards employees and customers, the way things are done in and around organisation, the basic assumptions and beliefs that are shared by members of the organisation (Robbins, 2009). Literature pertaining to organisation culture constantly reinforce that culture is imperative for organisational culture and change effort, deployment of human resources and to large extent aid in sustaining competitive edge (Raduan et al, 2008). Organisational culture is increasingly understood as a critical element in the creation of high performance workspaces. The advantage of knowing the company culture is that it provides an overarching structure that helps organize the sub cultural elements (Tharp, 2010). The organisation with higher degree of shared beliefs and values will be able to differentiate itself from the others. The organizations to promote a shared vision to individuals working in the organisation need leaders who have the ability to facilitate emotional involvement in that vision (Peter, 2004). Organizational culture and climate of the organization are the crucial variables to raise the motivation among the employees (Kaur, 2009).

Organisational culture is really a kind of image for the company which top management would like to project. The image of the organisation differs according to where you view it. Even in companies with strong cultures the social distance between senior management and lower level employees can be very wide. Cultures are hardly planned or predictable; they are the natural products of social interaction and evolve and emerge over time. So is it valid to allow such a notion of culture to give way to a version of managed consensus? Researchers have believed that cultures can be shaped to suit strategic ends; many highlighted the idea that organizations have the capacity to transform themselves from within. The literature reviewed so far suggested that organisational culture is an unavoidable rather most important component of any organisation which once nurtured effectively provides a competitive advantage to any organisation that makes it important for organisation to manage and develop the organisational culture within. Ahmad et al (2013) in their study on organisational culture of hotels in Kashmir highlighted that there is a significant variation between existing and preferred organisational culture in the hotels. They continue that hotels need to focus on the desired organisational values especially involvement, participation, organisational change and innovation and it is an important factor for hotels to be responsive to improve hotel revenue. Kondalkar (2007) discussed the model for managing organisational culture, which is quite similar to Robbins (2012) how organisational cultures form, shown in figure 1. Both the authors emphasize on the fact that organisational culture starts with the philosophical values, beliefs and attitude of the founder of organisation and further proceeds with his understanding of whether the members he is fitting into the organisation as top managers have the same values, beliefs and attitude or will adopt the same values, beliefs and attitude. The next step in framing of culture in an organisation is how the top management passes on these values, beliefs and attitude to the new employees who keep on joining the organisation through the times. When the values, beliefs and attitude of the founder, top management and employees merge together in an organisation organisational culture is formed for that particular organisation. The difference of opinion Kondalkar has about the model can be looked on as an improvement. The author's stress is on the fact that if the top management is aware of the power of organisational culture as strength of organisation in competitive environment it can be managed in the framing process though an element of further development in future should always be kept in mind.

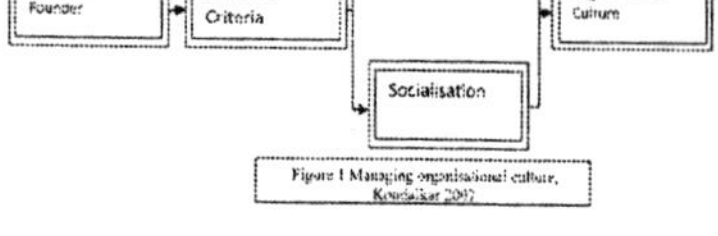

Figure 1 Managing organisational culture, Kondalkar 2007

Zdenko et al (2011) in their effort to study the impact of national culture on hotel organisational culture put stress on realization that organisational culture is not monumental, but there is a existing, prevailing culture and a number of subcultures which develop within a corporation as the interest group, formed on the basis of shared characteristics Ahmad (2013) highlighted that organisational changes have been proved most important, for hospitality organisations in this competitive era of rapid external and internal changes and development. He further states that in order to be effective hotel organisations should continuously develop the relationship between preferred organisational values and organisational outcomes. Shahzad et al (2012) also recommended through their study that mangers should focus on developing a strong organisational culture in order to improve the performance. The author related the development of organisation with employee's performance which he later related to the development of a strong organisational culture. Measuring organisational effectiveness was considered and important tool in development of organisational culture by Lee and Tseng(2005). Khan (2005) quoted that top management can promote the development of organisational culture by hiring people who share the same values and vision that the organisation represents. Employers can ensure this by making a new employee spend time with prospects before they enter the organisation as members. Once new hires are indoctrinated with the organisation's values, they will form an objective perception of the environment that will solidify the organisation's culture. Hotel organisations have to deal with employees and guest coming from different cultural backgrounds that makes it very important to develop a learning organisational culture. While dealing with the management and development of organisational culture, it is very important to identify the existing or new target culture in sufficient detail related to the attributes of the myths, symbols, rituals, values and assumptions that underline the culture.

Findings

After reviewing the selected literature in sufficient detail it was identified by various authors that organisational culture is framed in an organization with the values beliefs and attributes of the founder and how it is passed on to the top management for socializing in to employees which when institutionalized is considered as organisational culture. On the other side authors identified that culture is an invisible but strong factor for any organization which is when managed and developed accordingly creates competitive advantage for the organisation.

Suggestions

a) Leaders in hospitality can develop organisational culture through steady signals, systems of participation that encourage commitment, vibrant illustrations of normatively suitable or inappropriate behaviors, and the provision of rewards, both formal and informal, which will reinforce the desired attitudes and behaviors.

b) In order to develop Organisational culture the supervisor should show their keen interest in development of employee's skills and should develop a relationship of mutual trust.

c) A specific culture evolution program should be developed in each hospitality organisation the program will typically include a balanced mix of both formal and informal mechanisms.

1. Interventions will work best when incorporated into the "real" day-to-day work of the organisation.
2. The interventions selected must address the specific behaviors that the organisation wants to alter.
3. Interventions should be balanced and address both the rational and emotional side of the changes being undertaken.
4. All intervention mechanisms (formal and informal) should be reinforcing and consistent.
5. The program should occur at various levels of the organisation simultaneously and ensure cross organisational energy and support (e.g., it is vital that more junior-level employees see senior executives role-modeling the behavior types that they are being asked to perform).

Conclusion

The organisational culture and its perceived role in organisational success are matched on the basis of perceptions of culture either as a historical base, change-resistant, deep social system which underpins all organisational strategy and action, or as just one aspect of the total organisational system and this aspect of organisational system is transformable though surface structures such as rewards. The perspective adopted will determine the focus of the organisation, development and maintenance of organisational activities, that is, whether they are to involve the whole organisation, identified sub-cultures, or small cells brought together for specific projects. There are no definitive answers to questions about the most appropriate way to manage or develop organisational culture in order to provide for success or, indeed, whether management or development is required in a given context

References

Kumar, D. 2006. Impact of organisational culture upon employees and employer's behaviour. Thesis submitted to Mahatma Gandhi University

Luthans, F. 2011. Organisational behaviour an evidence based approach, 12th edition, McGraw hill publication, pp 71.

Robbins, S, P. Judge, T, A., and Vohra, N. 2012. Organisational Behaviour, Pearson publication, pp 506.

Lau, C, M., and Ngo H, Y. 1996. One Country Many Cultures: Organizational Cultures of Firms of Different Country Origins, International Business Review. 5(5):469-486.

Maclntosh, W. E., and Doherty, A. 2010. The Influence of Organisational Culture on Job Satisfaction and Intention to Leave, Sports Management Review.13: 106-117.

Abu-Jarad, I. Y., Yusof, N., and Nikbin, D. 2010. A Review Paper on Organisational Culture and Organisational Performance. International Journal of Business and Social Science. 1(3): 26-46.

Robert, G. E., Ioannis, I., and George, S. 2012. The Impact of a Corporate Culture of Sustainability on Corporate Behaviour and Performance. Harvard Business School, Working Paper.

Wang, G. L. 2012. A Study of How the Organizational Culture of International Tourist Hotels Affects Organizational Performance: Using Intellectual Capital as the Mediating Variable. The Journal of Global Business Management. 8(1): 189-201.

Edgar, S. 2004. Organisational culture and leadership. 3rd edition. published by Jossey-Bass Wiley imprint: 24.

Ahmad, L. M., Ahmad, F. S., and Ahamd, T. 2013. Organizational Culture in Hotel Industry: Perceptions and Preferences among Staff. Advances in management. 6: pp. 55-60.

Kondalkar, V. G. 2007, Organisational behaviour. new age international publisher.: 335, 337.

Robbins, S. P., and Mary, M. 2009. Organizational theory structure, applications and design. ISBN 9788131717301.

Raduan, C. Rose., Naresh K., Haslinda A., and Goh, Y. L. 2008. Organizational Culture as a Root of Performance Improvement: Research and Recommendations. Contemporary Management Research. 4 (1):43-56.

Tharp, B. M., Diagnosing Organizational Culture 2010, Organizational Culture White Paper Haworth.

Peter, J. J. 2004. Dealing With Organisational Change: Can Emotional Intelligence Enhance Organisational Learning?. International Journal of Organisational Behaviour. 8 (1): 456-471.

Kaur, P. 2009. Organizational Culture and Organizational Climate as a Determinant of Motivation. Journal of Management Research. ©3 8 IUP.

Shahzad, F., Luqman, R. A., Khan, A. R., and Shabbir, L. 2012. Impact of Organizational Culture on Organizational Performance: An Overview, Interdisciplinary Journal of Contemporary Research in Business. 3(9) .: 975-985.

Lee, T. Z., and Tseng, Y. F. 2005. A Study of the Relationship between Organizational Culture and Organizational Effectiveness of the Electronic Industries in Taiwan. Mathematics of Optimization: Methods and Practical Solutions. Departmental Bulletin Paper. :161-178.

Khan, A. 2005. Matching People with Organizational Culture, CEO Business Management Group. Inc. ©. : 6.

Pimapunsri, P. 2008. Factors affecting Learning Organization Culture and hotel managers' Leadership Styles in Thailand. Educational Journal of Thailand. 2 (1) : 34-43.

Zdenko, C., Sanda, G. K., and Marta, C. 2011. The Impact of National Culture on the Hotel Organizational Culture. 12th Management International Conference. : 1185-1198

CONVERTING INDIAN NUPTIALS INTO TOURISM PRODUCTS

Imosongla Jamir

Dept. of Tourism, Hotel, Hospitality and Heritage Studies, Jamia Millia Islamia, New Delhi 110025, India, amyxjamir@yahoo.com

Abstract: India is the country of rich culture, traditions history, civilization, and dazzling diversity is a heaven for those who want to wed the love of their life in memorable way.

The present paper examined the scope of wedding tourism business in India as a wedding. From grand palaces, forts, hills and temples to serene beaches, India has lot to offer to make your marriage a dream come true. Anyone can choose contemporary or traditional theme as per your preferences. The days will not be far away when Ministry of Tourism's campaign promote India as "Marriage Tourism" product as new destination in the world.

Indian marriages are known for the variety of color, boogie music, numerous traditions and customs, spectacular meals, flowers and an ocean of emotions. Every state of the India has different wedding ceremony.

Many married people visit India to explore the tradition with experience of magic of Indian marriage. The famous beach wedding destinations are Kovalam Kerala, Varkala, Kerala, Hotel Taj Exotica, Goa, Fort Aguada, Goa and Anjuna beach, Goa offering a grand fiesta. India has many palaces and forts where you can marry like a king and a queen. Palaces and forts have larger than life ambience and royal charm in India which includes Umaid Bhawan Jodhpur, Samode Palace, Jaipur, Taj Lake Palace, Rajasthan, Udaipur Devi Garh

Palace, Mandvi Palace in Kutch and The Palace, Utelia amongst others. This day certainly grasps a unique meaning in every one's life and if anyone want to celebrate his/her marriage in an Indian manner it sure means a lot of rites and rituals. Getting Married in India is undisputedly a very novel and unique affair and that makes me realize how better we can promote the wedding tourism in India. An attempt has been made in this paper to point out the experiences on the emerging potential in Wedding Tourism.

Keywords: wedding, marriage, culture, palace, Rajasthan, etc.

Introduction

Weddings and honeymoons tourism is a form of niche tourism international travel undertaken by tourists who are or were married or celebrating your wedding.

The main components of the wedding is for tourist destinations, accommodations and tourist services that attract tourists wishing wedding, people looking friendly travel destinations, traveling with people who want other people matter Traveling Wedding destination and travelers who are traveling around the cultural and security issues.

The wedding industry includes tourist destinations (tourist boards and CVB), travel agencies, hotels and hotel groups, tour companies, cruise lines, and advertising and promotions companies who sell these travel destinations to the gay community.

Growth Potential

It is expected that the growth of this segment of the industry in the next five years to be good. However, there are Certain elements of market experience wedding and honeymoon that will direct growth.

Second marriages, and those marrying later in life (age group 35-45), will generate demand for weddings and honeymoon tourism. Increased growing number of new marriages is, and must continue in September. Hence the number of seconds honey moons also increase.

The gay/lesbian market has significant potential. Generally doing much above the average annual income and have a willingness to travel Particularly That makes a strong demographic for honeymoons.

The gay travel destinations are popular gay tourism professionals as they usually have liberal or permissive attitudes toward gay, gay have prominent infrastructure (bars, shops, restaurants, hotels, nightlife, entertainment, media, organizations, etc..) the opportunity to socialize with other gays, and the feeling that one can relax with ease, including gay people. Gay tourist destinations are often the big cities, although not exclusively, and often coincides with the existence of gay neighborhoods. These municipalities and tourist offices often work actively to develop its reputation as a place for gay travelers in aligning Commonly Themselves local gay organizations. Travel analysts say that the existence of a population center often is gay friendly, the main catalyst for the development of a gay -friendly tourist destination.

Due to the demands of strenuous work, especially in the U.S. where vacation time is often used in the Un Certain times of the year section, there is a growing trend of steadily increasing newlyweds have a moon honey that suits your employer, give up the traditional holiday Malthus Immediately after the wedding. Therefore more inclined to travel farther and longer when the honeymoon is taken.

Markets destinations

The main favorable home market destinations in the world are:

- USA
- UK
- Germany
- Italy
- France
- Scandinavia
- India as tourist destination weddings

Wedding tourism an apparently new form of tourism that is causing much excitement in the tourism industry. In some cases it is known as "marriage tourism" of the "destination wedding". According to the wedding magazine, Conde Nast Bridal Group

Survey, wedding tourism worldwide has - has grown 400 % in the last 10 years. Europe-based partners are known to fly to foreign destinations such as Las Vegas, Hawaii, the Caribbean and Cyprus to get married. India as a country is a beneficiary of this trend. Both NRI and foreigners are choosing an Indian wedding with all its traditional rituals and interesting local. The Indian wedding industry already booming with revenues of Rs 50,000/- crore a year and a growth rate of 25,000 per year, is looking for a way to relate to the main hotels and travel agencies to attract this growing tourism segment. Though, in India, it is difficult to come across the exact statistics and figures on tourism industry, however, we can not ignore this segment. The wedding field of tourism in India is also explored

The day will not be far away when the Indian team promote Incredible India as a place for weddings. Currently many rich and famous from around the world have chosen India as a place for the perfect wedding.

The most recent weddings took place in India that is of singer Katy Perry and comedian Russell Brand married on October 23, 2010. There are several reasons why people choose India. A all a matter of choice, if a person likes to see a traditional Hindu wedding, would probably love to have one. Many married people go for a re-wedding in India just to experience the magic of the Indian wedding.

Most of the resorts in Rajasthan, Kerala, Himachal and other parts of India offer a complete wedding package for guests to make the task easier. Wedding in India is also considered auspicious by many, considering the statistics, a wedding in India will remain a lifetime more than any other though would have to do more with the traditions of India more than the good omen.

Wedding Tourism in India is becoming popular as more and more foreigners, NRIs and Indians are taking interest in the wedding functions held in great historical Forts and Palace of India. These traditions and rituals of India reflect the rich cultural heritage of the country. Wedding Tourism in India is gaining popularity due to the distinctive celebrations and religious ceremonies That in the course of a wedding are celebrated. Although there are great weddings and conducted in palaces and magnificent beaches in India, there are also small wedding ceremonies include several traditional rituals That. All kinds of Indian weddings have become a worldwide success .

Wedding Tourism in India offers much more than just the wedding rituals. Along with wedding ceremonies, one can enjoy and have a first hand experience of the wedding preparations are done by both parties. Wedding Tourism in India helps you explore the hidden facts of an Indian wedding and enjoy the warmth and hospitality that India has to offer.

Excellent facilities in hotels, better transportation, delicious cuisine and many more are an integral part of wedding packages. Special honeymoon packages also helps to have a glimpse of the lifestyle of the Indians and these packages also offer some nice moments that can cope with being memories for a lifetime. There are many small and large special tour packages that offer preferred wedding in order to make your wedding an unforgettable experience.

Special places:

We offer a dream destination of lush green farm to a five star hotel in your city to exotic locations to royal forts and palaces heritage as the wedding venue, find them all for you. Our services include venue search :

- Jodhpur
- Jaipur
- Udaipur
- Delhi
- Hyderabad
- Goa
- Kerala(House Boat)
- Samode
- Deogarh Mahal
- Devigarh Resort
- Shimla
- Manali
- Khimsar Fort
- Alwar and many more destinations.

It may also be in the Tiger Retreats, jungle safaris, wildlife areas, village Safaris, Nature Resorts, Spas, deserts, etc. River Escapes. These days also increase the growing trend is for wedding venues in having a romantic value mean Weddings Taj View Agra or the larger world

Ramoji Film City and also on cruise ships and Luxuries trains say Maharaja Express, Palace on Wheels Royal Rajasthan on Wheels, Deccan Odyssey, Royal Orient, and so on .

People are preferring to organize weddings in Holy Ghats of Ganges in Haridwar / Rishikesh in the backdrop of Holy Ganga Aarti, Sangam in Prayag. Kurukshetra in Haryana, Khajraho, Orchha in Madhya Pradesh for religious wedding venue .

People in small towns or cities are planning their wedding in metropolitan cities : such as wedding in New Delhi, Chandigarh, Ludhiana, Jaipur, Ahmedabad, Bhopal, Gurgaon, Bhubaneswar, Guwahati and so on.

Growth Potential

It is expected that the growth of this segment of the industry in the next five years to be good. However, there are certain elements of market experience wedding and honeymoon that will direct growth.

Second marriages, and those marrying later in life (age group 35-45), will generate demand for weddings and honeymoon tourism. Increased growing number of new marriages is, and must continue in September. Hence the number of seconds honey moons also increase.

Overall, this market is expected to increase by 75 % during the coming years.

Some Facts of Wedding Tourism in India

With the Liz Hurley - Arun Nayar wedding in India, we are hoping to promote marriage tourism in India. There are lot of exotic locales and several Germans have been coming with their girlfriends to get married in India.

Ordinary Germans are so excited about getting married in our country she said pointing out that it was not just the celebrity circuit which was sold on the big fat Indian wedding idea. The tourism ministry has gone a step further and even oragnised a mock Indian wedding with a willing German couple, who will exchange vows with two priests chanting shalokas in Sanskrit and German.

Rene Loichen, who works in marketing firm in Saxony, said "I think getting married on Indian beach is a good idea. There are so many landscapes, varieties of food to choose from". It is very interesting idea. I have been to India before and this would give me a chance to see the country.

When to get Married in India

The most popular time of year for weddings is from October to February, when the weather is dry and sunny. However, weddings are commonly held throughout the year from September to May. The peak months of December and January are extremely busy. As well as being much more expensive, hotels and availability are also scarce during this time.

Cost of a Wedding in India

The cost of getting married greatly depends on the time of year and how elaborate the occasion will be. The price soars around December and January, particular during the Christmas and New Year period.

During the off season, it's possible to have a small and simple wedding in India starting from around $500. Otherwise, during the season the minimum price is around $1,500, for less than 100 guests. This includes a party on the eve of the wedding, boat cruise, wedding ceremony, dinner on the beach, theme décor, music, and decorations.

Arranging Wedding in India

Most five star hotels offer spectacular wedding set-ups and special honeymoon packages. The five star hotels usually get their decor and planning done by wedding planners, but organize the banquet and table decorations themselves.

If you're not intending to get married at a luxury hotel, it's recommended that you hire a wedding planner to take care of the arrangements. This list of top wedding planners in India will point you in the right direction.

Legal Requirements for Getting Married in India

Getting legally married in India is a lengthy and time consuming process, and you should allow spending around 60 days in the country.

As a result, many people prefer to take care of the legal part of the wedding at home and just have the wedding ceremony in India.

For those that do want to make their wedding legal in India, here are the legal requirements for getting married in India.

Tips for Getting Married in India

- Plan your wedding at least a year in advance for the best options.
- Check out a range of options before you decide.
- Seriously consider hiring a wedding planner to take the stress out of organizing the event.
- A civil wedding can be arranged faster than a church wedding, although it also requires paperwork to be in order.

References

The Gay Vacation Guide: The Best Trips and How to Plan Them by Mark Chesnut; Kensington Books, 2002; ISBN 978-0-7582-0266-6.

http://www.onecaribbean.org/content/files/weddings.pdf

http://articles.timesofindia.indiatimes.com/2007-03-08/rest-of-world/27870021_1_tourism-ministry-german-couple-indian-wedding

http://www.lonelyplanet.com/usa/san-francisco/travel-tips-and-articles/76124.

The Complete Travel Detective Bible: The Consummate Insider Tells You What You Need to Know in an Increasingly Complex World! by Peter Greenberg; Rodale, 2007;ISBN 978-1-59486-708-8.

THE ROLE OF HUMAN RESOURCES EMPOWERMENT IN THE SUSTAINABLE DEVELOPMENT OF TOURISM INDUSTRY

Javeed Ahmad Teeli

Research Scholar, Department of HRM & OB, Central University of Jammu, J&K, jaaslords@gmail.com

Abstract: This article aims to study the role of human resource empowerment in the sustainable development in tourism industry. In this respect, the concept of empowerment, its importance and its role in sustainable development as well as objectives of tourism industry and winning customers' satisfaction in tourist environments by means of enhancing job satisfaction, innovation and creativity at work, problem solving,... are studied. The results from the research showed that there is a strong tendency in present organizations across the world to empower their personnel to increase efficiency and improve working systems. It was also suggested for the management and personnel to have short term, long term and on the job training.

Keywords: human resource empowerment, sustainable development, tourism industry. On the job training, Customer satisfaction.

Introduction

The concept of sustainable development was first given prominence at the UNCED (United Nation). In 1987, Sustainable Development was defined by the world commission on the Environment and Development (in the Brundtland Report) as "development that meets the needs of the present without compromising the ability of the future generations to meet their own needs". Unfortunately this definition remained vague and little guidance was offered on how countries could develop coherent sustainable development polices.

Sustainability in factors such as social, environmental and economic Balance in the long run is a vital concern of the present private and state organizations. Entering the twenty first century, this has become even more critical for modern societies.

One of the most important issues in everlasting progress of an organization or any business is the human resources involved in the businesses. Taking into account the constant achievements of organizations like Coca- Cola, Kodak, Intel, Phillips and the experience of countries that have been successful in tourism industry in the past few decades proves the core of their constant progress has been the evolution of their empowered human resources. Considering the multidimensional objectives set to develop the tourism industry, the human factor is of the most crucial element in attaining these objectives and the unrelenting success of these organizations.

Empowerment and its Importance

Empowerment has been described as a venue to enable employees make decisions (Bowen & Lawler, 1992) and as a personal experience where individuals take responsibility for their own actions (Pastor, 1996). The first definition puts the onus on management, and the second emphasizes the importance of the individual for successful application of empowerment. Whereas, earlier research focused on empowerment as a set of management practices to delegate authority (discretionary empowerment) (Blau & Alba,1982), recent research has centered on psychological empowerment ,focusing on employee experience (Corsun & Enz, 1999).

Empowerment research in hospitality and tourism is very limited (Erstad,1997). Managerial interest in employee empowerment in the hospitality industry has been associated with gaining competitive advantage through improvements in service quality (Hubrecht & Teare, 1993). Fulford and Enz(1995) suggested that different subject groups in the service industry should be studied to learn more about the concept and practice of empowerment.Going over the accomplishments of the developed countries, institutions and great corporations in the world reveals the fact that the innovative,expertise and motivated human forces and the way they are organized are the propelling forces behind all these achievements.

A glimpse at the improvements in offering generous supports, services and hospitality of countries such as France, Spain and Turkey available to tourists in recent years proves that the human resources are the key factor. In today's competitive world, for any industry to survive and ceaselessly grow, creative empowered human resources are the central pillars and in fact the real assets of any organization. This progress would have been impossible without the skilled empowered human farces.One of the most obvious obsessions of the present day businesses is the ability to employ and bring to together talented manpower who are in turn able to bring about changes in the organizations they work for, In fact, in a successful organization there is a combination of knowledgeable and well-endowed groups of people who feel they belong to the same family and by working passionately and ingeniously apply their experience and knowledge in teamwork to add prosperity and success to their organizations. Assuming responsibility, teamwork spirit, problem solving talents, bringing about change and variety, innovation and creative thinking and making proper decisions are of the most important characteristics of noble empowered human resources that are the prerequisite requirements of any business to remain consistently successful in the present era.

Functions of Empowered Human Recourses

The role that empowering human resources can play in tourism industry to sustain a constant success in different frameworks can be outlined as below:

- Providing standard services in tourist resorts and sights to satisfy the customers;
- Providing services according to the requirements of tourists;

- Better communication between the personnel themselves and thepersonnel and the management;
- Increasing job satisfaction and having a dynamic workplace within thetourist environments;
- Increasing productivity and efficiency of the private and public personnel
- involved in tourism industry;
- Taking advantage of creativity and innovation while working;
- Feeling the sense of belonging to the organization and doing teamwork;
- Improving the quality of doing the work
- Enhancing the services provided to the tourists in the tourist
- environments;
- Lowering the costs and increasing profitability of businesses involved in tourism;
- Improving the power of decision making within the personnel;
- Reaching the long term and short term goals set in tourism industry toearn more currency exchange and improve economic development.

The Objectives of Tourism Industry

Tourism industry is the most cultural issue of economy. Economic experts believe that tourism is only a part of the economy, which is greatly tied up with culture, because on one hand it provides desirably the introduction of cultures, civilizations, races, lands, tribes and different dialects with each other and on the other hand it can also be a resource of income for different countries. As tourism economy is the best stimulus for the countries that have a decreasing industry due to possessing a single product or limited sources of income, it is becoming one of the largest economic realities for developing countries (Padash and Esfahani, 2008). Today private and public tourist sectors aim at establishing fundamental transportation systems, creating tourist attractions, purposeful promotions, economic development, investing in the standard tourist products, earning exchange currency incomes, and planned dynamic regional and worldwide marketing. To accomplish all these goals, human resources in public and private sectors must be empowered.

Winning Customers' Satisfaction in Tourist Environments

One of the most important achievements in empowering the personnel is how to win customers' satisfaction. In fact, this will lead to sustainable progress in both private and public sectors (in market places, public services, hotels and restaurants). It is related to the mission of tourist organizations in creating the right jobs, educating and empowering the workforce in areas where tourists come and go. In order to win customers' satisfaction, good services must be provided. This will attract more tourists and lead to earning more income and, as a result, the increase in revenues will, in turn, help to develop economic activity in the region and create more productive jobs. In most of the successful chain hotels all over the world, one of the hotel's crew will ask the guests about their opinions about the services available to them, whether they need extra help or everything has been directed according to their requirements and if they are satisfied with the range of services provided. In fact these empowered crew can be personally responsible for particular requirements of their quests or their complaints. When the managers and personnel are authorized in the tourist environments, they can provide high quality services a reasonable costs. They know that the satisfaction of the customers is of the most important priority. Both public and private organizations that deal with tourists know that the provision of qualitative services to investors and any client in economic and tourist quarters play an important role in attracting new investors and tourists, and hence will result in the economic growth and future development of the region.

A second debate within the literature pertains to the relationship between service quality and customer satisfaction. Satisfied customers tend to be loyal to the company and more likely to return (Greenwell et al., 2002).Managers in tourism strive to improve the quality of their services and the level of customer satisfaction in the belief that this effort will create loyal visitors. Loyal visitors will return to the destination and recommend it to others (Tian-Cole & Crompton, 2003). Sparks and Westgate (2002) suggest that service failure can have devastating effects on an organization because customers frequently switch to a different provider when they experience a service failure. However, among customers who experience service problems, those who receive satisfactory resolution are more likely to remain loyal to the service provider. Services forces, such as taxi drivers, when briefed, can have pleasant encounters with tourists while they are entering a tourist zone, will have a tremendous positive impact on them and this will boost sustainableprogress in the same region. As a matter of fact, all the private and public sectors employees active in tourist environments should know that they are all the circle of chains joined together as a strong member of a system. Their coordinated cooperation to win tourists' satisfaction will help the constant success in the tourism of a particular region.

Provision of Optimum Services to Tourists

There is no doubt that providing good services to gain advantage over other businesses in the realm of economic activities are of the greatest factors. Tourist organizations aim at attracting tourists and entrepreneurs to tourist resorts or historical sights by empowering the human resources in the public and private sector tourist organizations is of the prime importance. In fact the whole burden of attracting tourists and foreign or domestic investors to a particular region lies on the shoulders of empowered personnel who, in turn, try to provide good services in order to make them their lifelong customers. An increase in the number of tourists and investors will obviously lead to improvements in employment, income and the development of the region and hence to sustained progress.

Enhancing Job Satisfaction

By providing efficient services and gaining clients' satisfaction, empowered employees will add their own satisfaction as well. In fact those who are the master of the job and can be more responsive toward their customers are more relaxed and feel less strain and enjoy their work and the working environment better than any other employees. Having happy and empowered employees is a blessing for an organization and will bring about abundance and everlasting success to it. In any position, if the employee is impotent and cannot fulfill expectations he will become bored and eventually dragged out of the system. People who do a job uninterestedly and work merely out of financial necessity (such as waiters in a restaurant or hotel crew) are not empowered because they lack the motivation and may therefore, be pernicious to the whole system. For this reason, organizations must plan to, motivate and empower their personnel if they want to succeed in a competitive market.

Teamwork and the Feeling of Belonging to the Organization

The empowered management and personnel do not consider themselves separate from the system that their organization is based on. They rather feel that what they do is a part of an integrated whole to sense the feel of belonging to an organization or subdivisions and having common interests and objectives with others leads to overall achievements of that particular organization and boosts the regions development. For instance, in the whole lot of hotels, shopping centers, tourist sights and wherever visited by tourists, if people involved are empowered by public or private organizations, the tourists or investors can have a pleasant memory from the region and this will encourage positive promotions abroad or in the country and attract many tourists and investors to that particular area and of course, again, it can increase employment, rapid regional development and sustained progress.

Innovation and Creativity at Work

Innovation and creativity is peculiar to human individuals and societies. In the present era, innovation is the most important criterion in corporate development. With the present rush to introduce new products and services to the markets, the organizations that cannot cope with everlasting changes that happen every second and do not have creative staff are bound to failure. Innovation cannot be sold or bought. It is a phenomenon potentially inherited by all human beings. People should welcome new ideas; organizations can creatively trigger this great hidden potential; and positive environment would motivate the personnel to think profoundly and unleash their creative abilities. Tourist organizations all over the world require highly innovative empowered manpower to attract tourists and investors to their regions. Nowadays the revenue from tourism industry account for the most part of same countries' annual budget. They not only invest in the provision of services but also encourage tourist organizations to employ and train innovative personnel.

Innovations in this field may take place inthe following forms

- Innovations in providing high quality services;
- Innovations in attracting national and international investments;
- Innovations in obliging hotels and resorts to provide the best possible
- services;
- Innovations in supervising public and private sectors to provide the
- tourists with the best services possible;
- Innovations in selling goods and services to domestic and foreign tourists at a reasonable prices;

These innovations and creative ideas in tourist organizations will pave the way for growth, development and sustainable progress.

Problem Solving

Empowering the personnel working in an organization will make them capable of finding solutions to problems or improve the existing set-ups. One of the first effects of empowering the personnel is the changes in their behavior for the better. These changes will naturally help to maintain a potential capacity to solve problems in the organization. The empowered personnel, whether they work form private or state tourist organizations, can have a holistic and cooperative outlook in detecting and shooting problems in different parts of their organization. Spotting the problems and finding quick solutions is no easy job; only the skillful and experienced people who believe in teamwork can find reliable solutions to the problems that are always faced by any organization. If the personnel are not trained and empowered to overcome difficult situations, they tend to whitewash the problems instead of solving them and this will certainly deter the situation and puts organizations in jeopardy. Constant growth and sustainable progress in the tourism industry can only be achieved by creative and empowered personnel, just as in any other industry.

Authorization

One of the most important accomplishments resulting from empowering personnel is authorization. Authorization will bring about ample benefits and advantages for organizations and people who are working for them, because in this way they will be able to increase output and make the organization grow faster.

By giving authorization:

- The human resources will feel free to think independently, track down the obstackles and difficulties for themselves and therefore increase output and the quality of their work;
- All the people will know what to do within the range of their authority and no one will baffled or confused;
- People who are given authorization are less prone to run into difficulties; ? Inefficient personnel can be identified and sorted out;
- Employees usually do teamwork and can improve their knowledge and gain more insights into what they are doing;
- The budget that is allocated to giving extra benefits and facilities can be invested in training groups of employees to maintain an increase in output and efficiency of the organization;

Intelligent and empowered management and giving authorization to personnel may lead to constant progress in tourist organizations.

Conclusion

There is a strong tendency in present organizations across the world to empower their personnel to increase efficiency and improve working systems. In this highly competitive world, countries and private organizations have begun to realize how innovative and empowered staff can help boost tourism industry in a particular region. Without this, one cannot expect higher employment, currency exchange revenues, high quality services, enhanced productivity and sustainable progress in tourist promotions to attract more tourists' areas. There are world wide and investment to areas worth sightseeing and entertainment. The management and personnel must have short term, long term and on the job training. The interaction of state owned organizations, private organizations, universities and other educational institutions, and local people can have accelerating effects on promoting the quality and quantity of services and consequent progress in tourist regions. The quality of services given by hotels, tourist resorts and facilities en route must be supervised by experienced and knowledgeable managers. There must be commitments to improve such facilities without delay. The authorities must try to inform people how to interact with foreign tourists. Some regions might still be unexplored in relation to their potential value to absorb tourists and investors. Sometimes a new archeological discovery can attract the attention of many tourists, provided there are enough promotions inside and outside the country.

References

Blau, J.R., & Alba, R.D. (1982). Empowering nets of participation Administrative Science Quarterly, 27(3), 363-379.

Bowen, D.E., & Lawler, E.E. (1992). The empowerment of service workers: What, why, how and when.Sloan Management Review, 33(3), 31-39.

Corsun, D.L., & Enz, C.A. (1999). Predicting psychological empowerment among service workers: The effect of support-based relationships. Human Relations, 52(2), 205-224.

Erstad, M. (1997). Empowerment and organizational change. International Journal of Contemporary Hospitality Management, 9(7), 325-333.

Fulford, M. D., & Enz, C. A. (1995). The impact of empowerment on service employees. Journal of Managerial Issues, 7(2), 161-175.

Greenwell, T. C., Fink, J., & Pastore, D. (2002). Assessing the influence of the physical sports facility on customer satisfaction within the context of the service experience. Sport Management Review, 5, 129-148.

Hubrecht, J., & Teare, R. (1993). A strategy for partnership in total quality service. International Journal of Contemporary Hospitality Management, 5(3), 1-

Pastor, J. (1996). Empowerment: What it is and what it is not.Empowerment in Organizations, 4(2), 5-7.

Sparks, R., & Westgate, M. (2002). Broad-based and targeted sponsorship strategies in Canadian women's ice-hockey. International Journal of Sports Marketing and Sponsorship, 4(1), 59-84.

Tian-Cole, S., & Crompton, J. L. (2003). A conceptualization of the relationships between service quality and visitor satisfaction, and their links to destination selection. Leisure Studies, 22, 65-80.

United Nations Conference on Environment and Development

OPPORTUNITIES & CHALLENGES FOR ECOTOURISM IN VALLEY OF FLOWER (UTTARAKHAND)

Lakhvinder Singh

Research Scholar, Department of Tourism & Hotel Management,Kurukshetra University, Kurukshetra
lakhvindersingh.kuk@gmail.com

Dinesh Dhankhar

Assistant Professor, Department of Tourism & Hotel Management,Kurukshetra University, Kurukshetra dd.dhankhar@gmail.com

Abstract: Tourism is the backbone of the economic development by great inflow to tourist but, at the same time it has given birth to several crucial issues related to environment degradation. Ecotourism is a dynamic and effective instrument that assimilates 'ecology' with 'economy'. Well-planned eco-tourism can benefit both protected areas and residents of surrounding communities by linking long-term natural conservation with local, social and economic development.The present paper critically analyses the Ecotourism in the Valley of flowers national park in Uttarakhand. The study was based on primary and secondary data sources. The study revealed that the study area has number of factors that are contributing to ecotourism such as are beautiful landscapes, peaks, lakes and tarns etc. But now-a-days the problem of Solid waste is increasing at an alarming rate because of the heavy arrival of tourists and improper management practices. The study also offered valuable suggestions that will help to facilitate the eco-friendly tourism in the Valley of Flower.

Keywords: Ecotourism, conservation, national park, solid waste, valuable,facilitate.

Introduction

The growing tourism is continuously affecting the natural resources which are under threat due to this such as loss of biodiversity and unflavored global climatic variation. Some international agencies such as WTO, UNEP etc. believe that ecotourism is a good idea for managing tourism impacts even if it is striving with many challenges (Global Ecotourism Conference, 2007).

Ecotourism, unlike its conventional counterpart, promotes environmentally responsible travel and seeks to ensure that visitors take nothing but photographs and leave nothing but footprints. Ecotourism is a combination of positive activities those accelerates economic growth, create large scale employment, alleviates poverty, generates revenue, earn foreign exchange, educates people, supports conservation and preserves cultural & natural heritage (Roy, 2007). Hence, the importance and scope of ecotourism is expanding globally day by day because the sustainability dimension of ecotourism doesn't only support for protection of the biodiversity but also put together many areas like social, cultural and economic issues (Weaver, 2001 quoted in Higham, 2007).

With an increasing anxiety for the protection of natural assets through protected areas, united with a strong aspiration to escape from the traditional vacation, many travelers are beginning to ascertain the benefits and advantages of ecotourism, which has become the fastest growing tourism market in the world (Agrusa& Guidry, 1999).

Recent tourism activities show an increasing crumbling of the tourist market and an increased demand for specialized types of tourism (Moghal&Agrusa, 1997). Tourists are starting to get away from routine tour packages and start takininterst in ecoutourism activities like sporting events, get in touch with ethnicity of destination visited and to explore alternate destinations (Boo,1990; lnskeep, 1991).

The growing interest of people for nature based tourism created a need for ecotourism. Besides, the understanding and the agreement with the principles of nature preservation and durability for a growing portion of the population took part in the evolution of the term "ecotourism" (Tiwari et al, 2010; Tiwari et al, 2011).

Ecotourism can be differently perceived by different societies. However, it can best be defined as travel to natural attraction areas that both conserve the culture and the environment while sustaining the wellbeing of the local community. It offers the opportunity to get the most out of their natural attractions and to gain all the economic benefits without losing their rich biological resources (Cater, 1993; World Conservation Union, 1996).

The increasing conception of ecotourism result in hiked foreign exchange and revenue earning, more employment opportunities, developed infrastructure, commercialization of local products and many other types of service facilities (Sherman, 1991; Himberg, 2005). As well as hosts are also move towards awareness regarding conservation and education enhancement.

Locals' participation is essential for sustainable development of protected areas and overall development of tourism industry. At global level, tourism is significantly contributing to sustainable development, alleviating poverty and the management of natural resources.

Tourist arrivals is increasing at very fast speed and it helps to boost economic condition. Garhwal region of Uttarakhand is set an example where tourism touched some of the most perceptive ecosystem of the high Himalayan region untrained and unguarded.

Valley of Flowers (VOF) National Park is one of the most beautiful mountain wildernesses of the Western Himalayas. Together, the parks preserve a transition zone between the eastern and western Himalayan flora, the ZanskarMountains and the Great Himalayas, long praised in Hindu mythology and for over a century by botanists and mountaineers (UNEP Report, 2005). The Valley of Flower is also having the religious significance for Hindus. It is associated with a legendary story, which described that this is the place where Lord Hanumanji collected 'Sanjeevni' herb to revive Lord Lakshman.

The biological significance of valley of flower lies in its wonderful floral and faunal biodiversity with myriads of fascinating flowers. To save the protected areas and to heighten economic development, suitableanalysis of ecotourism tourism development in the region must be put in place.

Objectives for the study

1. To evaluatethe eco-tourism opportunities in Valley of flower of Uttarakhand.
2. To find out the challenges for development of ecotourism in the study area.
3. To offer valuable suggestions to make Valley of Flower a hot ecotourism destination.

Research methodology

The present study is depends on both primary and secondary data sources. The primary sources include interviews, comments, observations, opinions, notes etc. of the person concerned i.e. host population, tourists visited there and government tourism officials existed in the study area. The secondary data for the study were collected from earlier published research works, government publications, magazines and various reports have also been gone through to derive information pertaining to the present study.

Study area profile

The Valley of Flower is discovered by Frank S. Smith, an English mountaineer while on an expedition on Mount Kamet. He described this place as a nature's gift to human being. It lies in the Chamoli district of north Indian state Uttrakhand and is booming bouquet of beautiful, lively and multihued flowers. It is among the nine zones or part of the Nanda Devi Biosphere Reserve (NDBR) in Himalayas, which is spread across an area of 5860.69 sq km. The Valley of Flowers is located at Latitude 30o 41' - 30o 48'N and Longitude 79o 33' - 70o 46'E with the VOFNP area being 87.50 sq km and altitude range being from about 3200 m to 6700 m above MSL. River Puspavati flows through the valley and there are many waterfalls enhancing the beauty of the place. The main valley portion of the Park runs in the east west direction along the banks of river Pushpawati. The splendour and the dazzling beauty of the valley beckons tourists from all over the world. The valley is declared as a National Park in the year 1982 and after that, grazing and camping is not permitted in the same. It was recognized as a world heritage site in 2005.

Opportunities existed for expansion of ecotourism in the area

Flora& Fauna

The Valley of Flowers National Park can bedivided into three broad eco-climatic zones viz. Subalpine (2800-3500 m asl.), Lower alpine (3500-3700m asl.) and Higher alpine (3700m asl.). The valleyhas an unusually rich flora of over 600 species withmany rarities. The species of wild flowers bloom in the valley when the snow started to melt but the flowers bloom were on peak during the mid July to mid of August. The magnificent natural vegetation of the valley attracts a large of number of nature lovers, environmentalist and tourist every year. The famous flora of the valley were Himalyan blue poppy, daisy, dianthus, calendula, whit & yellow anemones, Geranium, Marsh marigold, Morina, Strawberry and so on. The valley remains in bloom almost for three months. Most of the flowers have medicinal values too. The abundance of Asmanda fern in this valley is a rare sight than in other Himalayan valleys. Some species, such as Saussureaobvallata(Brahmakamal) are collected as religious offerings to Nanda Devi and other deities. By the month of September the shade of the valley starts changing and autumn bids farewell to flowers. The valley remains snow wrapped for the rest of year.

Apart from the flowers some species of Butterfly, Musk deer, Common langur, Presbytes entellus, Flying squirrel, Himalayan black bear, Red fox, Himalayan weasel, and Himalayan yellow marten, Tahr, Scrow, Blue sheep (Bharal), Himalayan birds & Snow leopard are also found in the park (UNEP World ConservationMonitoring center 2005).

Cultural Heritage and Pilgrimage Centres

The Valley of Flowers 07 kms south of the parkentrance, at Ghangrea, a track leads off to theHemkund Sahib shrine sacred to Sikhs, and theHindu temple to Lord Lakshman, (brother of LordRama), beside Lake Lokpal. About 400,000-500,000pilgrims visit them every year. (UNEP WorldConservation Monitoring center 2005). These have long been places of pilgrimage to both Sikhs and Hindus. The valley itself was formerly used by migratory villagers for grazing two to three herds of 700-1,000 sheep and goats each and for 40-50 local cows and buffaloes. In 1862 the valley was chanced on by Col. Edmund Smyth who praised the floral beauty of the region in various periodicals. In 1937 Smythe revisited the valley and next year published The Valley of Flowers, bringing it to world attention. There is the tombstone of a botanist from Kew, MargrettLegge, who died here in 1939.

The faith scapes of the region are recognized as rare attraction. The major pilgrimage sites in the area were:PanchBadri, ShriBadrinath, YogadhyanBadri, Briddhabadri, AdiBadri and so on.

Ethnic Society

The valley itself is uninhabited. The local people are mostly Bhotiya, non-tribal Rajput farmers and transhumant herdsmen, who winter their flocks at the area's main permanent village of Pulna 12km south of the Park and 1,750m lower in elevation. 5 km and 9 km south of the park entrance are the seasonal villages of Ghangrea (at 3,060m) and Bhiundhar (at 2,240m), occupied in summer to serve the pilgrims and tourists (when some 400 stalls line the pilgrim trail). The people of Bhiundhar who numbered about 330 in 1999, may no longer graze the valley and some families are still poor but others earn well from tourism and the pilgrimage and are very supportive of the Park (Srivastava, 1999). Withsupport from the Forest Department, the local communities have formed Eco-Development Committees (EDCs). The EDCs at Bhyundhar and Govindghat provide support to the parkmanagement and look after the waste disposal and management of visitor facilities along the trailoutside the National Park.

Landscape and Peaks

An attractive landscape is an asset on whichmountain tourism depends. It can be stated thatmountains are the foundations of the tourismindustry. The entire study area is mountainous. Therugged landmass is thoroughly and artisticallypunctuated with nature's superlatives. Here landscapes are mostenchanting. The actual attraction is the toweringsnow covered peaks that makes the scenerychallenging and beautiful to adventurers. The chainsof the high mountain peaks are divided into differentmountain groups by the mighty rivers of Garhwal.

The high peak of Bunderpunch (6302m asl), Kalanag(6387m asl) lie between the tons and Bhagirathirivers, Matri (6721 m asl), Chirbas (6525m asl),TrimukhParvat (6422m asl) lie between Jadh gangaand the Bhagirathi rivers.Another cluster of peaks lie between Bhagirathiand Saraswatiriver. Famous among the peaks areChaukhamba situated on the west of Badribath temple, Neelkanth (6600 m asl) and the SameruParvat (6350m asl).

Glaciers

There are numerous glaciers in the area. Valleysbetween 2000m asl and 3000m asl show the glacialfeature wherever knot blot out by fluvial action.Some of the glaciers, which need mention at thispoint, are:Doonagiri Glacier, Tiprabamak Glacier, Satopanth, Bhagirathi-Khark Glacier etc.

Water systems

It consists of rivers, Streams, Lakes, Tarnns andTorrents. The rivers are running deep into the gorgesfrom where it cannot be utilizerd for the purpose ofirrigation. The main rivers are-Alaknanda, Saraswati,Dhauli Ganga.Upper Garhwal Himalaya is famous for itstranquil tarns, which are found around 3000m asl.The landslide and heaps of debris, partly blocking therivers or streams forms most of these tarns, thoughsome are fed by the underground sources. Pluggingof valley by moraines deposited by ancient glaciersforms most glacial lakes. Mostly, they are sweetwater lakes but few are brine water too.Some of the Tals of the area are-,HemkundLokpal, Satopanth, Vasundhara fall, Deotal, Roopkund, Vednikund.

Visitor Facilities

The valley is very accessible and some of the many pilgrims to the nearby shrines travel on to see it. Where Nanda Devi Park is closely regulated for mountaineering and ecotourism, the Valley of Flowers is open to both. Should tourism and mountaineering come to pose a threat to the animals here, such activities in the Valley would be regulated too. In 1999, between 30 and 50 people visited the Park daily. In 2003-4, nearly 4,000 were recorded, 3,600 from India and 300 from abroad. Visits occur between May and early October, on foot once within the Park and guided by youths from the village to see that the flowers are not trampled. There is a Forest Department post and interpretation centre at Ghangrea near the entrance, with brochures, books and posters and where entry fees are charged. For the last two years this has been managed by members of the EDC who present slide and film shows for visitors.There are sign boards in the park and guided nature trails including a 19-kilometer trek. Regulations for trekking are being prepared. No camping is allowed in the valley. But mountaineering is allowed subject to permit and regulation, on two peaks, Rataban and Ghauri Parbat. There are some 25 visitor restthouses, lodges and hotels at Ghangrea near the park entrance and down the Bhiundhar at Govindghat on the Alaknanda, including a very large Sikh gurudwara. There are Forest Department guesthouses at both Ghangrea and Govindghat, and camping near Bhiundhar village.

Challenges for ecotourism development in the area

Given their significant and diverse natural, geographical, historical and cultural heritage assets, the Valley of Flower have vast potential for the development of nature based tourism. The problems of the litter piles up by the tone from the thousands of tourists that visit the place. A past threat to the forests surrounding the pilgrim route was the destruction of trees for firewood.. There is also a constant threat from local poachers. However, these problems, inter alia, can be summarized as follows:

- Unavailability of basic amenities for tourists.

- No provision of refreshments either at the entrance or near the entrance.
- The waste bins/cans are not installed at the entrance and park interiors.
- There is no adequate provision of drinking water inside park.
- The watch-towers are not in sufficient number and are also not sufficient in height.
- Trail paths are not well organized.
- The guides were locals but found to be inadequately conversant with the foreign languages.
- Lack of knowledge and awareness regarding implications of tourism and conservation among host and local community.
- Lack of technical know-how and weak promotional activity i.e. weak publicity promotion and mass media exposure.
- Lack of tourism-related infrastructures such as hotels and lodging services, transportation, safety and security and tourism information and communication services.
- Lack of tourism investments and finances.
- Lack of consistent tourism strategies and policies due to conflicts between the government departments and the tourism private agencies.
- Lack of effective administration, regulation and institutional frameworks of touristic activity.
- Lack of tourism diversification to keep pace with the rapidly changing and complex requirements of tourists.

Suggestion for the development

The attract ability of Valley of Flower is beyond doubt and it can attract the discerning eco-tourists.The strengths of park are relatively easy accessibility and abundance of natural resources including itsbeauty and tranquility.Following steps should be undertaken for managing the existing natural resources and for sustainable ecotourism:

- Protection, in-situ and ex-situ conservation and monitoring of flora and fauna.

- Provide educating and training to local people to improve the management of ecotourism in the area.
- Solid waste is important issue for managing the site. The litter piles up by tones generate by thousands of tourists that visit the area. The local people should be combined to clean this.
- Abundance of medicinal plant varieties should be combinedwith the rich ayurvedic tradition of Himalaya to promote health tourism as a priority segment for future development.
- The interpretation centre should be developed to act asa 'life-enrichment centre' where the link between the nature and human life are established increating a 'wholesome human being'.
- The waste cans / bins should be installed at major stop-overs / points and tourists should bediscouraged in carrying the plastic and polithin bags inside the park.
- Due to critical 'biological-structure' and plant & animal species of the park experienced and trained guide from local area should be hired to perform any kind tourist activity in the area.
- Keeping in pace with the tourist traffic, few refreshment centers can be planned in surroundings the parksmainly at the entrance and terminal point proposed in the itinerary.
- The watchtowers should be installed atadequatepoints where the wildanimals are frequently camping. The height of the existing towers also needs to be increased.
- The involvement of people living surrounding the park should be ensured to optimize the dual benefits of tourism development and conservationof Sanctuary and make arrangements for various financial schemes including microfinanceand poverty alleviation schemes can be made available to them in the process.
- There has to be a system of visitor statistics compilation which will help the facility development /improvement, regulation and monitoringactivities inside park.
- Tourism authorities must initiate special marketing campaigns to promote local agricultural products and facilities such as Catering, Home-stay accommodation, Transport and Guides etc.

- The government should establish sustainable tourism policies and regulations, ensuring responsibly zoned development; natural and cultural heritage and resource conservation and protection.

Conclusion

Valley of Flower is a paradise for the nature lovers with its rich bio-diversity. The number of tourists visiting Valley is increasing every season. Ecotourism in Valley of Flower can be regarded as one of the best approaches to promote sustainable developmentthat can be helpful to alleviate poverty by developing local economy and society and alsoconserving environment. At the same time it is also creating various adverse impacts such as environmental and social pollutions, deforestation, and many others. It should be promoted in a manner that it should not destroy the beauty of natural resources. Community participation has a key role to play in spreading awareness among the local villagers, tourists, etc for having a sustainable form of ecotourism. Proper publicity campaigns should be introduced to bring the facts to limelight, which is yet to catch up with the available avenues. The government should committed to develop integrated and innovative ecotourism policy, proper planning and implementation to benchmark this place as the main attractions for the tourists.

Refernces

Agrusa, J. and Guidry, J., (1999). Ecotourismand Sustainable Development of theMaya Rain Forest in Central America /First Pan-American ConferenceProceedings.

Boo, E., (1990). Ecotourism: The Potentials and Pitfalls. World Wildlife Fund: Washington, D.C.

Cater, E., (1993). Ecotourism in the Third World: Problems for Sustainable Tourism Development. Tourism Management, pp. 14, 2, pp. 107-115.

Higham, J. (Ed.), (2007). Critical Issues in Ecotourism: Understanding a Complex TourismPhenomenon. Elsevier, UK.

Himberg, N., (2006). Community-BasedEcotourism as a Sustainable Development Option in the Taita Hills, Kenya. Master' s thesis. University of Helsinki.

Inskeep, E., (1991). Tourism Planning: An Integrated and Sustainable Development Approach. Van Nostrand Reinhold: New York.

Roy, T.K.,(2007). Eco-tourism Development in Uttaranchal: An Opportunity But Challenge! In M. Chaudhary, K.K. Kamra, S.S. Boora, R. Bhushan, M. Chand and R.H. Taxak,(Eds.), Tourism Development: Impacts and Strategies, pp.277-291, Anmol Publication, New Delhi.

Sherman, P.B and Dizon, J.A., (1991). "Nature Tourism: Determining if t Pays." In T. Wheland (ed.), Ecotourism. Covelo, CA: Island Press.

Srivastava, S., (1999). Management Plan for the Valley of Flowers National Park. Wildlife Preservation Organization, Uttar Pradesh.

TIES (2007). Global Ecotourism Conference. Oslo statement on Ecotourism.

Tiwari, S.K., Tiwari, P.K. and Tiwari, S.C., (2010). A Review on the Future of Ecotourism in the Valley of Flowers National Park: A Case Study of Garhwal Himalaya, India, Nature and Science, 8(4), pp.101-106.

Tiwari, S.K., Tiwari, P.K. and Tiwari, S.C., (2011). An Overview of Potential Ecotourism Resources and Their Prospects inValley of Flowers National Park, Uttaranchal, India, Caspian Journal of Environmental Sciences, Vol. 9 No.1 pp. 105-110.

UNEP-World Conservation MonitoringCenter (2005). Under World Heritage sitesNanda Devi and Valley of Flowers NationalParks, Uttaranchal India.

Weaver, D.B., (2001) Ecotourism in the Context of Other Tourism Types. In D.B. Weaver (Ed.). The Encyclopedia of Ecotourism, pp. 73-83, CABI Publishing, Wallingford.

FOOD SAFETY AND PERCEIVED RISK: A STUDY OF HARYANA TOURISM COMPLEXES SITUATED ON NATIONAL HIGHWAY-1

Lakhvinder Singh

Research Scholar, Department of Tourism & Hotel Management, lakhvindersingh.kuk@gmail.com, Kurukshetra University, Kurukshetra

Dinesh Dhankhar

Assistant Professor, Department of Tourism & Hotel Management, dd.dhankhar@gmail.com, Kurukshetra University, Kurukshetra

Mahesh Sharma

Research Scholar, Institute of Hotel & Tourism Management, Maharashi Dayanand University, Rohtak mahesh972000hm@gmail.com

Abstract: Food safety is an important concern for holiday makers in tourist destinations. In fact, risk from food at tourist destinations has an influence on tourist perception. This risk can potentially affect physical health and lead to an inability to follow planned activities. The objective of this paper was to studythe tourists' demographics characteristics and their level of perceived risk towards food safety. A total of 111visitors during their stay at restaurants established inHighway tourism complexes of Haryana were used as the sample. Percentage, Mean, Standard deviation and Rank method test were utilized to achieve the objectives. The findings revealed variations in tourists' perceived risk of food safety in established restaurants.

Keywords: Food Safety, Visitors, Perceived Risk, Haryana Tourist Complexes.

Introduction

Modern tourists visited not only for the purpose of sight scene but they prefer to visit for the taste of a place. Nearly, all tourists and dine out. Food is a significant means to penetrate into another culture as it allows an individual to experience the 'Other' on a sensory level, and not just an intellectual one" (Long, 1998). Local food is a fundamental component of a destination's attributes, adding to the range of attractions and the overall tourist experience (Symons, 1999). This makes food an essential constituent of tourism production as well as consumption.

Food tourism has gained increasing attention over past years. Billions of tourists returning to familiar destinations to enjoy tried and tested recipes, or travelling further a field in search of new and special cuisine, gastronomy has become a central part of the tourism experiences. With food so deeply connected to its origin, this focus allows destinations to market themselves as truly unique, appealing to those travellers who look to feel part of their destinations through its flavours (Global Report on Food Tourism, 2012).

This is especially important in the face of rapid urbanization and shifts away from traditional economic sectors. With their proximity to food-producing lands, rural communities often enjoy a comparative advantage when it comes to serving up traditional fare. Tourism, particularly food tourism, allows these communities to generate income and employment opportunities locally, providing jobs for vineyard tour guides or local chefs, while fuelling other sectors of the local economy such as agriculture. It bringing together experiences from some of the world's top tourism destinations, as well as from food tourism experts, the report offers important insight and recommendations into this growing segment of tourism (Global Report on Food Tourism, 2012).

From an economic point of view, nearly 100% of tourists spend money on food at their destination. Data shows that more than two-thirds of table-service restaurant operators reported that tourists are important to their business, with check sizes of US$25 or above coming from tourists (National Restaurant Association, 2002).

According to Pyo et al. (1991), among all possible areas of expenditures while traveling, tourists are least likely to make cuts in their food budget. All these suggest that tourists' food consumption makes a substantial contribution to the local restaurants, dining places, the food industry, and thereby the destination's economy. This makes its essential to the study food related tourism.

Dining out is a growing form of leisure where meals are consumed not out of necessity but for pleasure, and the atmosphere and occasion are part of the leisure experience as much as the food itself. However, when it comes to tourists, dining out can both be a necessity and a pleasure. While some tourists dine to satisfy their hunger, others dine at a particular restaurant to experience the local food and cuisine, because for the latter these form an important component of their travel itinerary (Shenoy,2005).

Understanding consumer responses to various food safety issues is of crucial importance if effective food safety policy and risk communication are to be developed and implemented. In particular as food chains become global, there is a need to understand consumer risk perceptions and trust in food, and how these influence consumer behaviours. It is evident that consumers are make decision on the basis of risk and benefits associates with food choices.

The possibility of risk received from the consumption of unsafe food and drink is higher away from home. Food service providers and food sellers try to fulfil customers' satisfaction with fast service and food decoration. Nevertheless, with a number of tourists consuming at the same time, hygiene may be overlooked in the process of food preparation. The matter of physical health risk is important to tourists since health problems from unsafe food can lead to an inability to pursue their planned activities (Sonnenburg et al., 2000).

In an increasingly competitive world of tourism marketing, every region or destination is in a constant search for a unique product to differentiate itself from other destinations. Local food or cuisines that are unique to an area are one of the distinctive resources that may be used as marketing tools to get more visitors. This is particularly evident from the studies on wine tourism (Charters & Knight, 2002;

Hall &Macionis, 1998; Telfer, 2001), which have demonstrated that tourists travel to destinations that have established a reputation as a location to experience quality local products.

Existing and emerging food risks have been recognized by many governments' worldwide and other related organizations because these are responsible for communicating food risks and other safety matters to interested stakeholders, including consumers. Many efforts have been taken to improve food safety standards.

The present study is based on the restaurants situated at the highway tourist complexes of Haryana on NH-1. So, the researcher focuses on the study area to provide a basis for the study.The highway tourism of Haryana is famous for its unique food joints. Food joints facilities are those facilities which the passenger avails on road side to have food, rest, (rest for vehicles also) and other refreshment. There are five different kinds of food-joints in the study area i.e. hotels, restaurants, dhabas, wine-shops and other facilities (Singh and Kasuhik, 2012).

Restaurants located in the highway tourist complexes are famous touristic enclave in which many first time travellers to Haryana stop and spend some times before moving on to other locations of Haryana or nearby tourist attractions. The highway tourist complexes of Haryana usually occupied by a number of tourists year round. These spots are dotted with small guesthouses and lodgings, pubs, and restaurants, filling stations, saloons and parlours, souvenir shops and others vendors who cater to tourists. The Haryana is famous for its highway stop over with twenty-four hours availability of delicious food and recreation.

Such developments have spurred an interest in experiencing the unique and indigenous food, food products and cuisines of a destination, so much so that people are often traveling to a destination specifically to experience the local cuisines or to taste the dishes of its 'celebrity chef' (Mitchell & Hall, 2003).

Haryana is known as the "Green Land" of India and is known for its magnificent growth in the field of agriculture. Haryana has many interesting and unique tourism offerings i.e. Highway Tourism,

Farm Tourism, Golf Tourism, Pilgrim Tourism, MICE Tourism, Heritage Tourism and Adventure Tourism. The distinctive offerings of Haryana, makes it a perfect vacation destination for many a travelers (Ministry of Tourism, 2012).

Since highway tourism is the most popular type oftourism in Haryana, the major resource for that comes inthe form of highways passing through the State. Highway tourism signifies the availability of certain facilities for the tourists who commute between two destinations. These facilities range from food, entertainment, recreation, roadside attractions to shopping Malls, petrol stations, medical facilities etc.The increasing number of visitors bring s The strengths of Highway tourism complexes of Haryana attract large number of visitors which bring comprehensive development of the state contribute significantly to the State's economy(Haryana Development Report, 2009).

Understanding the growing importance of highway tourism and food joints the researcher decided to conducted a study with the following objectives:

- To study the demographic profile and travel characteristics of the tourists visiting Haryana highway tourism complexes.
- To measure the level of perceived risk towards food safety at selected tourism complexes of Haryana.

Literature review

Quality of food is an extremely important aspect of human life and people become more and more concerned about nutrition, food safety and environmental issues that determine their acceptance of food products. Good quality of food has not a constant definition but varies according to the food category and to the consumers' preferences. Food quality can be described to wholesomeness, freshness, nutritional value, texture, smell, colour, fragrance, and flavour. So, there is need to focus on evaluation of the factors, namely cultural, social, demographical, and consumer segmentation that appear to have constant influence on the consumer's food quality perception processes (Lazarova, 2010).

Cleanliness is an essential aspect of the restaurant industry. As dining-out rate has been increased, the issues of restaurant cleanliness and food safety have become increasingly emphasized from both managerial and customer viewpoint. Overall half of all food-borne illnesses were contracted from dining on food prepared outside the home and many of the food-borne illnesses happened because restaurants didn't follow proper food handling steps (Yu, 2012)

As such, providing safe and clean restaurant environment by reducing the burden of disease from food is the responsibility of restaurant owners, employees, country and related stakeholders. In addition, the restaurant industry is facing a stricter regulatory environment. They should offers guidelines aimed at prevention and reduction of food-borne illness and death from food produced at the retail level (Yu, 2012).

Therefore, researchers have noted that in a competitive service business environment, managers should understand their customers and provide service that increases their ability to attract new customers and to win the loyalty of existing customers, as well as increasing the positive word-of-mouth effect. In this manner, understanding the importance food safety and perceived risk the research decided to propose this study for successful restaurant management.

Food Safety

According to Food and Agriculture Organization of the United Nations in Collaboration with the World HealthOrganization (FAO/WHO, 1997), the main goal of food safety and risk management is to protect public health by controlling food risks as effectively as possible through the selection as well as the implementation of appropriate measures.

Kleefet al. (2006) stated that the way to increase consumers trust in food safety was to maintain these three practices: good risk assessment, risk management, and risk communication. Lepp and Gibson (2003) explained that there are seven risks factors perceived by international tourists which are health, political instability, terrorism, strange food, cultural barriers, a nation's political and religion dogma, and crime. Food risk perception was defined in Hohl and Gaskell (2008) by identifying three factors including adulteration and contamination, health effects, and production and hygiene. In the tourism industry, the food sector is one of the main facilitating sectors that support tourists' in situ experience. In many countries, food becomes the core tourism product that attracts tourists and can satisfy them.

Wongleedee(2012) studied international senior tourists in Thailand and his findings revealed that the majority of international senior tourists were apprehensive of their susceptibility to high risk of food and beverages in a foreign land. Nevertheless, the majority of international senior tourists rated the quality of food and beverage in Thailand as their highest level of satisfaction. However, food menus, sources of food and cooking premises may pose challenges to this industry, due to the heterogeneity of tourists' demographics. Health and hygiene factors become mattered and perceived differently by different demographics.

Miles et al (2004) studied about the public concern towards food safety by comparing the different opinions on food safety issues, and investigating whether there were any differences in demographic factors. The result regarding demographic differences revealed that there were differences among different genders, ages, and social classes. The research by Worsley and Lea (2008) examined the relationships between consumers' concerns about food and health and their personal values and demographic characteristics in South Australia. The findings showed a statistically significant relationship between the specific concerns and personal values, with an emphasis on the fact that demographic characteristics were important predictors. In Germany, Roosen et al.(2004) studied about food risk perception of German consumers during 1992 and 2002. They analyzed the consumers' general risk attitudes and their specific perceptions of food risks. The research discussed the socio-demographic variables, stating that female respondents were significantly more likely to be in the cluster of being concerned about natural food risks, while men judged risks as less important. Despite the fact that there are many studies discussing food safety in the literature, studies about foodsafety in the tourism industry are still limited. Moreover, little research regarding the extent of perceived risk in food products has been conducted (2004).

In regard to the fact that tourism is one of the industries in which diverse contacts between people appear. Many tourists from various countries gather together in particular places and do activities such as going out, having parties, eating and drinking. In this regard, it is essential to address the issue of tourists' health, food safety and hygiene.

Perceived Risk

Perceived risk is part of the consumers' behavior and marketing principles. It is a psychological factor that characterizes a buyer and determines the buyer's decision in the decision making process. There are many past studies in tourism that try to investigate the perceived risk of customers in order to reduce risk perception (2004). The literature mostly consists of studies on tourism risks in traveling aspects and risks related to diseases such as SARS, natural disasters such as Tsunami, and terrorism such as the 9/11 attack. Perceived risk has been defined in various academic fields and contexts of study. Moreover, perceived risk depends on individual consumer's engagement with a particular product or service purchase. It has been described from the simple definition to a more elaborated definition, especially when it is applied in the purchases of different kinds of products and services. Some academics defined perceived risk by pointing to its importance and role in the consumer's decision making process; as such, Reichel et al. (2007) defined perceived risk as an influential determinant that affects consumer behavior despite the fact that it may not be real. Some others have tried to narrow down the concept of perceived risk to their study contexts. Perceived risk can also be applied in the service industry as in the study by Bao (2009), in which it was explained as an influence on the level of perceived service quality, which afterwards shapes customer satisfaction. The later studies relevant to perceived risk propose perceived risk frameworks with a generation of different types of risks and risks in different types of products and services. Carroll (2009) studied about the spectators 'perceived risk during their attendance of a sport event proposing the definition of perceived risk as an individual's perceptions of the uncertainty and negative consequences constructed during attending a sport event, and will have impacts on future intentions to visit. The definition is broken down into psychosocial risk, physical risk, time risk performance risk, and financial risk. Griffin and Viehland (2011) in their study defined perceived risk in the context of online shopping by product categories assessed with demographic factor.

Lee et al. (2012) conducted a study to document consumer attitudes toward food safety in restaurant, specifically Asian and Mexican restaurants. Focus groups and an online survey were conducted to explore consumer perceptions of restaurant food safety and attitudes toward ethnic restaurants. The study revealed that kitchen cleanliness was the most important factor influencing safety followed by restroom cleanliness and cooking temperature. Food safety is an underlying factor in restaurant selection and continued patronage. Word of mouth and the internet were the most frequently cited sources of food safety information. Incorporating information about consumer attitudes into food safety training courses could help ethnic restaurant owners be mindful of their customers' expectations.

The present study is conducted in the state of Haryana, so the researcher also reviewed the existing literature related with the study area.

Singh (2012) in his research paper entitled 'challenges faced by tourism of Haryana' examines the major problem faced by Tourism Industry in Haryana and strategy and scope for tourism development in state. Anderson (2013) in her research paper entitled 'leakage the tourism system - a cost study of Zanzibar' examines the leakages in tourism system. The study seeks to trace the distribution channel of the tourist arriving in Zanzibar from generating market. The study was based on primary source. For this purpose 150 resorts were interviewed. The findings reveal massive internal and external leakages that only 16 percent of resorts' requirements were sourced within Zanzibar. Sharma (2012) conducted a study with Title 'Haryana tourism-Painted in different canvases. The main objectives of the study were to highlight the innovation of Haryana tourism and explain the highway tourism. Furthermore the study also focused on open golf tourism, pilgrim tourism and adventure tourism.

The most relevant studies was conducted by Singh and Kaushik (2012) showed the growth process and spatial pattern of food-joints along national highway-1, 2, 8 and10 falling in Haryana. The objective of the study was to analyse the spatial pattern and temporal growth of food-joints i.e. hotels, restaurants, dhabas, wine-shops and other facilities. The data have been analyzed with the help of simple statistical techniques. The study revealed tremendous growth of food-joints after 1991. The study points out that NH-1 and NH-10 have more concentration of highway food-joints facilities; however, the later has maximum number of facilities largely in big cities.

On the basis of extensive review of literature the researcher found that consumer perception of risk and their trust in risk information have been identified as important underlying determinants of consumer acceptance of new food as well as factors that influence consumer behavior in the context of food safety incidents. Therefore understanding consumer responses to various food safety issues is of crucial importance because food safety can be properly predicted if there is systematic understanding of the way in which consumer perceive risks, and benefits, associated with different food safety issues. Thus researcher decided to propose a study to measure the Food Safety and Perceived Risk: A Study Of Haryana Tourist Complexes Situtated On Nh-1.

Research methodology

The present study is conducted in Haryana which came in to existence on November 1, 1966. It shares boundary with Himachal Pradesh in the north, Delhi and Uttar Pradesh in the east, Rajasthan in the south and Punjab in the west. It encircles Delhi form three sides. The State Government has adopted a multi-pronged strategy to promote tourism. A total of 44 tourist complexes have been set up at strategic points along the highways passing through the State. The tourist complexes have been developed around Delhi with the interest of promoting leisure tourism and conference tourism.

Besides, tourists facilities have been set up at the district headquarters and in important towns to cater to the needs of tourist and local people some of the important tourist complexes are Surajkund and Badkhal Lake near Delhi, Sultanpur bird Sanctuary (Sultanpur), Sohna and Damdama in Gurgaon, Gauriya in Bahadurgarh, Myna and Tilyar in Rohtak Ethnic India in Rai, Blue Jay in Samalkha Skylark in Panipat, Oasis and Karna Lake in Karnal, Parakeet in Pipli, Kingfisher in Amabala and the fascinating pocket of pines in the Morni Hills and Pinjore Garden (Pinjore) etc.However, the present study is aimed at analyzing Food Safety and perceived risk at Haryana tourist complexes situated on NH-1 which include Kingfisher in Ambala, Parakeet in Pipli (Kurukshetra), Oasis/Karna Lake in Karnal, Skylark in Panipat, Blue Jay in Samalkha and Ethnic India in Rai (Sonepat).

The researcher consider various factors related to food hygiene and cleanliness as a key factor for the present study. While food hygiene can be a key factor in deciding where to dine (Ungku et al., 2011; Worsfold, 2006a), most people do not think of food safety when choosing a place to eat (Aksoydan, 2007; Leach, 2003). Customers who do consider safety often use aesthetics, visible cues, and restroom cleanliness to reflect the kitchen environment (Aksoydan, 2007; Barber &Scarcelli, 2009; Worsfold, 2006a). For what they cannot see, health inspectors' reports, specifically posted green, yellow, and red colours or A, B, C letter grades, can remind customers about the potential risk prior to entering the restaurant.

Study population for the present study was those visitors who visited the selected tourist complexes of Haryana and .To fulfill the objective carefully both primary and secondary techniques of data collection has been used. The secondary data was used to provide a baseline to the review of literature of study and it is collected from the library and online sources, books pertaining to the subject, journals and periodicals. For collecting primary data, a structured questionnaire was distributed to 150 visitors (25 each at selected tourist complexes) who stayed at the selected tourist complexes. Convenient sampling technique was used to record visitors' responses towards food safety and perceived risk at selected tourist complexes of Haryana. Out of 150 respondents 111 respondents were completely filled up the questionnaire.

Findings of the study

The findings of the study weredivided into 2 main parts: first, the respondents' demographic and travel information, and second, the level of perceived risk towards food safety based on 12 hygiene variables. The respondents were marked their perceived risk along five- point, Likert- type scale from very low risk to very high risk.

Demographic and Travel Profile of the Respondents

A total of 150 questionnaires were distributed for this research. After eliminating 39 ineffective questionnaires, 111 effective samples were usable. Table I describes the demographic and general travel information of the tourists. The gender mix is well balanced with 63.96 percent male and 36.04 percent were female. The majority of the respondents, 49.55 percent, were between the age of 21 and 30. The second and third largest age group was between 31 and 40 (18.02 percent), and 41 and 50 years old (17.12 percent) respectively. The respondents who were above 50 constituted only 15.31 percent of the study population. It is interesting to note that the education is mainly graduates (46.85 percent) whereas post graduates also shares a secondarily high percentage of 21.62. The respondents who were High school or secondary were 11.71 and 19.82 percent respectively. The respondents were also questioned regarding their income level. The highest income grout was the 5-10 lakh (47.75 percent) followed by 2-5 lakh (22.52 percent) and more than 10 lakh (29.73 percent).

Exhibit- I: Demographic Profile of Respondents

Variable	Characteristics	Percentage
Gender	Male	63.96
	Female	36.04
Age (in Years)	21-30	49.55
	31-40	18.02
	41-50	17.12
	More than 50	15.31
Education	High School	11.71
	Senior Secondary	19.82
	Graduate	46.85

	Post Graduate	21.62
Annual Income (in INR)	2-5 Lakh	22.52
	5-10 Lakh	47.75
	More than 10 Lakh	29.73

Regarding the frequency of visit the most common group is 2-5times which is 53.15 percent followed by first times (27.93 percent), and more than 5 times (18.92percent). Forthe question of stay at the tourist complexes the highest percentage falls to the 3- 5hours group (45.95percent), followed by 1- 2 hours (37.83 percent), and more than 5 hours (16.22 percent). The most common answer for the question"Have you ever been suffering from any disease during your visit/ stay at Tourism complexes of Haryana which is 90.99 percent, whereas "Yes" accounts for only 9.01 percent. The last question of the first part of the questionnaire addresses the information of whether they found any difficulty in finding a medical assistance to buy medicine if they became sick from food. A notably respondents present the answer "No" (88.29 percent) whereas only 11.71 percent were respond facing difficulty in finding medical assistance.

Exhibit- II: Travel Characteristics of the Respondents

Variable	**Characteristics**	**Percentage**
Frequency of Visit	First time visitor	27.93
	2-5 Times	53.15
	More than 5 times	18.92
How many times you spent at tourist complex (in hours)	1-2	37.83
	2-5	45.95
	More than 5	16.22
Have you suffering from any disease from food during your visit at tourist complex	Yes	9.01
	No	90.99
Do you find any difficulty medical assistance, if you suffer from disease from food at tourist complexes	Yes	11.71
	No	88.29

Perceived Risk for Food Safety by Hygiene Variables

Exhibit III reports levels of perceived risk for food safety using 7 hygiene variables and overall perceived risk. Mean (M) and standard deviation (SD) of the 7 variables is shown for the sample population of 111 tourists. Across all hygiene variables in the set of food and drink in established restaurants. Cleanliness of dining area attain first rank which has the highest risk score (M = 2.89, SD = 0.923), which is followed by cleanliness of food & drink served (M=2.89, SD=0.955) with second rank, cleanliness of dining utensils occupying third rank (M=2.88, SD= 1.033) and fourth rank booked by cleanliness of food seasoning and ingredients (M= 2.87, SD= 1.030). The cleanliness of food cooking method attains fifth rank (M=2.86, SD= 0.993), sanitation of food preparation area (M= 2.84, SD= 1.028), personal hygiene of food production staff working in the kitchen (M=2.81, SD= 1.093) occupying sixth and seventh rank respectively.

Exhibit- III: Perceived Risk for Food Safety by Hygiene Variables

Hygiene variables of food and drink in established restaurants if Selected tourist complexes of Haryana	**Mean**	**S.D.**	**Rank**
Cleanliness of food cooking method	2.86	0.993	5
Cleanliness of dining area	2.89	0.923	1
Sanitation of the food preparation area	2.84	1.028	6
Cleanliness of food & drink served	2.89	0.955	2
Cleanliness of dining utensils	2.88	1.033	3
Cleanliness of food seasoning and ingredients	2.87	1.030	4
Personal hygiene of Food production staff working in the kitchen	2.81	1.093	7
Personal hygiene of service staff working in the restaurant	2.72	1.025	8

Discussion

Previous studies in the food safety literature mainly showed the results and discussed in general food product consumer viewpoints. This study is useful in that it addresses food safety and perceived risk in the context of tourists. The findings may not be able to be generalized in other contexts. Yet it suggests that further studies of food safety and consumers in the tourism industry may be conducted with an emphasis onsocio- demographic and psychological factors such as types of tourists, which would be able to give a more clear answer of tourist risk perception on food and drink consumption during their holiday.

Food is part of the tourism industry whose intrinsic properties are heterogeneity and intangibility, implying that these properties can undermine consumers' confidence and result in an increased perceived risk (Mitchell, 1999). Restaurants 'owners, managers, and tourism authorities of Haryana tourism complexes may need to take this fact as an important matter and pay enough regard to cleanliness, even with small things as such the dining utensils or equipment and create a food safety atmosphere with physical evidence of cleanliness to food outlet. Furthermore, increasing higher standards on hygiene and making it tangible in the food preparation process, dining location and selling stalls, dining and cookingequipment's, as well as increasing hygiene knowledge and grooming of food and drink sellers and service providers, can ultimately be a way of enhancing the tourists' confident enjoyment and thereby generating income to this sector of food service.

Future research

Limitation of this paper is the area of the study. Due to time and cost constraints it is not possible to cover total tourism complexes of Haryana.Further research may compare tourists' income level, travel purposes, types of tourist, or existing knowledge of food safety with the level of perceived risk towards food safety. The use of different tourist sites for collecting data would add some value to tourism literature.

References

Aksoydan, E. (2007). Hygiene factors influencing customers' choice of dining-out units: findings from a study of university academic staff. Journal of Food Safety, 27(3), pp. 300-316.

Annual Report on Tourism Survey for Haryana (April 2011 - March 2012), Ministry of Tourism, Government of India.

Baker, G. A. (2003). "Food safety and fear: factors affecting consumer response to food safety risk," International food and agribusiness management review, Vol. 6, Issue 1.

Bao, C. (2009). "Air travel in the U.S.: an investigation of the influence of perceived risk in service quality," ProQuest Dissertations & Theses (PQDT),

Barber, N., &Scarcelli, J. M. (2009). Clean restrooms: how important are they to restaurant consumers? Journal of Foodservice, 20(6), pp. 309-320

Carroll, M. S. (2009). "Development of a scale to measure perceived risk in collegiate spectator sport and assess its impact on sport consumption intentions," ProQuest Dissertations & Theses (PQDT).

Charters, S., & Ali-Knight, J. (2002). Who is the Wine Tourist? Tourism Management, 23(3), pp. 311-319.

Chow, J. Alonso, Douglas, A. C. and O'neill, M. (2010). "Exploring open kitchens' impact on restaurateurs' cleanliness perceptions," Journal of retails & leisure property, Vo. 9, No. 2, pp. 93-104.

Cunningham, L.F. Gerlach, H., Harper, M.D. and Young, C.E. (2005). "Perceived risk and the consumer buying process: internet airline reservations", International journal of service industry management, Vol. 16 Issue 4, pp.357 - 372.

Dickson, T. and Dolnicar, S. (2004). "No risk, no fun: The role of perceived risk in adventure tourism," CD Proceedings of the 13th International Research Conference of the Council of Australian University Tourism and Hospitality Education (CAUTHE).

Dosman, M., Adamowicz, W. L. and Hrudey, S. E. "Socioeconomic determinants of health- and food safety-related risk perceptions," Risk analysis, Vol. 21, pp. 307-317.

FAO/WHO (1997). "Risk management and food safety".

Global Report on Food Tourism, 2012, A.M. Reports, Vol. II, UNWTO, Madrid, Spain.

Griffin and Viehland, D. (2011). "Demographic factors in assessing perceived risk in online shopping," 13th International Conference on Electronic Commerce - ICEC.

Hall, C. M., &Macionis, N. (1998). Wine Tourism in Australia and New Zealand. In R. W. Butler, M. Hall & J. Jenkins (Eds.), Tourism and Recreation in Rural Areas (pp. 197-224): Wiley.

Haryana Development Report, 2009.

Hohl, K. and Gaskell, G. (2008). "European public perceptions of food risk: cross- national and methodological comparisons," Risk analysis, Vol. 28, No. 2.

Kennedy, J., Worosz, M., Todd, E.C. and Lapinski, M.K. (2008). "Segmentation of US consumers based on food safety attitudes," British food journal, Vol. 110, No. 7, pp. 691-705, Emerald Group Publishing Limited.

Kleef E.V. et al. (2006), "Perceptions of food risk management among key stakeholders: result from a cross-European study," Elsevier. Appetite 47, pp.46-63.

Lazarova, R. (2010). Consumer's perception of food quality and its relation to the choice of food. A Master thesis submitted to Aarhus Universitet.

Leach, J. (2003). A guide to customer perceptions of food hygiene. London, England: Chadwick House Publishing.

Lee, L.E., Niode, O., Simonne, A.H., and Bruhn, C.M. (2012). Consumer Perception on food safety in Asian and Mexican Restaurants, ELSEVIER, Food Control 26, pp. 531-538.

Lepp and Gibson, H. (2003). "Tourist roles, perception risk and international tourism," Annals of tourism research, Vol. 30, No.3, pp.606-624.

Long, L. M. (1998). Culinary Tourism: A Folkloristic Perspective on Eating and Otherness. Southern Folklore, 55(3), pp. 181-204.

Mahon, D. and Cowan, C. (2004). "Irish consumers' perception of food safety risk in minced beef," British food journal, Vol. 106, No. 4, pp. 301-312.

Miles, S. et al. (2004). "Public worry about specific food safety issues," British food journal, Vol. 106, No. 1, pp. 9-22.

Mitchell, V. W. and Vassos, V. (1997). "Perceived risk and risk reduction in holiday purchases: a cross- cultural and gender analysis," Journal of Euro marketing, Vol. 6, No. 3, The Haworth Press, Inc.

Mitchell, V. W. (1999). "Consumer perceived risk: conceptualizations and models," European journal of marketing, Vol. 33, No. 1/2, 1999, pp. 163-195, MCB University Press.

Mitchell, R., & Hall, M. (2003). Consuming tourists: food tourism consumer behavior. In M. Hall, L. Sharples, R. Mitchell, N. Macionis& B. Crambourne (Eds.), Food Tourism Around the World. Oxford: Butterworth Heinemann.

National Restaurant Association. (2002). Travel and Tourism Facts [Electronic Version]. National Restaurant Association. Retrieved 9/27/2002.

Nyako, K. A. and Thompson, "Food safety risk perceptions and behaviour of consumers in the Southern Black Belt Region of the U.S.," unpublished.

Pyo, S. S., Uysal, M., &McLellan, R. W. (1991). A linear expenditure model for tourism demand. Annals of Tourism Research, 31, pp. 619-630.

Reichel, G. F. and Uriely, N. (2007). "Perceived risk and the non-institutionalized tourist role: the case of Israeli student ex-backpackers," SAGE Publications, Inc. Journal of travel research, Vol. 46, No. 2, pp. 217-226.

Roosen, J. S. (2004). Thiele and K. Hansen, "Food risk perceptions by different consumer groups in Germany,"working paper EWP 0407, Department of food economics and consumption studies, University of Kiel.

Sharma, A. (2012) 'Haryana tourism-Painted in different canvas' spectrum: A journal of multidisciplinary research Vol.1 issue 3

Shenoy, S.S. (2005). Food Tourism and the Culinary Tourist.A Doctoral Thesis submitted to the Graduate School of Clemson University,

Singh, S.P. and Singh, K. (2012). Growth Process and Spatial Pattern of Food Joints along Selected National Highways in Haryana: A Geographical Analysis. Asian Journal of Multidimensional Research Vol.1 Issue 2, pp.35-45.

Singh, R. (Nov 2012) "Challenges faced by Tourism Industry of Haryana" Volume 2, Isssue11, No-5, pp.1875-1880.

Sonnenburg, F. V. et al. (2000), "Risk and aetiology of diarrhoea at various tourist destinations," Elsevier. The Lancet, Vol. 356, No. 9224, pp. 133-4.

Symons, M. (1999). Gastronomic authenticity and the sense of place. Paper presented at the 9th Australian Tourism and Hospitality Research Conference for Australian University Tourism and Hospitality Education.

Telfer, D. J. (2001). Strategic Alliances along the Niagara Wine Route. Tourism Management, 22, pp. 21-30.

Tucker, M., Whaley, S. R. and Sharp, J. S. (2006). "Consumer perceptions of food-related risks," International journal of food science and technology, Vol. 41, pp. 135-146.

Ungku Fatimah, U. Z. A., Boo, H. C., Sambasivan, M., &Salleh, R. (2011). Foodservice hygiene factors e the consumer perspective. International Journal of Hospitality Management, 30(1), pp. 38-45.

Wongleedee, K. (2012). "Satisfaction: global senior tourists in Thailand," ICEMT Conference Proceeding, pp. 7-11.

Worsfold, D. (2006a). Consumer information on hygiene inspections of food premises. Journal of Foodservice, 17(1), pp. 23-31.

Worsley and Lea,E. (2008). "Consumer concerns about food and health: Examination of general and specific relationships with personal values and demographics," British food journal, Vol. 110, No. 11, pp. 1106-1118, Emerald Group Publishing Limited.

Yamane, T. (1967). "Statistics, an introduction analysis, 2nd ed., New York Harper and R.

Yeung, R. M. W. and Yee, W. M. S. (2002). "Multi- dimensional analysis of consumer perceived risk in chicken meat," Nutrition & Food Science, Vol. 32, No. 6, pp. 219-226.

Yu, S.A. (2012). Customer Perceptions of Restaurant Cleanliness: A Cross Cultural Study. Thesis submitted to the faculty of the Virginia Polytechnic Institute and State University.

Website:

- http://www.haryanatourism.gov.in/destination/highwaywise.asp retrieved on 05.10.2012 at 14:42.

DOES GREEN TOURISM SPEAKS BUSINESS?

Lipika Guliani

Assistant Professor, UIHMT, Panjab University lipika_b@yahoo.com

Syed Ahmad Rizwan

Assistant Professor, UIHMT, Panjab Universitye-syedahmadrizwan@gmail.com

Abstract: Green is the new word for business organization. Tourism businesses are no exception. For them too green does speak of environmental consciousness and represents responsibility of organization towards mother earth. Such initiatives will be life-long and more acceptable if it is related to business. Many businesses globally are encashing on this new concept. The current study delves into defining eco commerce and globally scrutinizing examples for organizations that how can this "greening" of business may yield profits for organizations in business terms.

Keywords: Eco-commerce, Green Hotels, Green, business, Green tourism.

Introduction

Tourism is recognized as one of the world's largest industries and continues to expand at a rapid rate (UNWTO 2006). Over 922 million people travelled in 2008 and it is estimated international tourism will increase to 1.1 billion by 2020 (UNWTO 2008). Tourism is also a profitable economic endeavor, making it an economically enticing industry and a form of development for many countries around the world. Indeed has the Travel and Tourism industry brings many positive impacts around the world but the fact that alongside with these advantages, other factors like climate change, Pollution and effects of tourism practices have also created a hot issue in the Tourism arena today. The negative impacts of tourism activities has resulted in an increasing demand of " green destination, meaning destination where there are visible efforts of protecting and sustaining the environment by dealing with issues like carbon emissions, bio diversity conservation, resources usage, water supply and waste management. It can be said that the tourism and the environment sustainability concept are visibly becoming natural partners.

Moreover, the hotel industry forms a large part of the tourism industry and if not managed properly, it has the potential to be detrimental to the social and natural environments within which it functions. Hotels are also resource intensive and in order to reduce their impact, it is imperative to go "green!". With increasing consumer focus on the environmental impact of everything, it's no surprise that travelers are seeking hotels that consider the environment too. Consumers who buy locally produced food, products with less packaging, and compact fluorescent light bulbs, want lodging that does the same."Going green is one of the hottest trends in the lodging industry," says Ray Burger, owner of Pineapple Hospitality, a green hotel product supplier and environmental/marketing consulting firm in St. Charles, Mo.This study examines various aspects of tourism and above all about green tourism, that how converting green can helps in increasing business??

Tourism business : income around the world

Worldwide, tourism generates annual revenues of nearly 11% of the global GNP (Gross National Product), making it the world's largest industry. Tourism is the world's largest income earner and was worth $ 500 billion in 2007 as tourism has become a popular global leisure activity. In 2008, there were over 922 million international tourist arrivals, with a growth of 1.9% as compared to 2007. It means every year the income from tourism is increasing.

A graph revealing approximate tourist arrivals in millions

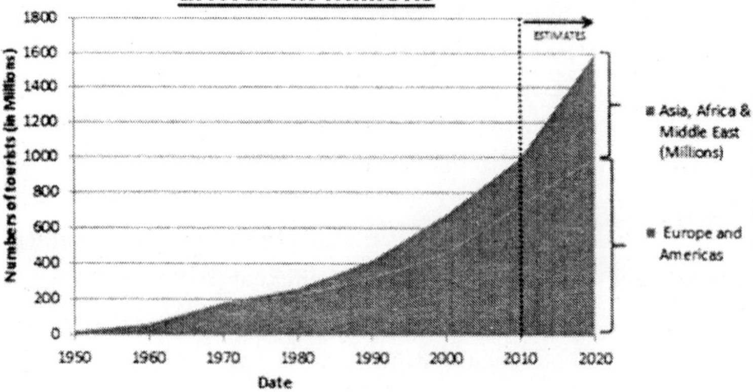

The graph above shows the last 60 years of tourist growth, increasing from just tens of millions in 1950 to 694 million in 2004. The other massive trend is the continued dominance of Europe as a destination, but also the massive growth in numbers to East Asia and the Americas.

It generates huge amount of wealth for countries and generates jobs at countries of all stages of development. The reliance on tourism as a source of income varies across the globe and can be measured as a percentage of countries GDP. Most Caribbean countries get at least half of their GDP from tourism. France, Spain, USA, China, Italy and UK are the most visited countries. This can be seen below;

International tourist arrivals in 2009 (millions)

In addition, it can be seen that many MEDCs also dominate the income earned by tourism;

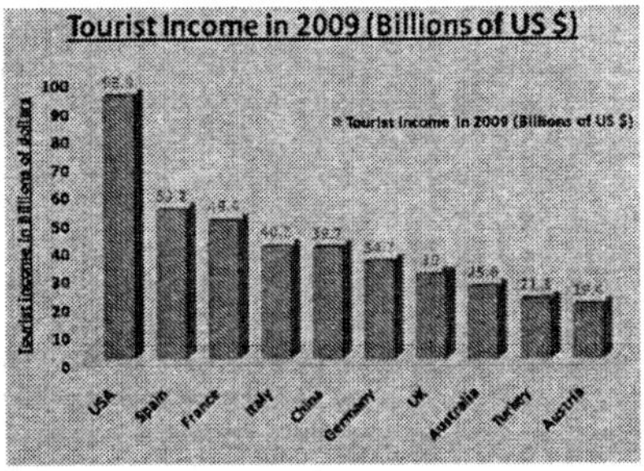

From above following points are evident

1) Wealthy nations such as the USA, Spain and France all have huge tourist numbers and consequently high amounts of money made from tourism as an activity. However, as a percentage of GDP the contribution of tourism is small (but not insignificant. These countries receive lots of people as tourists because they have the infrastructure (hotels, airports, visitor facilities) to allow tourists to have a great visitor experience. They are also politically safe places.
2) Poorer nations receive far fewer tourists and earn less money from tourism as an activity. However, tourism can often make up a huge percentage of countries GDP. This is because those countries have fewer other industries to make money, and this makes them vulnerable to changes in their tourism industry. This is especially evident in Island nations as shown on the graph above, where limited land space makes the development of other industries difficult.

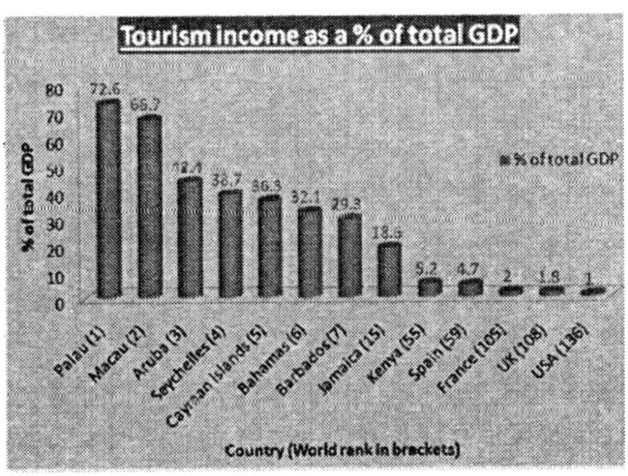

However, tourism generates jobs and a huge amount of foreign exchange too.

For Example,the Lake District National Park is England's largest park and includes Scafell Pike - its highest mountain, Wastwater - its deepest lake and thriving communities like Keswick and Bowness-on-Windermere. Current surveys show that at least 15.8 million visitors come to the Lake District each year spending a total of £925 million.

Green tourism or Ecotourism

Green tourism or ecotourism - is options, types and methods of cognitive journeys for which a major resource, and motivation is the environment, or its individual elements: landscapes, natural monuments, various natural systems. Ecotourism originated in the late 1970s when the negative impact of tourism started becoming obvious. Tourism was damaging the wetlands in the Yucatan Peninsula in Mexico. Hector Ceballos-Lascurain, a Mexican architect and environmentalist who coined the term "ecotourism," and his conservation group worked to protect these wetlands. They began talking to tourism professionals, government officials and others about the idea. These efforts led to a public awareness of ecotourism.

Ecotourism is the term applied to tourism and travel that pays special attention to environmental concerns. It is defined as responsible tourism focused on the natural world which has emerged as a concept that unites the interests of environmentalists and developers. Proponents of ecotourism see it as potential salvation of some of the world's most endangered ecosystems, and an opportunity for communities that possess biological resources to develop sustainable economic strategies, instead of pursuing environmentally-damaging patterns of resource use. However, finding a compromise between preservation and development is often challenging, and ecotourism can generate additional environmental problems for the very regions it is intended to protect. Ecotourism is a growing component of the larger tourism industry, and several factor indicate that it is likely to thrive over time. These factors include increased awareness of environmental problems among tourist populations, willingness of tourists to engage in socially -aware travel, and interest in visiting lesser- known countries like-Belize rather than traditional vacation gateway.

Ecotourism is intended to be sustainable, focused on the natural world, and beneficial to local communities. The IUCN (World Conservation Union) defines it as environmentally responsible travel and visitation to relatively undisturbed natural areas, in order to enjoy and appreciate nature that promotes conservation, has low negative visitor impact, and provides for beneficially active socio-economic involvement of local populations. The International Tourism Society (TIES) defines ecotourism as "Responsible travel to natural areas that conserves the environment and improves the welfare of local people." A relatively new travel model, ecotourism attempts to reduce negative human impact on sensitive ecosystems, on fragile cultures and third world economies.

Some examples of eco/green tourism

Ecotourism in Tropical Rainforests

Rainforest Expeditions in Peru is an example of ecotourism. It educates people around the world about the endangered Amazon Rainforest of South America. It also provides business opportunities for local groups of people, which helps with the conservation of the natural environment as well as economic stability of local communities.

Ecotourism in Africa

Conservation Corporation (CC) Africa is a group that works in six African countries to preserve the natural environment and benefit local communities. The group has successfully relocated 2,000 wild animals such as loins, rhinos, leopards and giraffes from other areas, thereby helping their survival as a species. Guests at Phinda Private Game Reserve (KwaZulu-Natal, South Africa) learn how to identify various creatures as well as discover the native culture and environment. CC Africa also provides training and jobs to the native people at the reserve, as well as money for schools and health-care clinics.

Ecotourism in the Galapagos Islands

One of the most unusual ecosystems in the world, this is a chain of 120 volcanic islands in the Pacific Ocean 600 miles (965 kilometers) off the coast of Ecuador. They are home to rare creatures, plants and flowers; giant tortoises, marine iguanas (belonging to the lizard family), sea lions and rare birds thrive here. Tourism is strictly controlled in terms of accessibility of areas. Tourists are accompanied by guides at all times.

Potential of green tourists

The growing economic importance of Green tourist cannot be ignored. According to a recent report published by the Green Hotels Association, "Companies with proactive environmental strategies have a 4 percent higher return on investment, 9 percent higher sales growth and 17 percent higher operating income growth than companies with poor environmental track records."

A study conducted by Virginia Polytechnic Institute and State University (Virginia Tech) and Lodging Hospitality (Watkins, 1994), indicated that frequent travelers would stay in hotels with environmental strategies. For example, Green tourism generates billions of dollars globally and is reported to be growing at a rate of 10% to 15% annually, the fastest growth rate in the travel market. Much of this growth has been in travel to developing countries (20%) that offer eco tourists pristine environments often coupled with indigenous cultural experiences. Surveys of tour operators consistently suggest that green tourists are willing to pay for these experiences, with 7 million U.S. tourists willing to pay between $2,000 and $3,000 for an green tour (World Tourism Organization 1994).

The Green Tourist demand and business do exist it is just the will of the stakeholders along with business acumen which is needed to make the Green Tourist move and contribute both to economy and environment. Following are the types of income generated from tourists :-

Eco commerce

Eco commerce is a business, investment, and technology-development model that employs market-based solutions to balancing the world's energy needs and environmental integrity. Through the use of green trading and green finance, eco-commerce allows for the further development of clean technologies such as wind power, solar power, biomass, and hydropower. Eco Commerce is an integrated ecological-economical model that provides a means to account for and value land management activities that improves the condition of natural capital and values the output of eco services. Eco Commerce is more comprehensive than a compilation or organization of ecosystems service markets as it provides the framework to build an ecological intelligence system that allows the public arena of commerce to define sustainability.

Green tourism & hotel industry

Individually, hotels do not have a significant negative impact on the environment. Collectively however, they can be very wasteful and consume huge amount of resources. It has been estimated that seventy-five percent of hotels' environmental impacts can be directly related to excessive consumption (Bohdanowicz, 2006). This is wasteful in terms of resources and it creates unnecessary operational costs. The Hotel industry in particular has recently received much attention, with awareness of the negative impact that are having on the environment (Kasim, 2004). Negative impacts include the extensive amount of laundry that hotels do on a daily basis, the use of disposable products, heated swimming pools, and the use of strong cleaning products by housekeeping departments (Gustin & Weaver, 1996). Some negative impacts include the extensive amount of laundry that hotels do on a daily basis, the use of disposable products, heated swimming pools, and the use of strong cleaning products by housekeeping departments (Gustin & Weaver, 1996). These impacts have urged many hotels to change or modify their practices so they are aware that this will not only help to sustain the environment but will also be advantageous to the hotel also in the long run. By doing and practicing environment friendly practices, hotels gain positive publicity, customer loyalty, hence a definite competitive edge over competitors. (Guskin & Weaver, 1996)

The increase concern of environment issues is certainly having an impact of hotel selection by visitors. A survey by the U.K.'s Devon County Council in 2009 shows that 54 % of respondents really consider environment issues before they book a trip to a particular destination. Further the survey also shows that 82 % of them were willing to paid more to stay in a green hotel which provides green services and hospitality. Indeed thus survey gives an idea of tourist's attitude about green hotel and green practices. In Mauritius many hotels like Beachcomber in Trou aux biches are going green. The green economic revolution is impacting the $90 billion U.S. hotel industry. Hoteliers and their vendors have the unique opportunity to increase revenue and market share by aligning themselves with their customers' emerging green focus.

One innovative leader is Habitat Suites in Austin, Texas. The hotel's motto is "Environmental consciousness in action." The hotel environment is free of toxic chemicals, has the largest hotel solar system in the continental U.S., and the property's organic fruit and vegetable garden is used for hotel food services and contributes to local food banks.

Why to go green?

Several studies have indicated that economic benefits can be gained in hotels through implementing environmental and social initiatives. In addition to cost benefits, there are also benefits to choosing an environmentally sustainable strategy. These include: Gaining competitive advantage by being a leader in the sector; Customer loyalty; Employee retention; Awards and recognition, Increased brand value etc. Green programs can provide a competitive advantage to leaders as long as green activities continue to be voluntary. Over time, however, green practices in the hospitality industry will become a baseline requirement, particularly as the cost of non-renewable energy continues to rise, regulatory pressure increases, and consumers become more demanding. Therefore, hotels with business models that revolve around green practices will have the strongest opportunity to achieve a competitive advantage by being ahead of the emerging sustainability curve. The term green hotel, which is the phrase most often used today, has "evolved to embrace all areas of sustainability and corporate social responsibility," according to the International Tourism Partnership [ITP] (2007, p. 1)

16 Feb 2011 Caribbean and international business leaders, including those involved in tourism, looking to cash in on green tourism to get practical answers at Sustainable Tourism Conference from 3-6 April in Bermuda. That's when the internationally recognized expert in sustainable tourism development and destination stewardship, Brian Mullis reveals the most powerful means by which tourism businesses and destinations can improve their bottom line through sustainable tourism. Mr. Mullis illustrate how Sustainable tourism has evolved from a grassroots movement or niche market into part of mainstream corporate and consumer culture and how businesses can make the practice profitable. The business case for engaging in green business practices is stronger than ever, said Mullis, who he has assisted hundreds of travel-related companies, including Fortune 500 companies, in the areas of sustainable tourism, business development, market access, carbon management, and standards development.

Case studies- green hotels & financial benefits

Hotel	Green Practice	Cost Savings	Benefits	Awards
Strattons Hotel (owned and managed by Vanessa Scott, is a 14 bedroom boutique hotel situated in the market town of Swaffham, Norfolk)	Waste Minimisation	£2,000 per year just in plastic reduction (The hotel reduced the amount of plastic bottles to landfill by 97% and saved £2,000 per	Saving money & reducing landfill. This monitoring has helped the hotel to keep its annual landfill waste to less than	Gold Star Award at the 2011 Green Tourism Awards

		year by switching to using refillable bathroom toiletries)	2% of its total waste output.	
Millbrook Cottages	Energy Saving	Reducing Carbon footprint and becoming more self sufficient	focuses on their co-mmitment to reduce dependency on fossil fuels by installing a number of different renewable technologies onsit (like-5kW wind turbine, 2.2kW array of photovoltaic panels, 750W hydro system). Millbrook Estate is enjoying the benefits of Feed-In Tariffs (FITs) from the energy produced from the	GOLD award(2007)

			wind turbine. With the Feed in Tariffs included, Millbrook estate is making enough financially to cover the cost of the site's electricity.
Waterton Park Hotel built on an island surrounded by a 26-acre lake and natural wildlife park	Energy Saving	£67,000 in total	A renewable energy heating system was designed by Yorkshire Renewable Energy Solutions (YRES) to use the latent heat within the lake to produce hot water and heating. Firstly, a NIBE 60kW heat pump system was installed to supply heat to the hotel's 39,000-gallon

swimming pool, as well as providing hot water for the showers in the leisure centre. This was successfully completed in 2009 and the initial savings on oil being in the region of £22,000 and equally important in ecological terms, a saving of around 168 tonnes of carbon per annum. Second phase of the project has reduced the carbon emmissions by a further 400 tonnes and taken away the overall

			annual oil costs of £45,000.	
Best Western Plus Blunsdon House Hotel (four star family-owned hotel in Swindon in Wiltshire.)	Waste Minimisation	£1500 per annum	Helps in reducing carbon impacts of the business by using biodiesel. Reuse of waste & money savings	GOLD Award
Battlesteads Hotel, owned and run by Richard and Dee Slade, provides high quality accommodation in Northumberland	Energy Saving	36% reduction in LPG and 12% energy saving	Increased revenue due to low energy costs. Reducing costs and overall carbon plus faster cooking times.	Gold Star Award at the 2011 Green Tourism Awards
Combe House Devon is an independent, privately run Grade 1 Elizabethan Country House Hotel & Restaurant	Energy saving Annual saving of 30%	Combe House Hotel & Restaurant has restore thc old Victorian Gardens and develop the fruit and vegetable project. This has brought	National award in 2010 for 'Most Excellent innovation in Sustainable Hospitality'.	

		about an estimated saving of 30% on the fruit and vegetable bill, giving a payback period of approxima-tely 3 years.		
One Aldwych Hotel in London	Water saving	80% of water has been saved since operation	This study focused on the Evac system whi-ch is a Sca-ndinavian vacuum operated drainage system minimising water wastage.	Gold GTBS award

Source: Compiled by authors from various sources

All the above case studies shows that more and more green hotels means more & more savings which leads to environmental as well as monetary benefits .

Other Benefits of Green Tourism

Energy and Sustainability

Long-distance travel requires energy: fuel for planes, trains, automobiles and boats. Many transportation companies are working to reduce their energy consumption; use alternative sources such as bio fuel and solar power; and offset their carbon footprint by giving back to charities.

Environmental Preservation

Ecotourism often takes travelers to exotic, untouched areas where nature still reigns over humans. While in pristine areas, conscious travelers take care to not disturb nature: staying on trails, controlling trash and fire, keeping chemicals out of the earth and water..

Voluntourism

More and more adventurers and long-term travelers are volunteering on farms, in schools and at building sites around the world.

Green Cuisine

Savvy eco tourists know that local food is sustainable food. By patronizing locally owned restaurants and hotels that work with farmers in the community, eco-travelers support local agriculture and reduce the environmental cost of shipping food over long distances.

Revenue

Ecotourism aspires to give indigenous peoples an opportunity to realize fair income and to raise them up from extreme poverty. According to Benefits of Ecotourism.com, eco tourist dollars could create an environment in which local residents enjoy the economic benefits of stretching natural resources. In reality, investors and corporations gain monetarily and local poverty often is not alleviated.

Conservation

Ecotourism does more than bring local and worldwide awareness to threatened regions of the world; groups such as TIES use funds generated from ecotourism to establish and maintain national parks and nature reserves.

Protection of wildlife

Ecotourism also helps to protect threatened wildlife and ensures that robust animal populations remain that way. Organizations such as the Nature Conservancy work with local resorts to help them build properties that will not harm the indigenous fauna. If you visit one of these eco-friendly lodges, you will know that your visit is not harming local animal populations.

Economic Advantages

Ecotourism destinations are often in economically depressed regions of the world. Organizations like TIES and the Nature Conservancy ensure that the hotels and lodges are built in ways that will benefit the local community---i.e., with fair and sound hiring practices---and help lead to economic stabilization. In addition, these organizations train locals in hospitality, tourism marketing and other facets of tourism that will help locals to operate their properties better and maximize profit.

Conclusion

Tourism & Hospitality industry is one of the biggest revenue generating industry around the world .According to Pizam's article (1982), the tourism and hospitality industry has been applauded by industrialized and developing countries for the number of jobs created. A large amount of position vacancy is generated within the tourism industry and the supported industries. As a labor-intensive industry, its contribution to employment is not only restricted to the area or country but it also provides those jobs to women, youngsters, unskilled, minorities and the socially disadvantaged who find it very hard to get any jobs (Pizam, 1982). Moreover going green has more advantages towards the society & the business as well. It helps in gaining competitive advantage, increase the brand value and employee retention which includes green hotels too. It is an environmentally conscientious operation that promotes and practices energy ,efficiency, conservation, and recycling, while at the same time providing monetary benefits to the hospitality industry.

References

Battlesteads (nd) Available at http://www.green-tourism.com/case-studies/battlesteads-hotel/case-18/. Accessed on 01 January 2014.

Bohdanowicz, P. (2006), 'Environmental Awareness and Initiatives in the Swedish and Polish Hotel Industries - Survey Results' International Journal of Hospitality Management, vol. 25, no. 4, pp. 662-668.

Brien, K.O (nd) Available at http://ezinearticles.com/?Green-Business-Travel---Increase-Sales-and-Save-the-Whales!&id=2371324. Accessed on 18 December 2013

Cool Geography (2014) Available at www.coolgeography.co.uk. Accessed on 19 December 2013

Eco Commerce (nd) Available at http://www.ecocommerce101.com. Accessed on 3 January 2013.

Gieseke Tim (2011). EcoCommerce 101: Adding an ecological dimension to the economy; Bascom Hill Publishing.Mpls.

Graci, S and Kuehel, J. (nd). How To increase your bottom line by going green. Accessed from greenhotels.combined.com. Accessed on 12December 2013.

Green Hotels (2008). Available at http://www.missouribusiness.net/eac/docs/green_hotels.asp. Accessed on 09 January 2014.

Grouch, A. (2012). Advantages of Ecotourism..ehow. Available at http://www.ehow.com/about_5434465_advantages-ecotourism.html.

Gustin, M. & Weaver, P. (1996). Are hotels prepared for the environmental consumer? The Cornell Hotel and Restaurant Administration Quarterly, 20(2), 1-14.

Hotel Combined (2008). Available at http://green.hotelscombined.com/Gyh-The-Business-Case-For-Sustainability.php. Accessed on 2 January 2014.

International Tourism Partnership (n.d.). Going Green: Minimum standards towards a sustainable hotel. Retrieved October 30, 2007 from -http://tourismpartnership.org/downloads/Going%20Green.pdf. Accessed on 5 January 2013.

Kasim, A. (2004). Socio-environmentally responsible hotel business: Do tourists to Penang Island, Malaysia care? Journal of Hospitality & Leisure Marketing, 11(4), 5-28.

Lindsay, H. E. (1998). Ecotourism:the promise &perils of environmentally-oriented travel.

OFGEM (2005). Available at http://www.ofgem.gov.uk/e-serve/RHI/Pages/RHI.aspx. Accessed on 12 December 2013.

Pizam, A. (1982). Tourism and crime: is there a relationship? Journal of Travel Research Issue 1.

Roth, B. (1998). Hotels are taking advantage of consumers' desire for eco-friendly vacation options.

Sen, D. (2012). Role of Ecotourism in Present Tourism.

UK Essays (2008) Available at http://www.ukessays.com/essays/tourism/green-research-within-the-hospitality-industry-tourism-essay.php#ixzz2qOVkVq3F. Accessed on 5 January 2014.

Watkins, E. (1994). Do guests want green hotels? Lodging Hospitality, 70-72.

WTO (2012) World Tourism Organisation Available at www.unwto.org. Accessed on 12 January 2014.

AYURVEDIC CUISINE: A WAY TO UNDERSTAND AHAR AND ANNA ACCORDING TO YOUR OWN CONSTITUTION

Mahesh Kumar

Research Scholar, Institute of Hotel & Tourism Management, Maharishi Dayanand University, Rohtak-124001 mahesh972000hm@gmail.com

Goldi Puri

Assistant Professor, Institute of Hotel & Tourism Management, Maharishi Dayanand University, Rohtak-124001 E-mail: drgoldipuri@gmail.com

Abstract: Ayurveda deals with area concerning the healthy and long life of human beings. Ayurveda does not only deals with natural medicines, it covers the whole aspects of life. It preaches that we live to eat and do not eat to live. Ayurveda places special emphasis on Ahar (diet) and Anna (food) and believes that healthy nutrition nourishes the mind, body andsoul. Ayurveda does not discriminate food to be good, or bad, instead it emphasizes various factors that influence food, such as its biologicalproperties, origin, environmental factors, seasons, preparation, freshness, and provides a logical explanation of how to balance food according toone's dosha and physical needs.There is no letter that is not a mantra, there is not a root that is not a food/medicine.There is not a man who is not useful. It is the coordinator of these elements who is a rare breed and is limited by hisher wisdom.

Keywords: Ayurveda, Taste,ThreeDoshas, Satyik, Rajsik, Tamsik.

Introduction

Annam BrahmeRaso Vishnu, PaktoDevoMahesarah EvamJnatvaTuYoBhunkte, Anna Dosho Na Lipyate.

The creative energy in the food is Brahma, The nourishing energy in the body is Vishnu, and the transformation of food into pure consciousness is Shiva. If you know this, then any impurities in the food you eat will never become a part of you.

Ayurveda is a way of healing and a way of life that always takes into consideration the whole person. According to the teachings of Ayurveda, every aspect of life contributes to overall health. Poor health seldom has a simple or single cause.

Ayurvedic cuisine derives from a 4000 year timeline. Most people believe that the origins of Indian history, and therefore the cuisine, dates back to Mohenjedaro and Harrapan civilizations. It is understood that the ayurvedic tradition of cooking, which is a complete holistic approach to cooking, evolved at this point in time. In Vedic times, a normal diet consisted of fruit, vegetables, meat, grain, dairy products and honey. Over time, some segments of the population embraced vegetarianism due to the ancient Hindu philosophy of ahimsa1000BC. The very famous phrase you are what you eatprobably is the origin of the teachings of ayurveda.

- From purityof food follows thepurity of the internal organ" - Chandogya Upanishad, Vii.6.2
- Of curd when it is churned, that which is its subtle part rises upward. That becomes clarified butter. In this very way, of food when it is eaten, that which is the subtle part, that rises upward, and that becomes mind" -Chandogya Upanishad, Vi.6.1 & 2

Objectives

The objectives behind the research article are: To study AyurvedicCuisine. To study vatta, pitta and kapha. To study satyik, rajsik and tamsik food.

Research Methodology:

- o In this research paper research methodology is qualitative analysis and source of data is secondary data.

Your Personal constitution:

Your personal constitution, which is your individual metabolic makeup, helps determine how much effect specific tastes have on you. This is why everyone who eats the same food does not necessarily suffer from exactly the same mental and physical effects from it. When all the members of a family enjoy a meal together, each individual tastes will be affected according to his/her own individual tastes. Your inborn metabolic pattern is called "prakriti", which also means Nature. You can learn how to prevent health imbalances and how to best treat them when they arise. You can know the prognosis of any disease you might contract, and you can determine which rejuvenation program will best for you. You can plan your aahar for your family according to what is best for each of their Prakrtis. (Svoboda RE, 1992).

The five great elements:

Ayurveda was designed by the Rishis especially for those who want to enjoy the world healthily. The rishi used the theory of the five great elements to explain how the internal and external forces are linked together. The five great elements are: Earth, Water, Fire, Air, and Space.

Earth: The solid state of matter, whose characteristic attribute is stability, fixity or rigidity. Earth is stable substance.

Water: the liquid state of matter, whose characteristic attribute is flux. Water is substance without stability.

Fire: The power which can convert a substance from solid to liquid to gas, and vice versa, increasing or decreasing the relative order in the substance. Fire characteristic attribute is transformation.

Air: the gaseous state of matter, whose characteristic attribute is mobility. Air is existence without form.

Space: the field from which everything is manifested and in to which everything returns; the space in which events occur. Space has no physical existence; it exist only as distances which separate matter.

The *Doshas*

One's sense of well-being reflects the inner state of health. Good health is the maintenance of one's unique combination of the doshas, a balanced condition of agni, of the seven body tissues, of the three waste systems(urine, sweat and feces), as well as balance in the mind, senses and consciousness. It is equally important to one's well-being to have love, happiness and clarity in daily living. Doshicimbalance governs internal biochemical changes that will eventually lead to either high or low metabolism. Pitta doshagoverns all physical and biochemical changes that take place within the body. Through this process foodstuffs are transformed into energy, heat and vitality. Pittaperforms these functions throughout one's life, but is especially prominent during the adult years. All these activities of

Pittadepend upon "digestive fire" or agni. Poor agnimeans poor health. Wrong diet such as hot spicy foods, wrong lifestyle such as living in a hot climate and repressed emotions can alter the normal function of pitta. Anabolism is the process of building up the body. It is the repair, growth and creation of new cells. This process is managed by kaphaand ismost active in the baby, child and teen years. Kaphadoshacan be disturbedby excessive intake of dairy, cold and oily foods.Catabolism is the destructive, but necessary, stage of metabolism.Larger molecules are broken down into smaller ones. This molecular deathis governed by vatadoshaand is most active in old age. Repeated intakeof vata-provoking food, such as salads and popcorn, and over-exercisingcan escalate vataand disturb health.(Svoboda RE, 1992)

Ayurveda revolve around the concept that our bodyis made up of these five elements-fire, air,earth, space and water. These five elements condense to the three dosha: Vata, pitta and Kapha, which are effectively Air, Fire and water respectively.

Vata: is the principle of kinetic energy in the body. It is mainly concerned with nervous system, and controls all body movement.

Kapha: is the principle of potential energy, which controls body stability and lubrication. The tissues and wastes of the body which vata moves around are Kapha province.

Pitta; controls the body balance of kinetic and potential energies. All of pitta process involve digestion or cooking; even if it is the cooking of thoughts in to theories in the mind. The enzymatic and endocrine system are pitta main field of activity.

Vata, pitta and kapha are all essential to life, but can cause great harm if they are allowed to fall out of harmonv with one another.How much of each Doshas produces in your body primarily depends on which tastes you consume. The tastes influence the balance of the Doshas in the body. Tastes have profound effect on all parts of the organism and not merely the tongue

Ayurveda classifies food in to the following Six Tastes (Rasas): one should be in a habit of taking all six 'Rasa' (tastes) in order to prevent nutritional deficiency disorders. Each taste stimulated by the food contributes to the nourishment of the body when consumed in appropriate quantity.

Sweet: Promotes life as a whole, provides overall strength, luster to the skin and is beneficial for the throat.However, excessive use will aggravate kapha and contribute to obesity, congestion and other diseases.

Sour: taste stimulates "agni" (proper digestive forces), provides energy, awakens the mind and stimulates salivation. Yet, excessive use will cause heartburn, indigestion, and water retention.

Salt: is heavy and oily and when consumed in moderation is antispasmodic, promotes energy and helps maintain water and electrolyte balance. However, when used in excess salt induces water retention, elevates blood pressure and induces vomit. Ayurveda commends the use of rock salt in the diet due to its mineral content.

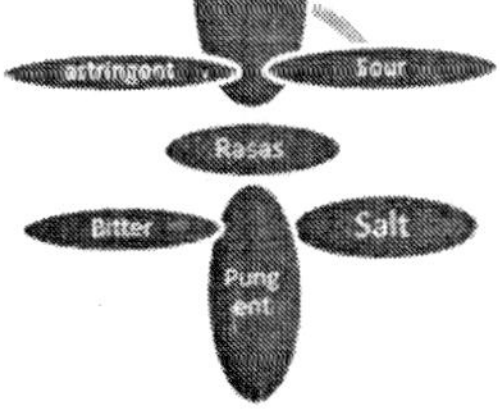

Six tastes

Pungent: in moderation, improves digestion, absorption and allows cleansing of sinuses, aids in circulation, and helps in elimination. It acts as a blood thinner and contributes to the vitality and vigor of the body. Yet excessive use may cause sterility, fatigue and excessive thirst.

Bitter: foods, like turmeric, dandelion, aloe Vera, fenugreek stimulate all other tastes. They act as antipyretic, tone the pancreas and reduce fat. Over consumption may cause dizziness.

Astringent: foods like unripe bananas, pomegranate, and chickpea aid in absorption and are binding. Excess use will induce griping, constipation and blood coagulation.Sharma HN(2005).

When different foods are taken in combination and their properties are not complimentary, indigestion, flatulence, and acidity can arise and toxins are formed in the body. Yet the same food when taken separately may be easily digested and may promote "agni." Ayurveda provides a guide on how to combine food for optimum nutrition and proper digestion. In addition, it recommends spices and herbs in ayurvedic cooking to help the food become more compatible for digestion. Thus, ayurvedic cooking is a great science of properly combining foods and food substances to maintain optimal health.

(charakSamhita, P V sharma(1985), Lad V D(1984,2002), Svoboda R E(1992)

The six tastes (rasa) of the food constitute: sweet (madhura), sour (amla), lavana (salty), pungent (tikta), bitter (katu) and astringent(kasaya). These six tastes also correspond to the six stages of digestive process (charakSamhita, P V sharma(1985).

Each taste plays an important role in the stimulation of the digestive and immune systems.

These six tastes are received on the different anatomical locations on the tongue.And correspond to specific digestive organs of metabolites.The sense of sweet is perceived by the tip of the tongue and is related to the corresponding organs,thyroid glands and apical areas of lungs. Pungent relates to the stomach and head; bitterto the pancreas, liver and spleen; astringent to the colon; sour to the lungs; and salt to the kidney.

Ayurveda also classifies food on the basis of its characteristics. These are as follows;

Rasa: Food is categorized on the basis of its taste as listed above. Rasa is a Sanskrit word which means the taste.

Veerya: This is the food that provides potency to the body. Meat provide energy and vigor and was hence given to warriors and kings. Brahmin and godly people were given food that did not provide heat to the body, thereby letting them meditate and stay in touch with God.

Prabhav: This is the food that has some special action on the body. This is known as tehseer in urdu and it implies hot and cold effect of food on the body. (Parvinder S Bali, 2009)

The types of food could be very similar in their rasa and veerya, but they still might differ in their prabhav on the body.Ayurveda classifies them as the following:

Types of Ayurvedic food

Ayurveda classifies food in three types:

- **Satyik:**satya means pure and hence a satyik person will be a highly intellectual person, with a curious mind. He/she will always strive for more knowledge and will try to live life on fair means satyik food promotes Sattva (that which induces clarity, harmony and balance).Satyik food is very conducive to health. Foods included in this category are fresh fruits and vegetables, salads, fresh fruit juices, cereals, herbal tea, fresh cow milk, dry fruits, nuts, jaggery, all spices and freshly cooked food.

  If you take satyik food the mind also will be satyik. The seven elements Dhatus of the body (Chyle, blood, flesh, fat, bone, marrow and semen) are formed out of food. Ideas and concepts are generated in the mind corresponding to these seven elements.
- **Rajasik:** this person will be the one who is basically doer. He/she will use almost any means to succeed. Rajasik food promotes Rajas (that which induces energy and action). Such foods include canned food, rice, sour cream, paneer, ice-cream, yeast, sugar, pickle, vinegar, onion, garlic and salted food.

- **Tamasik:**Tamsik on the other hand will have no desire to learn or expend his/her knowledge. He/she would also lack the intellectual capacity.Tamasik food promotes tamas (that which evokes darkness, inertia, resistance and grounding). Foods included in this group are alcohol, beef, chicken, fish,eggs, frozen food, microwave food, mushroom, drug, tea, coffee, fried foods and fried nuts. They fill the mind with anger, darkness and inertia.

Live a natural simple life. Take simple food that is wholly agreeable to your system. You should have your own menu to suit your constitution. You are yourself the best judge to select a satyik diet that suits your constitution" (from the Bhagvad Gita, Ch-16, and verse 16-17)

Time of Day and Time of Season

The body's biological clock is regulated by the doshas. The time of maximum activity of kaphais during early morning and early evening, 6 to 10 AM and 6 to 10 PM. The pittaperiod is during midday and midnight, 10 AM to 2 PM and 10 PM to 2 AM, while vatahours are dawn and dusk, 2 to 6 AM and 2 to 6 PM. Thus a pitta-type disease, like ulcers, may cause the most discomfort late at night in the pittatime of the bio-clock. The reverse is also true, in the sense that experiencing a sharp pain in the stomach region late at night may signify ulcers or another pitta-type aggravation.

Ayurvedic Cuisine and meat:

Although meat is mandated in ayurveda for debilitated patients, for warriors (Kshatriyas). It is very heavy for digestion putrefiesfaster than other foodsand produces Ama(Internal toxins) quickly. Unless you exercise strenuously. Regular meat eating will increase fat rather than flesh. It promotes speed rather than endurance. Which is not good forvata affected individual. Meat overheat the mind and warm the body, but even in cold climates. It should not be used to excess.

Today meat is also poor quality, full of antibiotics and other drugs taken from feedlot animals who never exercise so that all their Ama remain in their tissues.

Esoterically, the fear felt by the animal as it wait to be slaughtered and hatred as it feels for the human who slaughters it change the compositionof its flesh and increase fear and anger in whoever eats it. The more the violence involved in the collection of our food, the greater the violence in our lives.

Basics of Ayurvedic Cooking:

Ayurvedic cooking employs the knowledge of herbs, spices, vegetables, legumes etc. fromAyurveda which helps in maintaining the physical, mental, social and spiritual balance. The main factors affecting Ayurvedic cooking are:

- Ayurvedic foods are appetizing, flavorful, and aromatic in nature.
- The main objective of Ayurvedic cooking is to prepare food in a manner which can purify body from harmful toxins and revitalizes the body.
- Five elements, three doshas, three gunas, seven dhatus and six tastes form the backbone of Ayurvedic style and science of cooking.
- The method of cooking the food and the cook's mental disposition plays an important role in the quality of the food.
- Other such factors affecting the quality of the food are time for cooking and eating, surrounding atmosphere, compatibility of foods, and season of cooking.

Method ofAyurvedic Cooking:

The method of Ayurvedic cooking aims at making the food easily digestible. For this, following methods are employed in Ayurvedic cooking;

- **Heat/warmth:** The food should always be warm or hot as it increases the Agni and enhances the digestive power.
- **The Role of Spices in Ayurvedic Diet:** Herbs and spices play an important role in ayurvedic nutrition, for they are used to bring humeral balance in the food. For example, ginger neutralizes the heavy quality of the food thus adding ginger will convert the property of heavy food into a lighter state. Similarly, when combined with different food agents it will change its mode of action such as ginger when taken with rock salt will reduce vayuvata symptoms, with rock candy it will reduce pitta and when used

with honey it will reduce kapha. With its versatile qualities ginger is used for treating indigestion, flatulence, colic, vomit, stomach spasm, cold, cough and asthma. In addition to their medicinal qualities herbs and spices enhance the taste and flavor of the food and aids digestive secretions (Lad VD, 1984). Herbs and spices also provide mineral and vitamin supplements. The use of spices also breaks down the food, which helps in increasing breaking down the food, which makes it easier to be digested.

- **Processing of food:** Processes such as boiling, steaming, frying, sautéing, and seasoning. Pure Ghee is used for processing of food.
- **Avoid Contradictory Food:** Viruddhaaahar or contradictory food should be avoided in ayurvedic food. These can be opposite in taste (such sweet and bitter), potencies (milk-cold potency and salt-hot potency) and properties (dry foods and oleos food).Sour substance along with milk. Milk with salt. Cold and hot substance together. Banana with curd and buttermilks, chicken with curd, radish with jiggery, fish with jiggery
- **Fermentation:** fermentation of food lends them a hard to digest property and hence should be completely avoided in ayurvedic cooking. Digestive fire is maximum in winter and fermented products can be used to certain extent.

Cooking Equipment forAyurvedic kitchen

- One (at least) heavy cast-iron frying pan
- One chapati skillet, if possible (saucer-shaped, without steep sides)
- Two or three medium-sized pots with lids-stainless steel is best
- One soup pot with lid-also stainless steel
- One small metal pot for melting ghee
- One deep pot for frying-cast iron is best
- One heavy frying pan with lid
- Two or three mixing bowls, measuring cup and spoons
- Hand eggbeater
- Large metal spoon and soup ladle
- Blender
- Chapati, or other rolling pin, and cutting board

Quantity of food:

Generally half of the capacity of stomach should be filled with solids, 1/4th with liquids and rest kept empty for the free movements of body humors.

Sequence of consuming food:

Madhur (sweets) food like fruits are advisable to take in the beginning of meal, food with amla and lavana (sour and salty) rasa in the middle and katu, tikta, kashav(bitter, astringent and pungent) foods should be taken at the end of meal.

Raw food over cooked food:

Ayurveda recommends cooked food over rawfood. Ayurveda believes that if raw food is eaten then it will be cooked inside the body. The human body is not suited to easily digest raw foods. Raw foods such as raw fruits, vegetables, grains and legumes are difficult to digest as they require more energy to be digested properly.

Cooking is necessary to make the foods easily digestible and also to kill the bacteria. Most of the food should be eaten in cooked form. Raw food if it is to eaten should be only in the form of fruits, salads, nuts, sprouted beans and seeds. These should be consumed within an hour and a half of their preparation. Oil and lemons are used in raw foods before consuming to kill bacteria.

The ritual of Eating:

- Do not eat when angry, depressed, bored or otherwise emotionally unstable or immediately after any physical exertion.
- Bathe or at least wash your hands, face and feet before you begin to eat.
- Sit while eating in a clean area. Ensure that all your sense organ are satisfied by providing your dining room with pleasant music, fresh flowers.
- Avoid habitual use of restaurants'. Most people who sell you food are more concerned with their own profits than with your digestion.
- Only someone who loves youshould be permitted to cook foryou. Cooks in India are often selected from the Priestly class so that

there is at least some chance that while cooking some spiritually uplifting vibrations may be transferred in to the food.

- Prey, give thanks to nature for providing you with food and thank whichever deity you worship for being alive to eat it. Approach each food item with reverence and love.
- Before you begin your meal feed someone else. Traditionally in India a fivefold offering is made to the sacred fire, a cow, acrow, a dog and another human being, who might be a child, a beggar, or anyone else outside one's own family. This is a practical thanks to nature.
- Concentrate on your meal. No television or conversation should distract your attention.
- Observe silence while you eat. Chew each bite slowly and attentively many times.
- When feasible eat with your hands, so that your skin can send temperature and texture cues to your brain

Conclusion:

Ayurvedic cuisine has avery simple philosophy cook what is in the season with love and respect and share the food with people and enjoy life to its fullest. Ayurveda cooking is also called "annayoga" because Ayurvedabelieves that the act of cooking and eating is a way to protect our lives and support the 'prana' or lifeforce. It teaches us method to improveour lives by practicing life styles and food habits that improves our physical and mental wellbeing. Ayurvedic cooking does not present us with a rule book but provide us with a guidelines to understand nature and self. Recipe for ayurvedic cooking depend on the person, climatic condition of the region. Body type and health condition of the person. It sounds complicated at the beginning, however once you learn the basic principles you will understand they are all "Common sense" cooking.

References:

Charak. CharakSamhita (700BC), Sharma, PV. ed, and English vol 1-4. ChaukhambhaOrientalia, Varanasi, India. 1981-1985

Lad VD: Ayutveda: The science of self-healing. Lotus Light. Twin Lakes, WI. 1984

Lad VD: Book of ayurveda. Fundamental Principles of Ayurveda. NM. 2002

Parvinder S Bali, 2009(Food Production operation)

Pooja s banergee, 2012. A healthy way of cooking: ayurvedic Cooking

Sharma, HN: the Concept of Consciousness in Vedas. J Elements: Ayurveda and Health. vol3 (3) 4-5.2005

Sharma J. Guha A: Sankhya: The philosophy that Shaped the Tenets of Ayurveda. J Elements: Ayurveda & Health. vol 3 (3)4-5.2005

Svoboda RE: Ayurveda: Life, health and longevity. Penguin Books, New Delhi, India. 1992.

http://concioushealth.net/benefits of ayurvedic cooking.

IMPACT OF GREEN IMAGE ON GUEST SATISFACTION IN HOSPITALITY INDUSTRY

Manik Arora

Research Scholar School of Hospitality and Tourism Management University of Jammu manikarora1986@gmail.com

Suvidha Khanna

Assistant Professor School of Hospitality and Tourism Management University of Jammu urs_suvidha@rediffmail.com

Abstract: With every passing year masses are becoming more and more concerned about environmental issues and sustainable development. Green marketing is increasingly becoming a strategic tool that can enhance a hotel's competitive advantage. With the growing competition in the market the organizations are becoming increasingly sensitive towards overall customer satisfaction, as it is the key to turn a customer loyal. Hospitality arena is no different from this change. Things are more critical in developing economies like India where customers are primarily price sensitive. The primary objective of the study is to explore the impact of green image on guest's satisfaction. Although many studies have measured the effect of image on customer's satisfaction but none has explored the impact of the image of a green hotel on customer satisfaction levels in Indian context. The respondents of the study were guests staying in green hotel. The findings of the study show that there is a significant impact of green image on the guest satisfaction as per the results of the regression. The research methods used in the study are mean, Percentage and regression.

Keywords: Green Image, Eco hotels, Guest satisfaction

Introduction

Today, we are living in a society where firms are judged on their moral code, social accountability and socio-economic awareness as well as financial outcomes. As Consumers are becoming increasingly concerned about environmental issues, such as global warming, ozone depletion and habitat destruction, they now realise that their purchasing decisions directly influence the environment. This global trend guides hotels to move in a green direction. Also, the sales of services are crucial in hospitality industry because of the intangibility factor. Thus, creating an image among tourists about such concept also need a critical approach as the image is a conceptualisation that reflect the set of beliefs, ideas and impressions that public has of a product, service, destination, person, firm or brand (Kotler, Haider, & Rein, 1993). It also strongly influences a consumer's decision-making process and behaviour by offering mental shortcuts when processing purchase data (Kotler & Gertner, 2002). Image plays a vital role in the markets where it is difficult to differentiate products or services based on tangible quality features (Mudambi et al., 1997). Green hotel image becomes a powerful operational tool in attracting and retaining more guests. As it is been observed that after consuming/ buying green variant of any product or service, the guests feel the gratification that they have contributed towards preservation of environment, which adds to their self esteem also.

Increasing competition in the south Asian markets have made corporates neo sensitive towards customer satisfaction. The situation is more critical when talked of services because of their special features. As in the prevailing conditions, it is important for corporates to turn their existing guests loyal to save their share in the total market.

Several studies also revealed that environmental image not only can satisfy the customer's environmental desires and green needs, but can also increase their sales and enhance their competitive advantage (Hu and Wall, 2005; Corrigan, 1996; Chen et al., 2006; Porter and van der Linde, 1995; Chen, 2008, 2010). Previous studies have found that corporate image had a significant impact on customer satisfaction and customer loyalty (Abdullah et al., 2000; Zins, 2001; Park et al., 2004; Chang and Tu, 2005; Martenson, 2007). With this backdrop, the objective of the present study is to investigate the impact of green image of green hotels on guest satisfaction.

Background of the study

A brand requires a unique, favourable image to convey a strong sense of branding (Keller, 1993), which implies that a positive image is essential to brand power (Govers, 2003). Mudambi (1997) argued that image plays a vital role in the markets where it is difficult to differentiate products or services based on tangible quality features. Brand image includes symbolic meanings that associate with the specific attributes of the brand, and it can be defined as a consumer's mental picture of a brand in the consumer's mind that is linked to an offering (Cretu and Brodie, 2007; Padgett and Allen,1997). Brand Image is a set of perceptions about a brand reflected by brand associations for consumers (Cretu and Brodie, 2007; Keller, 1993). Therefore, Park et al. (1986) argued that brand image covers functional benefits, symbolic benefits, and experiential benefits. According to Chen (2009), "green image, "and defined it as "a set of perceptions of a brand in a consumer's mind that is linked to environmental commitments and environmental concerns." Various research evidences have found the impact of image on customer satisfaction. Satisfaction is a delightful degree of post-consumption evaluation or a pleasurable degree of consumption- related fulfillment (Oliver, 1996; Paulssen and Birk, 2007; Ruyter and Bloemer, 1999). Thus, satisfaction is a level of overall gratification perceived by a consumer, resulting from the quality of the product or service to fulfill the consumer's expectations, desires, and needs (Mai and Ness, 1999). Based on the above definitions, "green satisfaction," and defined it as a pleasurable level of consumption-related fulfillment to satisfy a customer's environmental desires, sustainable expectations, and green needs."

Hospitality sector has already started to brand their products green so as to satisfy their guest who are conscious towards environment. Furthermore, Hu and Wall (2005) asserted that the increase of environmental image can enhance the competitiveness of tourism. Similarly, green image is more significant for hotels especially with the rise of prevalent environmental consciousness of consumers and strict international regulations of environmental protection. Companies can embody the concept of green marketing in their products to obtain the differentiation advantages of their products (Chen et al., 2006; Peattie, 1992; Porter and van der Linde, 1995). In addition, Hospitality concerns investing many efforts in improving their brand images can, not only avoid the trouble of environmental protests or punishment but also enable them to enhance their customer satisfaction about environmental desires, sustainable expectations, and green needs. Because brand image is an important determinant of customer satisfaction, previous studies posited that there is a positive relationship between image and customer satisfaction (Chang and Tu, 2005; Martenson, 2007). According to the argument above, the more the green image is, the higher the pleasurable level of consumption-related fulfillment is to satisfy the customers' environmental desires, sustainable expectations, and green needs.

Hypothesis and data requirement

This study endeavour investigating the impact of green image on guest satisfaction in hospitality industry. For this, the hypothesis has been formulated that there is a positive impact of green image on guest satisfaction.

Data was collected from primary sources with the help of structured questionnaire, which was carefully prepared after a thorough review of literature. The survey instrument consisted of four major sections. The first section contains questions on personal profile of the respondents including gender, age, educational Status and marital status. Second section comprises 15 statements on green image of eco hotels which are based on literature from the fields of business, tourism and hospitality (e.g. Baloglu & McCleary, 1999; Beerli & Martin, 2004; Golden et al., 1987; Lin et al., 2007), Russel and Snodgrass (1987). This scale was been adopted by Lee,J.S., Hsu,

L.T., Han, H. & Kim, Y(2010).. Third section comprises 4 statements on guest satisfaction given by Oliver (1997) (2006), Bansal (2005), and Barnet (2007), and defined green customer satisfaction as the customer fulfilment of some need, goal, desire about environmental or green concerns and that this fulfillment was pleasurable. For each item, the respondents are given 7 point likert scale to respond from 1 being strongly disagree to 7 being strongly agree.

The sample for the study is collected from The Fern Residency, Chandigarh which is a certified green hotel. The sample size is determined by using the formula given by Krejcie & Morgan (1970). The average occupancy for the month of April, 2013 is 572. The data is collected for 3 days and the calculated sample size is 57 respondents out of which only 49 responses were found to be usable. The data were analysed with the help of SPSS (16.0). Regression equation was framed to find the impact of Green image on guest satisfaction.

Results

It was revealed from the study that 73% of the sample are males and 27% are females. The 72% of the sample are married and the rest representing 28% is single. The distribution of age is as follows; 53% of the respondents are from the age group 20 - 40 years, 37% are from age group 40-60. Whereas 64% of the respondents were graduate.

The statements regarding the green image of green hotels have been asked from the respondents on 7 point Likert scale. The mean scores ranged from 1.71 to 2.65. In the scale of 0 to 7, "The Price charged by green hotels is reasonable" had a maximum mean of 2.65, followed by "Services at a green hotel meet my needs and expectations" with a mean of 2.51. "Green hotels offers extra benefits" had the lowest mean of 1.71. This suggested that green hotels should offer some fringe benefits along with their products and services. While the statements regarding the guest satisfaction have been evaluated on the basis of 7 point Likert scale. The mean scores ranges from 1.51 to 2.16. In the scale of 1 to7, "I believe that I do the right thing in booking the room in this hotel" had a maximum mean of 2.16. "I feel that I contribute to the environmental protection and sustainable development" has the lowest mean of 1.51. The reliability analysis was done to measure the existence of internal consistency of the scale employed. Cronbach's alpha computed to 0. 823, which indicated a high level of internal consistency for the scale used in this survey.

According to regression results, the coefficient of determination, $R^2 = 0.505$. This implies that 50% of the variation in the green image is explained by the regression and the remaining 50% of the variation by error. Also, the coefficient of correlation r = 0.711. The Positive sign shows that there exists a positive direct relationship between the green image and customer satisfaction.

Regression Output for Job Involvement and Job Satisfaction

Multiple R 0.711

R - Square 0.505

Coeffient of Correlation; r = 0.711

Coefficient of Output

	Coeffient	Standard Error	t - stat	P - value
Intercept	0.477	0.221	2.157	0.036
X- variable	0.708	0.102	6.929	1.046

From Table 5, the regression equation as formed is:-

Job satisfaction = 0.477 + 0.708

The regression coefficient B = 0.708 shows that the customer satisfaction which is a dependent variable, changes by 0.7 units for each unit change in green image which is an independent variable. Thus, we find that customer satisfaction is influenced by green image of the hotel and the value of $r^2 = 0.505$ indicate that about 50% changes in customer satisfaction is due to green image of the hotel. Hence we can say that the hypothesis of the study is supported by the data.

Conclusion

In last decade, business ethics, corporate social responsibility, sustainable development, and environmental issues has been a concern of great importance among organisations. At the same time, customers in all major markets are demanding that companies produced higher quality products that are consistent with societal and environmental values if they wish to remain competitive in global markets. Miller (2003) illustrated this concept by describing how green consumers are most likely to purchase products that are of benefit to them as well as to the rest of the world. Hospitality industry is no different from this market shift. Therefore, hotels have increasingly paid attention to green concepts, such as green practices, green management, green marketing, green products, etc.

The aim of the present study was to investigate the impact of green image of eco friendly hotels on guest satisfaction. According to results of analysis, it can be concluded that the green image creates a premise for guest satisfaction and has a significant contribution, when it comes to guest satisfaction while the same has been supported by Chen (2010) that green image was positively associated with guest satisfaction. The overall findings suggested that a green hotel image gave rise to favorable guest satisfaction. Once the guest is satisfied to the level, the guest turns loyal towards a particular product and service, which in turn creates repurchase intention or in the case of hotels an intention to revisit. A hotel with a sound green image can achieve cost reduction from the use of energy and water, appeal to investors, attract and retain highly motivated employees and cultivate guest loyalty, thereby securing top market share and position (Green Hotelier, 2007). Although an awareness about green development or the use of green products/ practices is still at its initiation in Indian hospitality sector where majorly cost is the deciding factor when it comes to choosing a particular property but there has been an increase in the number of guest who consistently ask for eco friendly products. The increasing option of organic food in the hotel's menu is just a small indicator. Hence this study strongly emphasis that green image of ecotel creates a premise for guest satisfaction which in turn increases satisfaction among guests.

Limitations of the Study

This research study has few limitations, like the study area is limited only to "The Fern Residency", Chandigarh. The sample collected is small because it was collected by the author in three days, with larger sample the results may come clearer. The method used in the research in order to collect data is through Questionnaire method only. Other methods like group discussions, personal interview of customers etc could have also been employed for better results.

This study, very exploratory in nature, was conducted at a green hotel. As a result, the sample may be biased towards environmentally friendly activities. Many of the respondents were aware about the concept of sustainability. In addition, the results are not generalizable to the entire population. The sample in the present study is small and rather homogeneous. The results, therefore, cannot be applied to the general traveling population. They can however, provide stepping stones for future research

Future Research

The results of this study will help hoteliers and hotel developers to understand that what are the factors that can have the possible impact on guest satisfaction, which is always a priority for any business. By providing them with such a list, hoteliers can begin to understand that such dimensions are also important to their guests and can have an impact on their satisfaction levels. The study can be useful to the marketers involved in the hospitality business.

In addition to understanding marketing attributes, hoteliers have a new description of what a green image may encompass. It is a definition that they can incorporate into their own business practices. Hoteliers again can use this to their advantage by tapping into that market, i.e. the younger travelers. Because the research about green image of eco friendly hotel, or green hotels in general, is limited, the results of this study enable researchers to develop future research projects relating to the eco marketing of green hotel.

References

Abdullah M, Al-Nasser A, Husain N (2000). Evaluating functional relationship between image, customer satisfaction and customer loyalty using general maximum entropy. Total Qual. Manage., 11(6): 826-829.

Baloglu, S., & McCleary, K.W. (1999). A model of destination image formation. Annals of Tourism Research, 26(4), 868-897.

Bansal P (2005). Evolving sustainably: a longitudinal study of corporate sustainable development. Strateg. Manage. J. 26(3): 197-218.

Barnet ML (2007). Stakeholder influence capacity and the variability of financial returns to corporate social responsibility. Acad. Manage. Rev., 33(3): 794-816.

Beerli, A., &Martin, J.D. (2004). Factors influencing destination image. Annals of Tourism Research, 31(3), 657-681.

Chang, C.-H. and C.-Y. Tu. (2005). Exploring Store Image, Customer Satisfaction and Customer Loyalty Relationship: Evidence from Taiwanese Hypermarket Industry, Journal of American Academy of Business, 7(2), 197-202.

Chen, Y.-S., S.-B. Lai and C.-T. Wen (2006). The Influence of Green Innovation Performance on Corporate Advantage in Taiwan, Journal of Business Ethics, 67(4), 331-339.

Chen YS (2010). The driver of green brand equity: green brand image, green satisfaction, and green trust. J. Bus. Ethics, 92(3): 307-319.

Corrigan J (1996). How a green image can drive Irish export growth. Greener Manage. Int., 16: 87-95.

Cretu, A. E. & R. J. Brodie: (2007). The Influence of Brand Image and Company Reputation Where Manufacturers Market to Small Firms: A Customer Value Perspective, Industrial Marketing Management, 36(2), 230-240.

Green Hotelier. (2007, Summer 24). What does it mean to be a hotel? London, UK: International Hotels Environment Initiative.

Golden, L.L., Albaum, G.,& Zimmer, M. (1987). The numerical comprehensive scale: An economical format for retail image measurement. Journal of Retailing, 63(4), 393-410.

Govers, R. (2003). Destination image evaluation: Part II. Eclipse. The Periodic Publication from

Moonshine Travel Marketing for Destination Marketers, 10, 1-12.

Hu, W. and G. Wall: 2005, Environmental Management, Environmental Image and the Competitive Tourist Attraction,

Journal of Sustainable Tourism, 13(6), 617-635.

Keller, K. L. (1993), Conceptualizing, Measuring, and Managing Customer-Based Brand Equity, Journal of Marketing, 57(1), 1-22.

Kotler, P., Haider, D.H., & Rein, I. (1993). Marketing places: Attracting investment, industry,

and tourism to cities, states, and nations. New York: The Free Press.

Kotler, P., & Gertner, D. (2002). Country as brand, product, and beyond: A place marketing

& brand management perspective. Journal of Brand Management, 9(4-5), 249-261.

Krejcie, R & Morgan, D 1970, Determining Sample Size for Research Activities, Educational and Psychological Measurement, 30, pp. 607-610.

Lee, J. S., Hsu, J., Han, H., & Kim, Y. (2010). Understanding how consumers view green

hotels: How a hotel's green image can influence behavioural intentions. Journal of

Sustainable Tourism, 18, 901-914.

Lin, C.H., Morais, D.B., Kerstetter, D.L., & Hou, J.S. (2007). Examining the role of cognitive

and affective image in predicting choice across natural, developed, and theme-park destinations. Journal of Travel Research, 46, 183-194.

Mai, L. W. and M. R. Ness (1999). Canonical Correlation Analysis of Customer Satisfaction and Future Purchase of Mail-Order Speciality Food, British Food Journal, 101(11), 857-870.

Martenson, R. (2007), Corporate Brand Image, Satisfaction and Store Loyalty; A Study of the Store as a Brand, Store Brands and Manufacturer Brands', International Journal of Retail & Distribution Management, 35(7), 544-555.

Miller, G.A. (2003). Consumerism in sustainable tourism: A survey of UK consumers. Journal of Sustainable Tourism, 11(1), 17-39.

Mudambi, S. M., P. Doyle & V. Wong. (1997). An Exploration of

Branding in Industrial Markets, Industrial Marketing Management, 26(5), 433-446.

Oliver, R.L. (1997). Satisfaction: A Behavioral Perspective on the Consumer. Boston: McGraw-Hill.

Oliver, R. L. (1996). Satisfaction: A Behavioral Perspective on the Consumer (McGraw-Hill, NY, USA).

Paulssen, M. and M. M. Birk. (2007). Satisfaction and Repurchase Behavior in a Business-to-Business Setting: Investigating the Moderating Effect of Manufacturer, Company and Demographic Characteristics', Industrial Marketing Management 36(7), 983-997.

Padgett, D. and D. Allen. (1997). Communicating Experiences: A Narrative Approach to Creating Service Brand Image, Journal of Advertising, 26(4), 49-62.

Park, C. W., B. J. Jaworski and D. J. Maclnnis. (1986). Strategic Brand Concept-Image Management, Journal of Marketing, 50(4), 135-145

Park J, Robertson R, Wu C (2004). The effect of airline service quality on passengers' behavioral intentions. J. Air Transp. Manage., 10:435-439

Peattie, K.: 1992, Green Marketing (Pitman Publishing Corp., London, UK).

Porter, M. E. and C. Van der Linde (1995). Toward a new Conception of the Environment-Competitiveness Relationship, Journal of Economic Perspectives, 9(4), 97-118.

Russel, J.A., & Snodgrass, J. (1987). Emotion and environment. In D. Stockols & I. Altman

(Eds.), Handbook of enviromental psychology (pp. 245-280). New York: Wiley.

Ruyter, K. and J. Bloemer. (1999). Customer Loyalty in Extended Service Settings, International Journal of Service Industry Management 10(3), 320-336.

Zins A (2001). Relative attitudes and commitment in customer loyalty models. Int. J. Serv. Ind. Manage., 12(3): 269-294.

FOREIGN EXCHANGE EARNINGS THROUGH TOURISM IN INDIA

Manpreet Arora

Assistant Professor, School of Business & Management Science, Central University of Himachal Pradesh, Dharamshala, Kangra, Himachal Pradesh

arora.manpreet3@gmail.com

Abstract: The spread of education and the development of internet have widened the scope of tourism industry as now tourists can choose their destinations sitting at their homes. The foreign exchange earnings from tourism sector have a great impact on the developing country like India. According to ASSOCHAM the India's foreign exchange earnings from the tourism sector are likely to reach US 4 26 Billion in 2015 from the current balance of around $ 20 Billion. ASSOCHAM has also indicated that growing at a CAGR of nearly 7% the arrival of foreign tourists in India is likely to cross 80 lakhs by 2015. India is continuously in the process of improving its share in International Tourism Receipts during the past decade. So undoubtedly Tourism industry has a great potential to contribute more in the foreign exchange reserves basket of India. Rank of India in world for getting the tourists was 41 in 2012 and out of the total foreign tourist's arrival of the world India gets only 7% out of it. The heritage of India is so rich that it can set an example in front of world if this sector gets proper impetus. There is much more potential in this sector that if government gives right focus in policy framing and following a right approach in this direction can help in earning the foreign exchange to much more extent. This paper tries to find out the role of Tourism Industry in earning Foreign Exchange for

India. It also aims to study the contribution of Tourism Industry in the Foreign Exchange Reserves of India via analysing the foreign tourist arrivals in India in various years.

Keywords: Foreign Exchange earnings, Tourism

Introduction

The basic thrust of human beings for getting new knowledge and exploring new things is fulfilled by tourism. As the means of communication are developing and the countries are becoming more open and globalised the tourism industry has got new impetus and dimensions. The spread of education and the development of internet have widened the scope of this industry as now tourists can choose their destinations sitting at their homes.

The Internet has helped in the growth of the travel industry by providing on line booking facilities. It has also provided people with the power to explore destinations and cultures from their home personal computers and make informed choices before finalizing travel plans. With the immense information resources, the Internet allows tourists to scrutinise hotels, check weather forecasts, know about the local food and even talk to other tourists around the world about their travel experiences for a chosen destination.

Tourism accounts for around 6-7 per cent of global employment (direct and indirect) and 5 percent of global income as per the United Nations World Tourism Organization (UNWTO), Tourism Highlights 2012 edition. It is one of the largest generators of employment across the world and women account for 70 per cent of the workforce in the travel and tourism industry. Hence it generates more inclusive growth than other sectors. According to the UNWTO, international tourist arrivals surpassed the 1 billion mark for the first time in history in 2012, reaching a figure of 1.04 billion from 996 million in 2011 with 4 per cent growth despite the volatility around the globe, particularly in Europe which accounts for over half of international tourist arrivals worldwide. This new trend has made the tourism industry a very potential industry for earning foreign exchange for a developing nation like India, where the culture and history are in plenty to satisfy the tourists around the world. In India service sector is playing a dominant role in contributing towards foreign exchange and Tourism is one such area. India has shown tremendous increase in terms of FDI in this sector also, resulting to getting more foreign exchange.

According to Economic Survey of India In 2011-12, FDI inflows to the services sector grew at 57.62 per cent to US $ 12.14 billion compared to the growth of overall FDI inflows at 33.6 per cent. However, in 2012-13 (April-November), overall FDI inflows fell by 43.3 per cent to US$ 15.85 billion from US$ 27.93 billion in the corresponding period of the previous year. Following this trend, FDI inflows in the top five services also fell by 9.7 per cent to US$ 8.19 billion. Among them, while FDI inflows to the top four services sectors fell in the range of 14 to 97per cent, FDI inflows to the hotel and tourism sector increased by a very high 328 per cent over the corresponding period in the previous year. Not only FDI but there is a continuous increase in the inflow of tourists from around the world to India thereby contributing towards foreign exchange reserves.

Review of literature

Padamshree and Bharti (2011) studied the growth of foreign tourist arrivals and foreign exchange earnings into India through the Indian tourism industry. They examined the share of the Indian Tourism Industry in the World in general and especially the Asia Pacific region. It is evident from this study that the India Tourism Industry is growing significantly each year at a rate of 7% in foreign tourist arrivals. In addition, India is currently experiencing a steep jump in its position in terms of tourism growth and is continuously moving upward.

Tourism sector holds immense potential for Indian economy. It can provide impetus to other industries through backward and forward linkages and can generate huge revenue earnings for the country. Sandeep Das (2011) in his article explains that tourism provides opportunities of job creation directly and indirectly. So this sector should be provided with incentives for sustainable and overall economic growth along with creation of jobs. Premlata Kumari (2012) found out that Tourism is one of the largest industries in the world today. It generates employment at all skill levels. In India tourism sector has proved to be a powerful mechanism for generating direct and indirect employment. She found that the direct employments due to foreign tourists in India for 2002 and 2008 are 17.44 and 28.79lacs. During the same period of times employments by domestic tourists are about double respectively 37.33 and 57.00 lacs. Krishna Kumar (2011) studied that International tourism is an extremely tempting proposition in terms of potential of business especially foreign exchange earnings, for India. He is of the view that further to benefit from the international tourism business, India has to think strategically and gear up internally to bridge the strategic gaps and develop appropriate physical, human resource and other organisational infrastructure in an integrated manner, which can meet the varied needs of international tourists.

The Travel & Tourism industry provides tremendous opportunity to India in terms of contribution to its GDP and employment generation (Akhilesh et al 2012). FDI is playing a great role in the tourism sector and is helping to earn foreign exchange. The Travel & Tourism industry provides tremendous opportunity to India in terms of contribution to its GDP and employment generation.

Objectives

1. This paper tries to find out the role of Tourism Industry in earning Foreign Exchange for India.
2. It also aims to study the contribution of Tourism Industry in the Foreign Exchange Reserves of India via analysing the foreign tourist arrivals in India in various years.

Methodology

The study was based on a range of secondary data collected from various government sources such as the Ministry of Tourism, the Government of India, the World Tourism Organization and other relevant websites. In order to study the specified objectives, statistical tools like Compound Annual Growth Rate (CAGR), and Percentages were used. The data of various reports have been compiled to get the periodic information. Various news articles and press releases of ASSOCHAM have also been reviewed for getting the statistics.

Incredible India Campaign and its Effects on Tourism Industry

The launch of incredible India campaign by the tourism ministry in the last decade has resulted in a very visible positive effect on the flow of foreign tourists into India and the earnings there from grew at double digits. A 2011 forecast of the World Travel and Tourism Council (WTTC) predicted that FTA's will cross 11 million by 2021 which is approximately one percent of the global tourist population. It is a notable fact that foreign tourists tend to spend more time in India than almost any country in the world. There are very positive signs for the tourism industry thereby earning foreign exchange for the economy as a whole.

It indicated a significant potential for the improvement of foreign exchange reserves for the years to come. The growing impetus of the foreign travellers towards India is because of the natural flora and fauna, religious reasons and above all medical tourism is playing a great role in this area. A report by FICCI indicates that in 2011, travel for leisure, recreation and holidays accounted for just over half of all International tourist arrivals. In India most of the FTA's report travelling for business and professional purposes and for visiting friends and relatives, religious reasons, pilgrimages, health treatment etc. for these tourists who come for holidays, heritage and culture is the dominant factor for giving priority to India as a holiday destination.

The tourism ministry is playing an important role in the development of the industry. The launch of the Incredible India program has proved to be a great success. It has helped to promote India's culture and tourist attractions in a superb way by projecting India as a country of customs traditions and religions. The Incredible India campaign was launched in 2002 to encourage the visitors around the world to experience India to get a colourful, vibrant image in the minds of tourists around the world. After that India experienced a great inflow in the tourist arrivals resulting to contributing to a great extent in the foreign exchange reserves.

Contribution of Tourism Sector towards Foreign Exchange

Foreign exchange is critical to global business transactions. For India earning and monitoring foreign exchange has always been a critical issue. Foreign exchange reserves show the financial strength and the stage of development of the economy. The acceptance of currency at a predetermined rate makes the international trade easy. The foreign exchange balances of a country directly affect the rates of exchange. A hard currency nation has stability in foreign exchange rate. The rising foreign exchange balances of a nation increases its credit worthless in the international capital market. India has always been striving hard to get a good ranking in the International market. As service sector is getting much momentum after the liberalisation measures taken by India, role of tourism industry in contributing towards the foreign exchange earnings is getting great impetus. Day by Day India is becoming a favourite destination of tourists around the world and helping the economy to earn more foreign exchange. The following table shows the number of tourist arrivals and the foreign exchange earnings from the year 2000 to 2012.

On an average the numbers of foreign tourist arrivals in India follow a good growth pattern except few years. It is an interesting fact that despite in some years the number of tourists arrival have decreased as compared to the last year, the resulting foreign exchange earnings have continuous growth trend after 2002. According to ASSOCHAM the India's foreign exchange earnings from the tourism sector are likely to reach US 4 26 Billion in 2015 from the current balance of around $ 20 Billion. ASSOCHAM has also indicated that growing at a CAGR of nearly 7% the arrival of foreign tourists in India is likely to cross 80 lakhs by 2015.

India is continuously in the process of improving its share in International Tourism Receipts during the past decade. It is about 0.64% in 2002 to about 1.65% in 2012. India's rank in world's ranking has also improved to 16th in 2012.in the Asia Pacific Region India's share has grown to 5.5 % in 2012 and its ranking has also improved to the 7th in this regard. The growth rate in foreign exchange earnings from tourism in rupee terms in Feb 2013 over Feb 2012 was 19.8%.Foreign Exchange Earnings (FEEs) from tourism in rupees terms in October, 2013 increased by 4.40%. to Rs.8513 crore as compared to Rs.8154 crore in October, 2012 said a statement issued by the government. Foreign Tourist Arrivals (FTAs) in October, 2013 were 5.89 lakh as against 5.56 lakh in October 2012 showing a growth of 5.94 %.FEEs during the month of October 2013 were Rs.8,513 crore as compared to Rs.8,154 crore in October 2012 and Rs.7,019 crore in October 2011. The growth rate in FEEs in rupee terms in October 2013 over October 2012 was 4.4% as compared to 16.2% in October 2012 over October 2011. FEEs from tourism in rupee terms during January to October 2013 were Rs.83,727 crore with a growth of 12.8%, as compared to the FEEs of Rs.74,215 crore with a growth of 22.1% during January to October 2012 over the corresponding period of 2011.FEEs in US$ terms during the month of October 2013 were US$1.382 billion as compared to FEEs of US$1.538 billion during the month of October 2012 and US$ 1.424 billion in October 2011.

Foreign Tourist Arrivals and Foreign Exchange Earnings During the years 2000-2012

Year	Foreign Tourist Arrivals (in nos.)	Percentage Change Over Previous Year	Foreign Exchange Earnings in Crore	Percentage Change Over Previous Year	Foreign Exchange Earnings (Million US$)	Percentage Change Over Previous Year
2000	26,49,378	6.7	15,626,	20.6	3,460	15.0
2001	25,37,282	-4.2	15,083	-3.5	3,198	(-)7.6
2002	23,84,364	-6.0	15,064	-0.1	3,103	3.0
2003	27,26,214	14.3	20,729,	37.6	4,463	43.8
2004	34,57,477	26.8	27,944	34.8	6,170	38.2
2005	39,18,610	13.3	33,123,	18.5	7,493	21.4
2006	44,47,167	13.5	39,025	17.8	8,634	15.2
2007	50,81,504	14.3	44,360	13.7	10,729	24.3
2008	52,82,603	4.0	51,294	15.6	11,832	10.3
2009	51,67,699	-2.2	53,700*	4.7	11,136*	(-)5.9
2010	57,75,692	11.8	64,889#	20.8	14,193#	27.5

2011	63,09,222	9.2	77,591#	19.6	16,564#	16.7
2012	66,48,318	5.4	94,487#	21.8	17,737#	7.1

Advance Estimates *Revised Estimates

Source: Ministry of Tourism, Annual Report 2012-13

The growth rate in FEEs in US$ terms in October 2013 over October 2012 was negative growth of 10.1% as compared to the growth of 8.0% in October 2012 over October 2011.

Conclusion and Suggestions

Undoubtedly Tourism industry has a great potential to contribute more in the foreign exchange reserves basket of India. The rank of India in world for the tourist's arrival was 41 in 2012 and out of the total foreign tourists' arrival of the world; India gets only 7% out of it. The heritage of India is so rich that it can set an example in front of world. There is much more potential in this sector that if government gives right focus in policy framing and following a right approach in this direction can help in earning the foreign exchange to much more extent.

India should enter into agreements with various countries through embassies and High Commissions to strengthen tourism cooperation aiming at destination development, promotion, marketing and capacity building. India can also benefit by strengthening ties to ASEAN countries. It has already signed MOU with ASEAN in 2012, which would serve as a key instrument for more action oriented cooperation, encouraging both the parties to cooperate.

India is also emerging as a favourite destination for Saudi countries, it should strengthen their ties with such economies where people are ready to spend good amount for leisure and tourism purposes. Another initiative taken by Tourism Ministry is Go Beyond campaign which promotes lesser known destinations to the International Tourists which if tapped properly can give good advantage to the industry. Government should continue to focus on innovative marketing strategies to tap more FTA'S. To boost inbound foreign tourists government can waive tourist visa fees in selected destinations.

References

Meyer, D, Foreign Direct Investment in Tourism - The Development Dimension - Expert Advisory Committee (2005-2006). Funded by United Nations Conference on Trade and Development, Geneva, Switzerland.

Meyer, D. (2006) FDI in Tourism: The Development Dimension. Case Study Sri Lanka. Geneva: UNCTAD

Usha C.V. Haley, (2001), Tourism and FDI in Vietnam, Haworth Press, pp 67-90

Das, Sandeep(Sep,2011), "Indian Tourism Sector: A Growth Story", Yojana, pp-49-51.

Barnaa maulick, "Enlarging the Potential of Rural Tourism in India" Kurukshetra, May 2012. Pg no 13-16.

India Tourism Statistics, 2012

Web Sources

http://www.adbi.org/working-paper/2011/09/30/4727.global.economic.crisis.

impact.services.india/contribution.of.the.services.sector.to.indias.growth/

http://www.ehow.com/about_6558572_define-foreign-exchange.html#ixzz2p3rVwonA

http://www.pib.nic.in/newsite/erelease.aspx?relid=92572

http://indiabudget.nic.in/es2012-13/echap-10.pdf

http://economictimes.indiatimes.com/news/economy/indicators/indias-gdp-growth-likely-to-be-around-5-this-fiscal/articleshow/24259347.cms

http://incredibleindiacampaign.com/

http://164.100.47.134/intranet/TourismSectrinIndia.pdf

http://tourism.gov.in/writereaddata/CMSPagePicture/file/marketresearch/Ministry%20of%20tourism%20English%202013.pdf

http://mospi.nic.in/mospi_new/upload/SYB2013/ch26.html

http://tourism.gov.in/writereaddata/Uploaded/RFD/050220121004071.pdf

ORGANIC FOOD AND HOSPITALITY

Mou Roy

Lecturer, Ranjita Institute of Hotel Managemnt, Bhubaneswar. (Affiliated to National Council for Hotel Management & Catering Technology, Noida) Bidyanagar, Mahura, Janla Bhubaneswar - 752054 Orissa dutta_mou@yahoo.com

B. Srinivas Rao

Project Manager Shailja's Organic Products Pvt. Ltd. Bidyanagar, Mahura, Janla Bhubaneswar - 752054 Orissa srinivastevia@gmail.com

Abstract: Through this paper authors would like to understand the feasibility, necessity and challenges in implementing the above model in our cities. Main emphasis of this paper would be on understanding the dynamics involved in an organic restaurant, which can source its inputs locally. Authors would like to understand the dynamics of making the producers an important stakeholder in our business. We would also like to look upon providing additional income to the producers by raising carbon credits. We also would like to understand the current models of organic restaurants and the hospitality they provide in Indian context. Our final objective is to come up with a prototype of a organic restaurant which sources all its raw materials within a radius of 15km. The idea is to promote a green organic hotel industry where producers form a major customer base thereby reducing the carbon footprint.

Keywords: Organic Food, Hospitality

Preface

The crisis in Cuba in the early 90s mostly affected the food in urban areas, as 80% of Cuba's food was imported. The urban dwellers were largely dependent on the food supplied in the market from the rural areas and majorly from the imports. The rising food prices had a telling impact on the nutritional requirements of the population. This paved the way for a revolutionary idea of urban agriculture devoid of any chemicals or pesticides. City dwellers started to produce vegetables in whatever space they had inside or outside their houses called as huertos or gardens. Some people even utilized their balconies, porches and back yards of their houses for vegetables and other food production. This not only made them self reliant but also reduced the carbon foot print. Presently Havana the pioneer in urban agriculture is able to meet nearly 80% of the food demand.

We would initially collect data from various primary and secondary sources on the existing models of organic restaurants. Our primary sources would include both the practitioners of organic restaurants and also their customer base. We would also try and interact with the government officials about the incentives that they can provide to the above model. We will also ponder upon different strategies on raising awareness about organic food and the concept of carbon foot print. We will adopt systems thinking through our paper so that the perspectives of all the stakeholders will be recorded.

Introduction

Since the revolution of 1959, being able to eat sufficient food has been asserted as a basic human right by the Cuban Government. One of the ways by which the

government secures access to food is a distribution system guaranteeing basic food packages at subsidised prices. Since 1959, much work has been done to develop the national agricultural sector into a highly mechanised sector, with intensive use of agrochemicals. Most attention was paid to the production of sugarcane and other export crops. In the mid-1980s, over 50% of the total foodstuffs consumed in Cuba was imported. The imports were made possible by the favourable terms of trade of the socialist bloc(especially for sugarcane), as well as by cheaply provided Russian oil, of which part was re-exported.

When the Socialist Bloc disintegrated, Cuba lost access to cheap fossil fuels, direct food imports and the agricultural inputs on which it so heavily depended for its export production. Imports dropped: in 1993/94 supplies for agriculture dropped by 67%. Cuba was thrown into a severe crisis, commonly referred to as the "special period". The crisis was further compounded by the further tightening of the US embargo. Food shortages occurred, most severely in Havana. It has been estimated that food availability declined as much as 60% between 1991 and 1995. Extensive food rationing was instituted to ensure equitable distribution.

Before 1989, urban agriculture was almost non-existent in Havana. There was no need, not even for the poorest residents, to grow food, as food was distributed by the State. However, because of the food crisis, urban agriculture emerged. President Fidel Castro proclaimed that no piece of land should be left uncultivated. So even on the front lawn of the Ministry of Agriculture (MoA), crops were planted.

The strongly urbanised district of Havana was not exempt from the search for non-conventional food-supply programmes. A start was made to decentralise production and to link production directly to transportation and consumption patterns. The self-supply (autoconsum) plan, initiated in the late 1980s, was expanded. This plan to increase local food self-sufficiency reduced the need for transport, refrigeration, storage and other resource-demanding activities. All over Havana, urban gardens were started. For the residents, it was not so much a question of whether, but rather how, they could produce food or raise animals.

The main idea of urban agriculture in Havana can be described as "Production in the community, by the community, for the community", which refers to the cycle of producers, products, marketing and consumers. Urban agriculture is very much seen as a way to bring producers and consumers closer together in order to achieve a steady supply of fresh, healthy and varied products directly from the production site to the consumer.

What India can learn from Cuban model?

Various studies conducted on migration show that more than 80000 farmers migrate to cities every year and the number is only increasing. It is expected that by 2020 nearly 70% of TamilNadu farmers, 65% of Punjab farmers, 55% of UP farmers would have moved to cities. There is also a growing concern over the shrinking of the cultivable land, and close to million hectares has been lost over the past five years for industries and infrastructure projects. The pollution in our modern cities is tormenting and only makes things worse. One thing that the urban residents usually overlook is the pollution caused by the food they eat. Our Urban cities have become centers of mass consumption and very little is being produced in these places. Majority of them do not even know the place of origin of the food they eat and the food miles associated with it. Going by the current trends it looks like the situation will only get worse in the coming days.

In order to prevent a disaster we feel India can learn a lot from the cuban model of agriculture. The food miles travelled by the food that we eat can be considerably reduced by following this model. The cities can be made green and more liveable. The strategies that we might have to use can be debated but there is no second thought on making our urban consumers producers as well. In our report we have tried to come up with a model which can help in not only reducing the carbon foot print but also increase the incomes of the urban residents.

Philosophical underpinnings of organic farming

Albert Howard in his book "An agricultural testament" talks about the regenerating capacity of the nature. According to him little or no consideration is paid in the literature of agriculture to the means by which Nature manages land and conducts her water culture. The crops and the livestock look after themselves. Nature has never found it necessary to design the equivalent of the spraying machine and the poison spray for the control of insects and fungus pests. There is nothing in the nature of vaccines and serums for the protection of the livestock. It is true that all kinds of diseases are to be found here and there among the plants and animals of the forest, but these never assume large proportions. The principle followed is that the plants and animals can very well protect themselves even when such things as parasites are to be found in their midst. Nature's rule in these matters is to live and let live.(An agricultural testament, 1995, pp1-4).

In one straw revolution Fukuoka says, it is difficult to understand nature and one who claims that he understood it has only an idea about the nature which is far from understanding. It is impossible for specialists to see nature as a whole rather they are interested in dissecting the nature into parts that interest them the most and make these parts a universe in itself. He claims that understanding nature is beyond the reach of human's cognitive capacity and science has only helped in showing how small human intellect is. "A scientific testing method which takes all relevant factors into account is impossibility." He has also criticized "Green Revolution" and "the Good Rice Movement" saying that these encouraged cultivation of weak and feeble seed varieties which needs application of various chemicals to give satisfying yield.

Taking the example of food pollution he has also advocated the concept of systems thinking saying that "A problem cannot be solved by people who are concerned with only one or another of its part". He articulates that devising counter measures for a problem further aggravates it, as the focus invariably remains on the symptoms of the problem rather than on the source. He has also not parted with the role of consumers in the whole process of agriculture. He argues that the consumers also have contributed to agricultural pollution by demanding products of uniform shape, size and colour instead of caring about the quality. Various chemicals which had no role to play in this sector are being blindly used to satisfy their demands. He says, "until there is a reversal of the sense of values which cares more for size and appearance than for quality, there will be no solving the problem of food pollution." He also negates the common belief among the consumers that natural food should be expensive. He argues, foods that are grown naturally use external inputs their price must be low that those grown using modern techniques and if the seller is asking for higher prices for the natural food then he is taking excessive profits.(One straw revolution, Fukuoka, 1984)

Wendell Berry in less his book, The unsettling of America: culture and agriculture talks about the disease of modern character which is specialization, in detail. He feels, the hazard of the specialist system is that it produces specialists- people who are elaborately and expensively trained to do one thing. Specialization is thus seen to be a way of institutionalizing, justifying, and paying highly for a calamitous disintegration and scattering out of the various functions of ; workmanship, care, conscience, responsibility. The specialist system, he feels fails from a personal point of view because a person who can do only one thing can do virtually nothing for himself. In living in the world by his own will and skill, the stupidest peasant or tribesman is more competent than the most intelligent worker or technician or intellectual in a society of specialists. Under the rule of specialization he feels the society becomes more and more complex, it has less and less structure. It becomes more and more organized, but less and less orderly. He gives the example of a doctor who is interested in the disease but not in health, clearly in the same category with the conservationist who invests in destruction of what he otherwise intends to preserve, where both of them have the comfort of job security but at the cost of ultimate futility.

"The earth has enough for everyone's need but not enough for everyone's greed", said Mahatma Gandhi. Venkat also echoes similar views when he attributes the destruction of the biosphere to the "rapacious needs of a social order based on greed, power, profit and exploitation". He criticizes the consumerist way of life that guzzles more energy than what it generates and calls for a cooperative and non-exploitative relationship with the biosphere. Permaculture which initially aimed towards creating self-sufficiency in food at the household and community level gradually evolved to include 'care of the earth' and 'care of the people 'as its principles. This means that there should be provision for all life systems to continue and multiply and at the same time there should be provision for people to access all those resources necessary for their existence. The most striking point about Permaculture is that it very correctly recognizes agriculture as a human intervention and not a natural phenomenon. This is why to make it sustainable it should be kept as near to nature as possible and without trespassing the laws that govern nature. For this lessons can be learnt from nature itself. Observing the temperate and tropical forest systems which have sustained and self-managed themselves over years can offer valuable lessons in this regard.

Community managed organic restaurant

We are trying to propose a organic restaurant which will source majority of its inputs within a radius of 30kms. The idea is to promote urban farming through kitchen gardens, terrace gardens, landless gardens etc and link the produce to a organic restaurant in the nearby locality. All the residents supplying the inputs to the restaurant will be members of the same and will have their say in decision making through their elected representatives. Like for instance most of the urban residents are organised into colonies and every colony has a elected body which is in-charge of solving their issues. We plan to approach these elected bodies through volunteers and convince them on the importance of organic food and other issues related urban agriculture.

Our modern cities also have thriving slums. The slums can also be taken into the fold by encouraging landless gardens, which need very less land. There are many non-governmental organisations already working in the slums and our strategy would be to reach the slum dwellers through these channels. This will not only increase the incomes of these poor slum dwellers but also ensure nutritional security to some extent. But one constraint is that only creepers can be grown in these landless gardens.

The restaurant will be mainly run by the volunteers who are passionate to work for this cause. The Aam Aadmi phenomenon has unleashed the power of volunteerism in this country and we are quite confident that if a right cause is being promoted people will surely join. The governance structure for this community managed restaurant needs to be researched but a strong leadership at the helm is vital.

What is Organic?

Organic farming, a term used inter-changeably with Ecological Farming (farming that adopts agro-ecological approaches), occasionally reaching the level of 'do-nothing' or 'natural' farming, manifesting itself as 'bio-dynamic farming' at times, 'zero-budget' farming at other times in its adoption by lakhs of farmers in India, rests on the following:

"Organic agriculture as a holistic production management system that avoids use of synthetic fertilizers, pesticides and genetically modified organisms, minimizes pollution of air, soil and water, and optimizes the health and productivity of interdependent communities of plants, animals and people". - Codex Alimentarius, International Food Standards.

"Organic agriculture is a holistic production management system which promotes and enhances agro-ecosystem health, including biodiversity, biological cycles, and soil biological activity. It emphasizes the use of management practices in preference to the use of off-farm inputs, taking into account that regional conditions require locally adapted systems. This is accomplished by using, where possible, cultural, biological and mechanical methods, as opposed to using synthetic materials, to fulfill any specific function within the system". - FAO

According to IFOAM (International Federation of Organic Agriculture Movements), organic agriculture is based on the following.

- **Principle of health:** Organic Agriculture should sustain and enhance the health of soil, plant, animal, human and planet as one and indivisible.
- **Principle of ecology:** Organic Agriculture should be based on living ecological systems and cycles, work with them, emulate them and help sustain them.
- **Principle of fairness:** Organic Agriculture should build on relationships that ensure fairness with regard to the common environment and life opportunities
- **Principle of care:** Organic Agriculture should be managed in a precautionary and responsible manner to protect the health and well-being of current and future generations and the environment.

Because of the clearly laid down and accepted principles, standards and practices, organic farming ends up promoting use of local natural resources, avoids synthetic chemicals in farming and cuts down on fossil fuel use by different ways. Soil and water conservation are an integral part of this model along with enhancement of biodiversity and eco-system restoration. (Odisha state organic farming policy, draft prepared by organic farmers association).

Challenges

The main challenge for us woudl be to produce all the inputs required for this restaurant to be operational. For instance grains like rice, wheat pulses, some fruits, spices etc, cannot be grown in a urban setup so we have to source these inputs from outside. The items in the menu will be limited since we can only grow seasonal vegetables and fruits in the sorroundings. Serving non- vegetarian items will not be possible. The other important challenge is the problem of certification. The conventional modes of certification are quite expensive and we are planning to take the route of people's guarantee scheme(PGS) and we are not quite whether this scheme can be extended to urban residents. If the people in the locality can create a level of trust among the consumers that what they grow is completely organic then we do not think certification will become a major problem. The other major challenge would be raising enough finances to make the model functional. Preparing elaborate business plans would also be a challenge and also forecasting the demand is also not very easy. The responsiveness of the residents about urban agriculture is also a matter of concern. We are banking on volunteers to take up this challenge but are not sure about their motivational levels.

Avenues to promote urban agriculture

Urban dwellers usually live either in independent houses, apartments or in slums. In case of independent house they usually have a small backyards which can be utilised for growing vegetables and fruits. Many of the colonies in Bhubaneswar already have functional kitchen gardens. Our conversations with residents revealed that the idea of kitchen garden is very old one there's nothing new about. The only problem is that we are slowly forgetting these traditions. Many of them even have compost pits in their backyards to convert their kitchen waste into organic manure. Targeting these households in the initial stage would make things work.

The second lot is the ones living in the slums. The Agha khan foundation in Bihar came up with this idea of landless gardens specially for the urban slums. Here they use gunny bags which are filled with a mixture of soil and manure. Holes are being made in different directions and seeds of creepers are placed in these holes. Then the bag is placed at a place where it gets ample amount of sunlight. There are many non-governmental organisations which are already working with urban slums on the issues of health and education. We plan to tie-up with these organisations to promote our idea of landless garden. This not only helps our cause but also ensures some income for these poor households.

The third lot being the residents who reside in the apartments. There are some voluntary organisations which are already working with residents of Bangalore on terrace farming. We feel that we ask for their help in promoting terrace farming which needs high levels of motivation. The residents need to be given some initial training before we start terrace farming.

Responses from the people

We actually wanted to test our idea with our actual stakeholders, so met some of these people to understand what they feel about our idea. Mrs. Shailja Rout, currently working as the Finanace director of the CV Raman group of institutions was very much buoyed by the idea of an organic restaurant. Being a plant lover herself she said that they already have a kitchen garden in their backyard and would love be part of our idea. But working as the head of a department she had some doubts on the effectiveness of the idea if it lacks strong leadership. She feels that we should come up with more clarity on the governance structure that we need to put in place. She felt that there were some short comings on a community based enterprises but was quite confident that a strong leadership can neutralize them.

She also feels that many of her friends are aware of the negative impacts of the chemical food and most of them are ready to pay a premium price for organic food.

When we talked to a housewife about the idea of growing vegetables in their kitchen garden she was not very surprised. She bshowed her backyard where they already grow vegetables. They also have a compost pit where they put all the organic wastes of the kitchen. She was not very excited about the idea of a organic restaurant but was ready to supply vegetables for the same. She was very much aware of the ill-effects of the chemical food but was not awarte of the concept of carbon foot print. She said that she is ready to volunteer in promoting the idea of urban kitchen gardens.

When we asked the same questions to some of the engineering students they were putting up blank faces and were not much interested in the discussions. None of them were aware about carbon footprint but some of them had some idea about organic food.

Hospitality

An organic restaurant in a hotel can be promoted as a unique selling point & a special feature of a hotel, especially for tourists who are interested in eco-tourism and sustainable tourism.

- To follow the market and customers' tastes, it can be a great marketing strategy for hotels to sell organic food or establish organic restaurants.
- Hotels that use organic food actually enjoy a relatively low premium.
- In order to generate the quality of the organic food, hotels can choose to buy locally.
    - o A method for hotels to save expenditures on food costs.
- Green hotels are coming up in the urban areas.
    - o In order to be 'green', then organic food can be very attractive for the hotels to use in their restaurants.
- Hartman Group's surveys are widely used to analyze the reasons why consumers choose organic food.

- Consumers bought organic food due to the superior taste, environmental benefits and nutrition health concerns.

  (Whole food market, 2004, Hartman, 2002)
- Consumers are either :-
  - o Environmental militants
  - o Traditional
  - o Dietaries
  - o Youthful
- Environmental militants buy organic food since they believe that organic food is much more eco-friendly than conventional food.
- Traditional are people who are loyal to the original taste of the food.
- Dietaries choose organic food for dietary reasons, since they are fighting to keep fit, as they consider organic food are better for the diet.
- As for youthful, most of them prefer organic food just simply because of the concept and they think it is kind of cool to do like this.

Children under 18 are more likely to buy the products, as parents consider it is required for the growth of their children.

Basically, organic food represents for less pesticides and chemicals.

Some people turn to organic food, because they want to fight with diseases.

Decision factors include internal and external factors, such as personality, disposable income, health, lifestyle, past experience, attitudes, opinions and perceptions.

For example - If there are two opinions for a tourist who is living a 'green life' - a normal hotel and an eco-friendly hotel, normally the tourist will choose the eco-friendly one due to internal factors.

External factors can be - suitable products, words of mouth, recommendation of friends/families, special promotions and climates. Internet and social media also play an important role to attract consumers.

Some say that organic products are sold for a higher price because of the organic label and not because organic products are tastier or because they are well made, i.e. not for the quality, but the image & the concept.

We have guidelines to achieve a good eco sustainable programme which are as follows:-

- Reduce - Reuse - Recycle - Right way of segregating waste at source point.
- Sewage treatments plant clarifies water and the same can be used in gardens.
- Encourage guests to have menus as per seasonal availability. Allow guests to order half portions to reduce wastage.
- Wind mill owned by the hotel located off-property helps reduce carbon footprint and generate renewable clean energy.
- Active participation in eco-friendly events of the city and bearing partners in promoting such events for general awareness.

According to Schnoll, travel decision process includes:-

- Travel stimuli
- Personal & social determinants
- External variables - (prospective travelers' confidence in the service provider, destination image, learning experiences.....)
- Destination characteristics

As the green trend in all the industries grow, it is possible that hotels all over the world will more/less use organic food.

- Selling organic food is not only about the quality of the products, but also the image & concept of the products.
- It is my important for hotels to make consumers to have the idea of organic food always relate to a healthier life style.
- Properly use different marketing tools to promote for the organic food is also necessary for hotels.
- Clearly, analyzing consumer of making decisions & then following consumer's taste is essential.

- For most hotels, process and the high costs & the availability of organic food are the two main obstacles for the development of organic food in the hospitality industry.
- The future development of organic food in hospitality industry is still continued to be very potential.

Conclusion

No doubt an argument for agrarian life will sound old fashioned. Most of us, after all are urbanites, and so represent the culmination of a migratory trend that is unparalled in the human history. The exodus from country to city, now accomplished in the developed countries and well on its way in the rest of the world, is seen by many as the prerequisite for human freedom and progress. But given the enormity of implication and consequence that follows from a loss of intimate and practical connection with the earth and the general ignorance about our interdependence with other organisms, we have become completely insensitive to nature. Our idea behind this project was less about an academic accomplishment and more about finding these connections.

The whole idea of an organic restaurant is not a new one. But trying to sources majority of the raw materials in and around it is a challenging task. Involving the community in your day to day business is also not very easy. Though our report doesnt talk in depth about these issues but through this paper we tried to propose a model which can be researched and tried out as a pilot. This idea can be easily tried out in a city like Bhubaneshwar since people here are already having kitchen gardens in their back yards. The important issue that urban dwellers are facing is the unclean and polluted environment in their sorroundings. This idea of urban agriculture can help in transforming the ambience and making it clean and green..The role and contribution of green practices in hospitality and tourism industry leads to a greener Indian economy.

References

Fukuoka (1975), One straw revolution.

Wendell Berry, (1975),The unsettling of America - Culture and agriculture

Venkat, (2012), Permaculture

Narendranath,(2010),Dilemmas in Agriculture

The organic farming reader, edited by Claude, Vandana Shiva, Sultan Ismail, k. Vijayalakshmi, Korah Mathen, Bernard Declercq (2006)Sustaianable agriculture, A pathway out of poverty for India's rural poor

Wendell Berry(2012), The art of common place, The agrarian essays of Wendell Berry

Sukhpal singh (2012),Organic produce supply chains in India,

Vandana Shiva(1992),The violence of green revolution.

Organic boom(2013), Down to earth.

AR Vasavi(2012), Shadow space.

Sainath(2011), In 16 years farm suicides cross a quarter million, article in Hindu

Centrality of agriculture to India's economic development,(2006), Economic and political weekly.

Orissa agricultural policy, 2008.

C.Shambu Prasad and Sumita Sindhi(2010), Coping with complexity-Mapping sustainable agriculture in Orissa using the RTD frame work..

Source: Organic Food Market-India report, research on India, Netscribes (India)

Rajesh Gopalakrishnan, (Hotel Scapes, 2013)

TERRORISM AND TOURISM: AN INDIAN PERSPECTIVE

Kumar Nilmani

Academic Associate, Economics at Indian Institute of Management, Kashipur. kumar.nilmani@iimkashipur.ac.in,

Ranu Chauhan

Assistant Professor, Indian Institute of Tourism and Travel Management (IITTM), Gwalior. chauhan.ranu7@gmail.com

Abstract: The tourism industry is one of the most vulnerable industries in the world because of its nature and characteristics. There are many vital forces that are shaping the tourism industry and tourist influx in any particular country and terrorism is most prominent among them. India's rank on Global terrorism Index (GTI) is four in the year 2012 and only Iraq, Afghanistan and Pakistan had fared badly then India. Terrorist activities have great significance and ramification in the number of foreign tourist arrivals in India. Terrorism not only affects the number of tourists, but has a wider impact on social, political life and economy of that nation. This paper tries to discuss in detail the impact of 26/11 and other terrorist incident and its aftermath on the tourist influx and tourism industry in India.

Keywords: Terrorism, Global terrorism Index, Tourist Influx, 26/ 11.

Introduction:

Tourism is a social, cultural and economic phenomenon which entails the movement of people to countries or places outside their usual environment for personal or business/professional purposes. These people are called visitors (which may be either tourists or excursionists; residents or non-residents) and tourism has to do with their activities, some of which imply tourism expenditure.

As such, tourism has implications for the economy, on the natural and built environment, on the local population at the destination and on the tourists themselves. Due to these multiple impacts, the wide range and variety of production factors required to produce those goods and services acquired by visitors, and the wide spectrum of stakeholders involved or affected by tourism, there is a need for a holistic approach to tourism development, management and monitoring. This approach is strongly recommended in order to formulate and implement national and local tourism policies as well as the necessary international agreements or other processes in respect of tourism.[1]

According to World Travel and Tourism Council Travel & Tourism's direct contribution to world GDP and employment in 2012 were US$ 2.1 trillion (2012 prices) and 101 million jobs. Taking account of its combined direct, indirect and induced impacts, Travel & Tourism's total economic contribution in 2012 was US$ 6.6 trillion in GDP (2012 prices); 260 million in jobs; US$ 760 billion in investment (2012 prices); and US$ 1.2 trillion in exports (2012 prices). This total contribution represents 9% of total economy GDP in 2012, 1 in 11 jobs, 5% of total economic investment and 5% of world exports.

Global Performance and Outlook: 2012 and 2013

Despite on-going challenging economic conditions, global Travel & Tourism direct contribution to GDP grew by a robust 3.2% in 2012. This was faster than the growth of the world economy as whole (2.3%), and also faster than the growth of a number of broad industries including manufacturing, financial & business services and retail. Total Travel & Tourism employment, including those working in the industry's supply chain and supported by the spending of

1 Understanding Tourism: Basic Glossary, World Tourism Organization UNWTO

their employees, increased by 4.0 million jobs in 2012 as compared to previous years. While Travel & Tourism GDP growth slowed throughout 2012 and was weaker than forecast one year ago, visitor exports exceeded expectations, rising 4.7% year on year.

In percentage growth terms, Asia, Latin America and Sub-Saharan Africa were amongst the fastest growing destination markets in 2012. Though in absolute change terms, visitor exports growth in North America and Europe exceeded expectations in 2012 and explain most of the growth in global visitor exports. In terms of outbound spending, Asia and Latin America were the fastest growing origin markets in 2012, but in absolute change terms, it was again Europe and North America, along with North East Asia, that accounted for the overall above expectations growth.

In contrast, growth in both domestic Travel & Tourism spending (2.8%) and Travel & Tourism investment (2.4%) in 2012 was weaker than expected a year ago.

Looking ahead to 2013, the slowdown in Travel & Tourism international demand growth observed in the second half of 2012 is forecast to continue. But offsetting this is an improving macroeconomic environment, where the imminent prospect of a Eurozone break-up has reduced, and risks are shifting to the upside. A quick return to robust growth, especially in the Eurozone, will remain elusive in the short-term, however.

Global Travel & Tourism contribution to direct GDP in 2013 is forecast to grow by 3.1%, compared to 3.2% in 2012. Travel & Tourism are again forecast to outpace growth of the total global economy (2.4%) in 2013. Visitor exports growth is forecast to slow from 4.7% in 2012 to 3.1%, with domestic Travel & Tourism spending forecast to grow by 3.2%, a marginally better outturn than 2012. Total Travel & Tourism employment is projected to expand by 4.4 million jobs in 2013[2].

2 Economic Impact of Travel & Tourism 2013 Annual Update: Summary (World Travel and Tourism Council)

The above report by WTTC provides us with a panoramic view of the tourism industry as a whole. From Asia to Latin America, from Europe to North America tourism is from Sub-Saharan Africa to North East Asia tourism is a force to reckon with, and find the prominent place in employment and contribution to GDP.

Tourism: A Booming Sector in India

The direct contribution of Travel & Tourism to GDP in 2012 was INR1, 919.7bn (2.0% of GDP). This is forecast to rise by 7.0% to INR 2, 053.3bn in 2013.This primarily reflects the economic activity generated by industries such as hotels, travel agents, airlines and other passenger transportation services (excluding commuter services). But it also includes, for example, the activities of the restaurant and leisure industries directly supported by tourists.

The direct contribution of Travel & Tourism to GDP is expected to grow by 7.8% pa to INR4, 360.6bn (2.1% of GDP) by 2023. The total contribution of Travel & Tourism to GDP (including wider effects from investment, the supply chain and induced income was INR6, 385.1bn in 2012 (6.6% of GDP) and is expected to grow by 7.3 % to INR6, 853.7bn (6.7% of GDP) in 2013. It is forecast to rise by 7.9% pa to INR14, 722.3bn by 2023 (7.0% of GDP).

Fig. 1

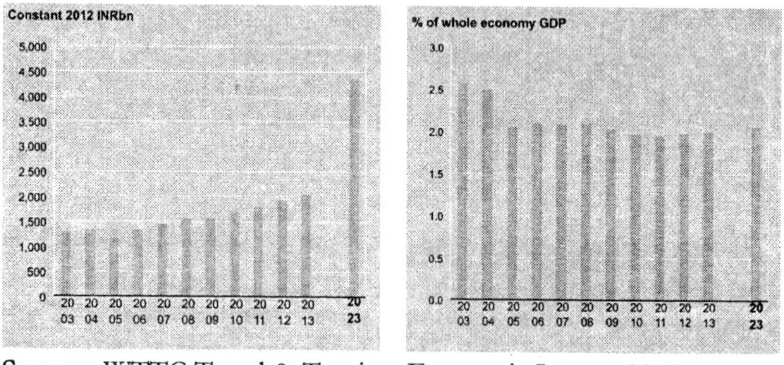

Source: WTTC Travel & Tourism Economic Impact 2013

Travel & Tourism generated 25,041,000 jobs directly in 2012 (4.9% of total employment) and this is forecast to fall by 0.6% in 2013 to 24,899,000 (4.8% of total employment). This includes employment by hotels, travel agents, airlines and other passenger transportation services (excluding commuter services). It also includes, for example, the activities of the restaurant and leisure industries directly supported by tourists. By 2023, Travel & Tourism will account for 30,631,000 jobs directly, an increase of 2.1% pa over the next ten years.

The total contribution of Travel & Tourism to employment (including wider effects from investment, the supply chain and induced income impacts, see page 2) was 39,512,000 jobs in 2012 (7.7% of total employment). This is forecast to fall by 0.2% in 2013 to 39,420,500 jobs (7.6% of total employment). By 2023, Travel & Tourism are forecasted to support 48,592,000 jobs (8.0% of total employment), an increase of 2.1 % pa over the period.

Visitor Export[3]

Visitor exports are a key component of the direct contribution of Travel & Tourism. In 2012, India generated INR1, 004.6bn in visitor exports. In 2013, this is expected to grow by 8.7%, and the country is expected to attract 7,518,000 international tourist arrivals. By 2023, international tourist arrivals are forecast to total 13,699,000, generating expenditure of INR1, 892.0bn, an increase of 5.7% pa.

From the data mentioned here it shows that tourism has a great contribution in Indian economy. It's the backbone of earning of foreign money, at the same time one of the largest source of employment. It provides tax revenue both direct and indirect. Tourism provides job directly to hotel, restaurants, nightclubs, tour operators, taxis and the shop who sells souvenir and other related product. It indirectly provides jobs to the people who involve in logistics like providing goods and services required for tourism related activities.

Terrorism: A Curse on Tourism Industry

The events of September 11, 2001 in USA and 26/11 in India, serves a grim reminder of the fragility and vulnerability of the tourism industry. This industry doesn't recognise as a significant means to

3 WTTC Travel & Tourism Economic Impact 2013, all values are in constant 2012 prices & exchange rates.

bring peace and harmony among nations and international politics, it nevertheless requires peace, harmony and stability for its survival and nourishment.

Tourism destination and tourist by their very nature has always been 'soft target' for terrorist activities. In his work on terrorism and tourism Sonmez, Apostolopoulos, and Tarlow (1999) propagates that for a terrorist organization, tourism destination are vulnerable enough to easy to infiltrate, act against tourists and have guaranteed international media attention aftermath impact of attack can be gargantuan, and in overall tourism destination have been utilized as platform to deliver a cost effective message of ideological/political opposition (Page-15). They also mention experts (Atkinson, Sandler, & Tschirhart, 1987; Jenkins, 1988) predicting that attack will be more indiscriminate, brutal and terrorism will become institutionalized as a means of armed struggle which spread across geographies and the world will witness more terrorism than ever in in the coming years due to global media coverage and attention. The recent attack on the Sochi Olympic venue is again a part of the biggest agenda by terrorist because of the global media coverage and the influx of foreign tourist as they are always soft target.

The terrorist attacks in Volgograd on December 29 and 30 are an ominous sign that the decision to hold the 2014 Winter Olympics in Sochi may lead to one of the greatest catastrophes in the history of the Olympics. Many of the 120,000 persons expected to visit the Olympics do not realize that they are walking into what effectively is a war zone[4].

Citing a new "surprise package" for Russia and Olympic spectators, Islamist militants in the North Caucasus on Sunday launched a new threat to the Sochi Olympics with a purported "martyrdom" video by two suicide bombers who attacked a transit hub 400 miles away.

"We'll have a surprise package for you," one of the men said in the militants' video. "And those tourists that will come to you, for

4 CNN - Attacks show Sochi Olympics under grave threat, By David Satter, Russia analyst, December 31, 2013

them, too, we have a surprise. If it happens [the Olympics], we'll have a surprise for you. This is for all the Muslim blood that is shed every day around the world, be it in Afghanistan, Somalia, or Syria, all around the world. This will be our revenge[5].

The above mentioned news and statements shows that, how a particular tourist event is a prime target for terrorists to exert their political and ideological views to express in such a manner it find global media attention and coverage. Again the soft target is tourists.

Fig. 2

World Travel & Tourism Council TSA Research Findings (1990 Constant US $ Billion)
(1997-2002 & 2012)

Particular	1997	1998	1999	2000	2001	2002 (E)	2012 (P)
Travel & Tourism - 1990 Constant US$ Billion							
Personal Travel & Tourism	12.02	13.93	14.35	15.53	16.34	17.27	38.33
Business Travel & Tourism	2.11	2.29	2.44	2.59	2.31	2.07	5.19
Govt Expenditures - Individual	0.14	0.17	0.19	0.20	0.21	0.23	0.35
Visitor Exports	3.23	3.41	3.50	3.66	3.48	3.48	11.76
Travel & Tourism Consumption	17.51	19.81	20.48	21.98	22.34	23.04	55.63
Govt Expenditures - Collective	0.33	0.39	0.43	0.46	0.49	0.52	0.81
Capital Investment	6.24	6.50	7.05	7.56	7.97	8.48	16.53
Exports (Non-Visitor)	1.25	0.98	1.09	1.28	1.44	1.42	4.25
Travel & Tourism Demand	25.32	27.67	29.06	31.28	32.25	33.47	77.23
Gross Domestic Product							
Travel & Tourism Industry	9.70	10.89	11.13	11.66	11.84	12.21	27.36
Travel & Tourism Economy	21.90	23.81	24.86	26.24	27.12	28.20	61.10
Travel & Tourism - Rs. in Billion							
Personal Travel & Tourism	394.08	495.44	535.50	602.96	653.81	726.03	2825.16
Business Travel & Tourism	69.24	81.28	91.02	100.46	92.42	86.91	382.38
Corporate	63.01	73.38	81.58	89.95	82.59	77.62	349.53
Government	6.23	7.90	9.44	10.51	9.83	9.29	32.85
Govt Expenditures - Individual	4.66	5.98	7.02	7.78	8.60	9.50	26.09
Visitor Exports	105.78	121.10	130.72	141.94	139.34	146.17	866.57
Travel & Tourism Consumption	573.76	703.80	764.25	853.14	894.17	968.60	4100.20
Govt Expenditures - Collective	10.86	13.73	16.10	17.85	19.73	21.79	59.85
Capital Investment	204.41	230.87	263.15	293.41	319.19	356.55	1218.29
Exports (Non-Visitor)	40.80	34.76	40.64	49.61	57.52	59.67	313.45
Travel & Tourism Demand	829.84	983.15	1084.14	1214.01	1290.61	1406.61	5691.79
Travel & Tourism Industry Aggregates (Direct Impact only)							
Employment ('000)	10359.20	11241.00	11240.50	11243.70	11060.50	11017.60	14419.90
Gross Domestic Product	317.87	385.82	415.37	452.60	473.82	513.24	2016.12
Travel & Tourism Economy Aggregates (Direct and Indirect Impacts)							
Employment ('000)	21889.00	23098.00	23343.00	23530.30	23561.40	23662.80	29950.60
Gross Domestic Product	717.60	845.89	927.53	1016.40	1083.31	1165.28	4502.76

Source : World Travel & Tourism Council.

Year: Period of fiscal year in India is April to March. e.g. year shown as 1990-91 relates to April 1990 to March 1991.

Units: (a) 1 Lakh (or Lac) = 100000.

(b) 1 Crore (or Cr.) = 10000000.

Some part of the footnotes/units may not be applicable for this table.

---

5 Abs News-Terror 'Surprise' for Sochi Olympics? Purported Suicide Bombers' New Threat, Jan. 19, 2014, By BRIAN ROSS and JAMES GORDON MEEK

Every time a terrorist attack happened in a tourist destination, tourism demand declines and industry faces slowdown. Another phenomenon that has been visibly noticed from past terrorist attack in several countries, as well as major terrorist attack like 9/11 in the USA and 26/11 in India, is that devastating attack of terrorism not only confined only to particular tourism industry, but because of the higher multiplier effect of this industry the entire economy suffers. Evidence suggests that the attack on the world trade Centre not only demolished the economy of Florida, Nevada and Hawaii which are largely dependent on tourism industry, but also have a snowballing impact on the economy of the whole of the USA. Thus a single incidence of terrorism has the potential to cause a global devastating attack.

Reason and impact of Terrorism on Tourist Behavior.

The definition of terrorism opens a Pandora's box of intellectual discussion over the years with matter pertaining to who is a terrorist and who is a freedom fighter. A one nation terrorist is a freedom fighter for the other-depending on their morality and legality. How state sponsored and bon state sponsored terrorism can be distinguished and defined (Chomsky, 2001; Cooper, 2001; Jenkins, 2001; Lizardo & Bergesen, 2003; Schweitzer, 2002). Ruby (2002, pp. 10-11) in a brilliant analysis of various definitions isolate five defining criteria: motivation for the terrorist act (political or other), target towards which it is directed (non-combatants), actors (sub-national groups or clandestine agents), objective (creation of a fearful state of mind) and intended audience (larger than the immediate victims). Enders and Sandler (2002) use the very same criteria when they offer the following definition:

Terrorism is the premeditated use or threat of use of extra normal violence or brutality by subnational groups to obtain a political, religious, or ideological objective through intimidation of a huge audience, usually not directly involved with the policy making that the terrorists seek to influence (Enders & Sandler 2002, pp. 145-146).

Apart from their immediate media flash, tourism destinations have recently been attacked as terrorist considers its fight against their ideologies which they think these tourists represents. Politically an attack on tourist of a particular nation considers an attack on their nation and governments (Richter & Waugh, 1986). As the tourist industry for many nations such as Egypt, Israel, Greece, Sri Lanka and Indonesia is a major source of economic prosperity, the terrorist manages to damage their economy and Governance by attacking on their destinations. (Aziz, 1995), in his study of terrorist incidences in Egypt in 1990, establish the relationship that tourist attack are used as symbolic resistance on the government and try to destroy the one the major source of earning of economy. The objective to create a fear factor in the mind of tourists is the prime reason behind these terrorist acts, this can be scholarly articulated and presented in the earlier work of Sonmez and Graefe (1998a, 1998b). Terrorist attack risk and concern about safety and security are major influential factors in travel decisions, even among experienced tourists. Enders and Sandler (1991) in their pre 9/11 study in Spain analyse the impact of terrorism on tourism. He concluded that a typical terrorist act resulted in a subsequent reduction of 140, 000 tourists. In a later study of the of the impact of terrorism on tourism in Greece, Italy and Austria and other western countries, they assert that terrorism not only affect the influx of tourist in the particular nation where the terrorist incidence has happened but it also impact it's neighbouring country where the fear psychosis prevails (Enders et al., 1992).On the contrary Mansfled (1996), suggest that Cyprus, Greece and Turkey have benefitted from conflicts in Egypt, Israel, Jordan, Lebanon and Syria as the tourist tries to replicate the east Mediterranean touch so they are looking for other similar destinations which they perceive them as safer. Recently, Drakos and Kutan (2003) in their study of terrorist incidences in Greece, Israel and Turkey between 1991 and 2000 concluded that, due to terrorist attack in a particular nation the neighbors may act as a substitute but in the long run there is a negative impact on the wider region.

Tourists as they are not expert in terrorism incidence analysis always predict the worst scenario, when they plan to travel (Viscusi

& Zeckhauser, 2003), they are not assessing the probity of attack rather than the horrific outcome of the incidence (Sunstein, 2003). But, this negative impact rather does not last for long, and tourism destination may recover from the terrorist shock (Aly & Strazicich, 2000; Narayan, 2005) but Pizam and Fleischer (2002) warn that repeated terrorism incidences have a long lasting impact and has the potential to lead to complete collapse of a tourist destination. One of the most amazing finding is that, the effect of repeated terrorist attack on domestic tourists is much less as compared to foreign tourists. Yechiam, Barron, and Erev (2005) found significant behavioral differences in tourist behavior that Intifada had on occupancy of Israeli hotels. The rise of attacks on Israel, there was a drop of 60% occupancy from foreign tourist, but it is only 10% in the case of domestic tourist. In the subsequent years the drop of room demand is 80% for foreign tourists, but surprisingly there is 20% rise in occupancy from domestic tourist demand. It seems that repeated terrorist attack reduces the risk sensitivity and fear among domestic tourists.

Major Terrorist attacks in India.

India in recent history has witnessed a series of vicious terrorist attack. It causes an immense damage to the precious life as well as economy of the nation. Mumbai is always a prime target for terrorist as it in India's financial capital and most cosmopolitan among all the states. That's why Mumbai is repeatedly targeted by terrorists as they got immediate international media attention at the same time they are able to hit hard on the economy of the nation.

When it comes to economic issues, Mumbai - the country's financial capital - is likely to feel the impact of the terrorist attacks, much as New York City did after September 11, 2001. "Mumbai brings in 40% of foreign trade, 60% of customs duty collections, 40% of income tax collections, 20% of central excise collections and $10 billion in corporate taxes," says Rangar of IndusView. Chakrabarti notes: "The Mumbai terror attack has been the most dramatic in a long series of terror events in India. It involved foreign hostages and places where business leaders, executives and foreigners frequented. It has therefore been a much more potent media drama than any of the previous terror events. This grabbed worldwide attention and there is certainly a negative impact on India's risk and security perception. It will dent foreign investors' views of India. This will lead to a drop in investments, but I expect it to be marginal[6]."

So it is clearly evident that why Mumbai has been attacked subsequently.

Fig. 3

Incidents of Bomb Blasts/Terrorist Attacks in India (As on 01.01.2008 to 01.08.2012)

Date	Incidents	Casualties		Compensation Paid to the Victims	
		Killed	Injured	Compensation Paid to Deceased (N OK in Lakh)	Compensation Paid to Injured (In Lakh)
07.12.2010	Bomb Blast in Varanasi (UP)	2	20	2.00	11.75
19.09.2010	Jama Masjid (Delhi) Firing and Explosions	-	2*	-	-
17.04.2010	Chinnaswamy Stadium Blast,Bangalore	-	20	-	3.90
13.02.2010	Bomb Blast in Pune	17	64	85.00	22.00
16.10.2009	Margao Blast	2	-	-	-
26.11.2008-28.11.2008	Terrorist Attacts in Mumbai	174	292	-	-
29.09.2008	Bomb Blast at Malegaon, Maharashtra	6	29	-	-
29.09.2008	Bomb Blast at Subarkantha, Gujarat	1	10	-	-
27.09.2008	Bomb Blast at Mehrauli, Delhi	-	-	-	-
13.09.2008	A Series of 5 Bomb Blasts in Delhi	22	131	-	-
26.07.2008	A Series of 18 Bomb Blasts in Ahmedabad	57	157	-	-
25.07.2008	A Series of 8 Bomb Blasts in Bangalore	1	8	-	-
13.05.2008	Serial Bomb Blasts at Jaipur	68	150	-	-
01.01.2008	Attack on CRPF Group Centre at Rampur	8	3	-	-
07.09.2011	Bomb Blast High Cort, New Delhi	15	67	134.00	149.80
13.07.2011	Serial Bomb Blasts inMumbai	27	127	75.00	47.30
13.02.2012	Blast in a Car of Embassy of Israel	-	4	-	-
01.08.2012	Serial Bomb Blast in Pune	-	1	-	-

Note: *: Persons Injured in Firing Incident.

Source: Rajya Sabha Unstarred Question No. 253, dated on 23.02.2011, Rajya Sabha Unstarred Question No. 2280, dated on 25.04.2012 & Rajya Sabha Unstarred Question No. 2691, dated on 05.09.2012

6 KNOWLEDGE@WHARTON - Terrorist Attacks Will Further Weaken a Slowing Indian Economy

Terrorist choose to attack Taj and Oberoi hotel where they can get maximum no. of foreigners. They attack Nariman house to show a symbolic attack on state of Israel. India a land of diversity is in harmony with several religions living side by side. Its beauty of India to unity in diversity terrorist attack on Varanasi and places like this is premeditated attack to destroy the very fabric of Indian society by spreading communal hatred among societies.

Impact on Foreign Tourist arrival

Fig. 4

Number of Foreign Tourist Visits in India (1997 to 2013-upto September 2013) (In Million)		
Year	No. of Foreign Tourist Visits	Percentage (%) Change over the Previous Year
1997	5.50	9.3
1998	5.54	0.7
1999	5.83	5.3
2000	5.89	1.1
2001	5.44	-7.8
2002	5.16	-5.1
2003	6.71	30.1
2004	8.36	24.6
2005	9.95	19.0
2006	11.75	18.1
2007	13.26	12.8
2008	14.38	8.5
2009	5.17	-2.2
2010	5.78	11.8
2011	63.09#	9.2
2012	66.48#	5.4
2013-upto Sept.	47.41#	3.8

Note: #: In Lakh.

Source: Ministry of Tourism, Govt. of India

From the data it is clearly evident that there is sharp reduction in the number of foreign tourist influx in India because of the Mumbai attack. It is one of lonest terrorist attack which is continues for three days and the whole government mercenary is working to subdued it. It was a complete disaster with the loss of 174 precious life 292 injured and economy suffer enormously because of this.

Month wise analysis of data also reflects that there is a significant reduction in the number of tourists from the month of December, 2008 when a terrorist attack takes place, to the further month of Jan, Feb.... 2009.

But there is very noticeable trend to be identified that despite the terrorist attack India's ranking on the global list of recipients of tourist is and has been improved in subsequent years. In year 2008 when India has been severely impacted by the Mumbai terrorist attack and the next year it retain the same rank of 40 and in year 2010, 2011 India constantly improves his rank. Improving of the India's ranking established the theory that after a particular time period a destination has the capacity to emerge from terrorist shock and India is not an exception to this theory.

Fig. 5

Month-wise Foreign Tourist Arrivals in India
(January 2003 to September 2013)

(In Number)

Month	Jan.	Feb.	Mar.	Apr.	May	Jun.	July	Aug.	Sept.	Oct.	Nov.	Dec.
2003	274215	262692	218473	160941	141508	176324	225359	204940	191339	260569	290583	319271
2004	337345	331697	293185	223884	185502	223122	272456	253301	226773	307447	385238	417527
2005	385977	369844	352094	248416	225394	246970	307870	273856	257184	347757	423837	479411
2006	459489	439090	391009	309208	255008	278370	337332	304387	297891	391399	442413	541571
2007	535631	501692	472494	350550	277017	310364	399866	358446	301892	444564	532428	575148
2008	511781	611493	479765	361101	304361	341539	431933	383337	341693	450013	531683	533904
2009	481308	469787	442062	347544	305183	352353	432900	369707	330707	458849	541524	615775
2010	568719	552152	512152	371956	332087	384642	466715	422173	369821	507093	608178	680004
2011$	5.38	6.36	5.50	4.17	3.55	4.12	4.76	4.28	4.17	5.60	6.70	7.37
2012$	6.81	6.77	6.23	4.52	3.72	4.33	4.86	4.46	4.12	5.76	6.90	7.50
2013$	6.99	6.88	6.40	4.52	3.84	4.44	5.24	4.74	4.36			
% age Change												
2004/03	23.0	26.3	34.2	39.1	31.1	26.5	20.0	23.6	18.5	18.0	32.6	30.8
2005/04	14.4	11.5	20.1	11.0	21.5	10.7	13.0	8.1	13.4	13.1	10.0	14.8
2006/05	19.0	18.7	11.1	24.5	13.1	12.7	9.6	11.1	15.8	12.5	4.4	13.0
2007/06	16.6	14.3	20.8	13.4	8.6	11.5	18.5	17.8	1.3	13.6	20.3	10.2
2008/07	-4.5	21.9	1.5	3.0	9.9	10.0	9.0	6.9	13.2	1.2	-0.1	-10.5
2009/08	-6.0	-19.9	-7.9	-3.8	0.3	3.2	0.2	-3.6	-3.2	2.0	1.9	15.3
2010/09	18.2	17.7	15.9	7.0	8.8	9.2	7.8	14.2	11.8	10.5	12.3	10.4
2011/10	9.7	15.1	7.4	17.7	7.0	7.2	10.1	5.3	8.7	10.4	10.1	8.4
2012/11	9.4	7.9	16.3	1.3	3.1	6.9	2.2	4.0	1.4	3.0	3.0	1.7
2013/12	2.6	1.6	2.8	-	3.2	2.5	7.9	6.4	5.8			

Note : $: Figures are In Lakh.
Source : Ministry of Tourism, Govt. of India.

Fig. 6

Nationality-wise Classification of Foreign Tourist Arrivals (FTAs) According to Purpose of Visit in India (2011)						
Country of Nationality	**FTAs (In Number)**	**Business and Professional**	**Leisure, Holiday and Recreation**	**Visiting Friends and Relatives**	**Medical Treatment**	**Others**
North America						
Canada	259017	15.3	23.0	45.0	0.3	16.4
United State of America	980688	21.6	18	42.8	0.2	17.4
Total	**1239705**	**20.7**	**18.7**	**43.1**	**0.3**	**17.2**
Central and South America						
Argentina	9391	19.5	50.2	13.6	0.1	16.6
Brazil	17268	46.1	24.8	12.8	0.2	16.2
Mexico	10876	37.2	34.7	12.3	0.1	15.7
Others	23453	24.5	32.2	20.6	0.5	18.3
Total	**60988**	**32.6**	**34.3**	**15.8**	**0.3**	**17.0**
Western Europe						
Austria	36483	31.1	32.1	19.9	0.8	16.2
Belgium	40478	35.1	30.2	20.1	0.1	14.5
Denmark	34683	44.1	32.6	10.8	0.3	12.2
Finland	23730	42.5	32.2	10.6	0.1	14.6
France	231423	26.2	36.6	19.1	0.2	17.9
Germany	240235	43.2	29.8	12.9	0.5	13.5
Greece	7253	32.1	38.1	12.0	0.3	17.4
Ireland	22089	32.6	27.4	24.9	0.1	15.0
Italy	100889	41.1	34.9	9.6	0.3	14.1
Netherlands	75153	14.6	31.6	13.8	0.2	12.9
Norway	24578	34.4	32.4	16.9	0.7	15.6
Portugal	24061	17.7	30.9	33.5	0.3	17.7
Spain	71405	30.9	38.3	15.1	0.2	15.5
Sweden	48690	37.2	36.9	13.8	0.3	11.7
Switzerland	46332	27.1	38.9	18.2	0.9	15.0
United Kingdom	798249	23.1	26.7	34.0	0.2	15.9
Others	12964	28.1	34.7	13.7	0.5	22.9
Total	**1838695**	**29.3**	**3.2**	**24.8**	**0.3**	**15.5**
Eastern Europe						
Czech Rep.	11256	47.0	31.5	9.0	0.3	12.2
Hungary	6900	41.2	36.4	9.8	0.2	12.3
Kazakhstan	9810	18.6	40.6	8.6	4.1	28.2
Poland	28499	30.9	40.9	12.9	0.1	15.2
Russian Fed.	144312	17.0	50.9	8.6	1.8	21.8
Ukraine	23467	24.7	36.9	10.2	1.3	26.9
Others	50354	31.8	32.8	13.5	0.9	21.0
Total	**274598**	**26.6**	**41.6**	**10.6**	**1.1**	**20.0**
Africa						
Egypt	8791	51.2	17.5	9.3	0.7	21.3
Kenya	30045	22.5	24.7	27.3	4.4	21.2
Mauritius	22091	13.6	47.4	17.4	3.8	17.8
Nigeria	33537	33.2	14.1	9.4	36.8	16.5
South Africa	58430	20.2	41.5	24.5	0.5	13.3
Sudan	2328	15.3	12.8	8.6	8.5	54.9
Tanzania	19470	17.6	27.0	21.4	11.3	22.8

Source: Ministry of Tourism, Govt. of India. (14012)

India offers a paradox as in Global terrorist index it is one the most vulnerable nation at the same time being a fastest growing nation in the world offers an abundance of opportunities which can be evident from the data provided above for the purpose of visit to foreigners.

Fig.7

Nationality-wise Quarterly Foreign Tourists Arrivals in India (2011)

Country of Nationality	Aarrivals (In Number)	Quarter-wise Share (%)			
		1st Quarter (Jan-Mar)	2nd Quarter (Apr-June)	3rd Quarter (July-Sep)	4th Quarter (Oct-Dec)
North America					
Canada	259017	27.7	17.5	17.3	37.5
United State of America	980688	23.7	24.4	20.6	31.3
Total	**1239705**	**24.3**	**23.4**	**20.1**	**32.2**
Central and South America					
Argentina	9391	39.3	12.1	15.5	33.1
Brazil	17268	30.6	18.9	21.7	28.8
Mexico	10876	27.0	21.9	21.8	29.3
Others	23453	29.2	21.7	23.5	25.6
Total	**60988**	**30.8**	**19.4**	**21.5**	**28.3**
Western Europe					
Austria	36483	31.3	18.8	20.0	29.9
Belgium	40478	26.0	19.6	22.1	32.3
Denmark	34683	34.2	18.4	18.6	28.8
Finland	23730	42.1	18.5	12.2	27.2
France	231423	29.3	21.3	22.2	27.2
Germany	240235	30.1	19.1	18.9	31.9
Greece	7253	27.0	20.4	20.0	28.6
Ireland	22089	25.3	24.0	21.0	29.8
Italy	100889	31.1	17.7	20.5	30.8
Netherlands	75153	30.0	19.3	21.3	29.4
Norway	24578	31.7	20.3	18.8	29.2
Portugal	24061	29.4	21.8	21.7	27.1
Spain	71405	23.3	17.8	28.8	30.2
Sweden	48690	35.1	15.6	13.1	36.2
Switzerland	46332	29.6	16.6	20.8	33.0
United Kingdom	798249	31.8	17.8	18.8	31.6
Others	12964	29.2	14.6	22.2	34.0
Total	**1838695**	**30.8**	**18.6**	**19.7**	**30.9**
Eastern Europe					
Czech Rep.	11256	32.2	17.4	19.6	30.8
Hungary	6900	35.8	16.3	19.7	28.2
Kazakhstan	9810	38.2	12.3	21.7	27.8
Poland	28499	31.7	14.8	19.4	34.2
Russia	144312	45.5	11.2	15.0	28.3
Ukraine	23467	38.3	16.4	16.5	28.7
Others	50354	32.1	17.7	18.8	31.4
Total	**274598**	**38.1**	**14.4**	**17.3**	**30.1**
Africa					
Egypt	8791	23.8	23.0	22.0	30.3
Kenya	30045	26.2	19.4	19.5	34.8
Mauritius	22091	26.2	20.8	21.7	31.4
Nigeria	33537	23.4	22.3	28.0	26.3
South Africa	58430	27.8	18.2	17.1	36.8
Sudan	2328	20.0	21.8	31.4	26.7
Tanzania	19470	25.1	22.1	21.7	31.1
Others	57694	25.1	21.4	25.2	28.4
Total	**232386**	**25.6**	**20.4**	**22**	**32.0**
West Asia					
Bahrain	9587	17.9	24.7	33.1	24.2
Iraq	30800	23.3	19.6	32.4	24.8
Israel	48089	29.0	17.8	22.7	30.5

Source: Ministry of Tourism, Govt. of India. (14012)

Most of the tourists who visited India are from nations from American continent and Europe and they are very much worried about their safety and security. Their embassies also issue guideline and terror alert from time to time to visit a particular nation. Despite all this India is emerging as a favourite destination for tourist arrival.

Conclusion and Recommendation:

The present study investigates a relationship of the impact of terrorism on tourism by using time series data for a long period. It is undeniable that impact of terrorism on tourism industry is detrimental, but its capacity to bounce back and rejuvenate is immense. Despite impacted by all the negativities of terrorism activities India has vast potential to overcome this, and Developed gradually which is very much evident from our research. There is a direct correlation between terrorist attacks and the number of tourist arrivals to a particular nation and destination. One thing that has also been found that impact of terrorism on growth of economy is negative, but not has that much impact as war or other internal conflict on the destination and the economy of the nation. The nature and political and ideological objective of national and international tourism is quite different. The national or home grown terrorism confined only to a particular region and territory and have regional political objectives which is isolated from one another is most of the cases. On the contrary, Global terrorism has very different focus like religion, social economic organization in the nation. However, both kinds of terrorism manifest them in ugly form and imbibe fear fact, in the citizen's state of mind.

This study has limitations also, as the extent to which nature of terrorism has evolved which is extremely difficult to detect with data. We may not rely on past and historical evidence with much confidence as a guide of the impact of terrorism in future. At the same time interpreting the result, finding might not be generalized for the general population and destinations.

References

S.F. Sönmez, Y. Apostolopoulos, P. Tarlow Tourism in crisis: Managing the effects of terrorism Journal of Travel Research, 38 (1) (1999), pp. 13-18.

S.E. Atkinson, T. Sandler, J. Tschirhart Terrorism in a bargaining framework, Journal of Law and Economics, 30 (1) (1987), pp. 1-21.

H. Aziz Understanding attacks on tourists in Egypt, Tourism Management, 16 (2) (1995), pp. 91-95.

N. Chomsky, USA leading terrorist state, Monthly Review, 53 (2001), pp. 10-19.

H.H.A. Cooper, Terrorism: The problem of definition revisited, American Behavioral Scientist, 44 (2001), pp. 881-893.

B.M. Jenkins, Terrorism and beyond: A 21st century perspective, Studies in Conflict and Terrorism, 24 (2001), pp. 321-327

O. Lizardo, A.J. Bergesen, Types of terrorism by world-system location, Humboldt Journal of Social Relations, 27 (2003), pp. 162-192

G.E. Schweitzer, A faceless enemy: The origins of modern terrorism, Perseus, New York (2002)

C.L. Ruby, The definition of terrorism, Analyses of Social Issues and Public Policy, 2 (1) (2002), pp. 9-14

W. Enders, T. Sandler, Patterns of transnational terrorism, 1970-1999: Alternative time-series estimates, International Studies Quarterly, 46 (2002), pp. 145-165

L.K. Richter, W.L. Waugh, Tourism politics and political science: A case of not so benign neglect, Annals of Tourism Research, 10 (3) (1986), pp. 313-315

S.F. Sönmez, Y. Apostolopoulos, P. Tarlow, Tourism in crisis: Managing the effects of terrorism, Journal of Travel Research, 38 (1) (1999), pp. 13-18

S. Sönmez, A.R. Graefe, Influence on terrorism risk on foreign tourism decisions, Annals of Tourism Research, 25 (1998), pp. 112-144

S. Sönmez, A.R. Graefe, Determining future travel behavior from past travel experience and perceptions of risk and safety Journal of Travel Research, 37 (1998), pp. 171-177

W. Enders, T. Sandler, Causality between transnational terrorism and tourism: The case of Spain, Terrorism, 14 (1991), pp. 49-58

W. Enders, T. Sandler, G.F. Parise, An econometric analysis of the impact of terrorism on tourism, Kyklos, 45 (4) (1992), pp. 531-554

Y. Mansfeld Wars, tourism and the 'Middle East' factor, A Pizam, Y. Mansfeld (Eds.), Tourism, crime and international security Issues, Wiley, New York (1996), pp. 265-278

K. Drakos, A.M. Kutan, Regional effects of terrorism on tourism: Evidence from three Mediterranean Countries, Journal of Conflict Resolution, 47 (5) (2003), pp. 621-641

W.K. Viscusi, R.J. Zeckhauser, Sacrificing civil liberties to reduce terrorism risks, Journal of Risk and Uncertainty, 26 (2-3) (2003), pp. 99-120

C.R. Sunstein, Terrorism and probability neglect, Journal of Risk and Uncertainty, 26 (2-3) (2003), pp. 121-136

Aly, H. Y., & Strazicich, M. C. (2000). Terrorism and tourism: Is the impact permanent or transitory? Time series evidence from Egypt and Israel, Working paper 2010, Ohio State University, Columbus, OH: Department of Economics. Available at: ?http://www.bus.ucf.edu/wp/content/archives/2010_a.pdf? (24 July 2006).

P.K. Narayan, Did Rabuka's military coups have a permanent effect or A transitory effect on tourist expenditure in Fiji: Evidence from Vogelsang's structural break test, Tourism Management., 26 (2005), pp. 509-515

A. Pizam, A. Fleischer,Severity vs. frequency of acts of terrorism: Which has a larger impact on tourism demand? Journal of Travel Research, 40 (3) (2002), pp. 337-339

E. Yechiam, G. Barron, I. Erev,The role of personal experience in contributing to different patterns of response to rare terrorist attacks, Journal of Conflict Resolution, 49 (3) (2005), pp. 430-439

World Travel & Tourism Council "Economic Impact of Travel & Tourism 2013 Annual Update: Summary"

World Travel & Tourism Council "Benchmarking Travel & Tourism in India" How does Travel & Tourism compare to other sectors? Summary of Findings, November 2013

World Travel & Tourism Council "Travel& Tourism, Economic Impact" 2013, India

BLENDING YIELD WITH TECHNOLOGY: A STUDY OF LOW-COST CARRIERS IN REFERENCE TO SCENARIO OF INDIAN AVIATION INDUSTRY

Nurmahmud Ali

Assistant Professor, School of Hotel Management and Tourism Lovely Professional University Phagwara, Punjab, Pin - 144401

Contactnur23@lpu.co.in,.

Sidharth Srivastava

Assistant Professor, School of Hotel Management and Tourism Lovely Professional University Phagwara, Punjab, Pin - 144401.

sidharthsrivastava2011@yahoo.in

Abstract: India's aviation sector has become the fastest-growing in Asia in terms of flight operations and the rise in domestic airlines. This huge rise is mainly due to increasing low-cost flights that have been attracting substantial number of new customers. The 'low cost carriers' is not a new concept in abroad and has shown phenomenal growth across the globe and has exemplified the use of technology in managing yield. In India and China alone, demand for low-cost travel has skyrocketed, with domestic flight operations in this segment showing a remarkable jump of 466% and 254%, respectively according to the OAG report. The main question at this point that is raised is whether these low cost carriers (LCC's) are working on strong economic principles and business models to make them sustainable in long run too. The objective of this paper is to review the strategies of low cost carriers and their impact on Civil Aviation Industry in India. The paper will try to present the strategies adopted by low cost carriers to maximize revenue with the use of technology. The impacts made by LCC's on fares, costs and profitability will also be examined the low cost strategy when is exposed to the passengers, it results in growing passenger numbers and further the revenue for both airlines and airports. Airlines at the same time wants to grab a decent pie from the transportation sector and further employ Cost Leadership, lower their operating cost structures, employ advertising and branding to further increase their market share. These strategies results in competition among the airlines. These strategies and their impacts will provide an insight of the key variables for assessing the competition among the airlines.

Keywords: Low Cost Strategy, Low Cost Carriers (LCC's), Technology, Competence, Civil Aviation.

Introduction

The early travel started with the basic needs of the human being, which was to survive the harsh weather, protection from wild beasts and forage food, it continued with crossing of oceans for which they built ships, which was evolved further with the invention of engines and railways mark an important point in the transport history. Then the dreams to fly became a reality. Further, to save time and for a hassle free journey aircraft were invented. This industry has redefined comfort, safety, security and aversion of hassle. It is now the easiest travel experience where one can cover long journeys within few hours from one destination to another. So this industry is the new passion for the people to travel, according to their needs and their choice and satisfy them in exchange of money. Before 1953, all the airlines in India were private ones. In 1953, the government of India under the Air Corporations Act, nationalized and merged the eight private airlines that existed then and created two state-run airlines out of them. In 1991, the Indian economy began to liberalize. It became more open and market-oriented, and the process of deeper integration with the world economy had begun. These reforms were extended to the civil aviation sector in 1994 when the Air

Corporations Act of 1953 was repealed. This enabled the entry of private carriers who could now offer scheduled services (Natrajan 1991).

Flying has become more affordable in India, where the number of people traveling by air in a day is nearly equal to the number of people traveling by train on a day. India recorded a 25% growth in air passenger traffic in last year alone. There are six to seven million air passengers in the country, and industry watchers say their numbers could easily rise nearly tenfold in five years. This has meant a revival in the entire tourism and aviation industries, with increasing job opportunities for trained flying professionals not only with domestic airlines, but also international ones.

A Brief introduction about the Low cost carriers:

A low cost airline or carrier is one that offers air travel at normally very low rates by cutting down on expensive customary in-flight passenger services. This low cost airline is also known as no-frills air-lines.

Civil Aviation sector is a key contributor to the nation's economy and provide a platform for India to compete effectively in the global economy depending critically on air transport. During last decade, Aviation sector witnessed unparalleled growth, domestic air traffic has tripled and international traffic doubled. National Aviation Company of India (NACIL), which runs flag carrier Air India (AI), has gone back to the drawing board to study new domestic routes and to introduce low cost arm Air India Express in phases. The first phase of low cost expansion is estimated to cash in on the boom of low cost travel in India and the airline might deploy more capacity in North region.

The Indian Aviation market is growing exponentially and each operator can grab a decent pie from it. Private carriers such as Jet Airways and Kingfisher Airlines already have low cost service, thereby propelling existing competition among discount airlines like Delhi-based low fare carriers Spice Jet and Indigo. LCC's have a smaller fleet as compared to full service carriers; these numbers signify the growth in the low cost space.

With the advent of technology and with increase in number of domestic travelers the purpose of enhancing the travel promotional programs has increased over the period of time. Which have directly created an impact on the yield of the company as well. Due to the symbiotic relationship between the technology and growth in standard of living of people we have witnessed a boom in the low cost airlines. To save time people are selecting faster routes, thus the demand for cheap domestic airlines has increased. As per the reports of DGCA Indigo airlines hold the maximum market share of 29.5%1.

Some airlines resort to very innovative practices. While many airlines these days are working with aircraft manufacturers, AirAsia for example goes a step further, working with airports to develop specially designed low cost terminals that require far less maintenance and overhead. The lower maintenance cost for the airport is passed on to the airline, and in turn to the customer. With increase in the service technology the customers are also benefited and thus, provides an additional edge in the to the schematic yield management for the LCC.

All financial instruments compete with each other in the market place. Yield is one part of the total return of holding a security. A higher yield allows the owner to recoup his investment sooner, and so lessens risk. But on the other hand, a high yield may have resulted from a falling market value for the security as a result of higher risk.

Yield levels vary mainly with expectations of inflation. Fears of high inflation in the future mean that investors ask for high yield (a low price v/s the coupon) today. Yield management is a variable pricing strategy, based on understanding, anticipating and influencing consumer behavior in order to maximize revenue or profits from a fixed, perishable resource. The maturity of the instrument is one of the elements that determine risk. The relationship between yields and the maturity of instruments of similar credit worthiness is described by the yield curve. Long dated instruments typically have a higher yield than short dated instruments.

The yield of a debt instrument is generally linked to the credit worthiness and default probability of the issuer. The more the default risk, the higher the yield would be in most of the cases since issuers need to offer investors some compensation for the risk.

Over 600 million people fly each year, not to mention the millions bags which go along with them. The number of passengers in the Domestic sector alone has increased from334.06 Lakhs in 2010 to 396.31 Lakhs in 2011. Air travel is an essential part of our daily lives. Apart from growth in the number of passengers, air freight too showed a growth of 6.9% over the previous year and is predicted to increase by 7.5% by the year 2015.

The Aviation industry is therefore, no longer considered a safe, non-political global transportation system moving goods and people safely from one place to another, but rather a potential liability that exposes all nations to the threat of a terrorist attack. The high concentration of people on large airliners, the potential high death rate with each single attack on an aircraft, and the ability to use a hijacked airplane as a lethal weapon does provide an alluring target for terrorism. Apart from the threat of terrorism attacks, the other issues faced by Indian airports are criminal activities such as the trafficking of drugs and contraband.

According to the study carried out by aviation consultancy firm CAPA and prominent aviation IT solution provider SITA, facilities like provision of wi-fi on-board planes, greater usage of mobile technology, self-check in kiosks and biometrics and e-passports for border protection should be introduced in newly-modernised airports in India.

Yield management involves strategic control of inventory to sell it to the right customer at the right time for the right price. This process can result in price discrimination, where a firm charges customers consuming otherwise identical goods or services a different price for doing so.

Origin of low cost carriers:

The concept originally incepted in the US in early 1990s.

Business Model of Low Cost Carriers:

- A single Passenger class.

- A single type of airplane reducing training and service cost.
- No frills such as free food/drinks, lounges etc.
- Emphasis on direct sale of ticket through Internet avoiding fee and commission paid to travel agents.
- Employees working in multiple roles.
- Unbundling of ancillary charges to make the Headline fare lower.

SWOT analysis of the Low cost carriers:

In formulating a marketing strategy and action plan it is important to identify the different prospects in relation to the current status and factors that could influence the future of Low cost carriers. The following SWOT analysis will helps to formulate the strategies and actions required for the better procurement of LCC.

Strengths:

- It makes travel the easiest.
- It is not too expensive and it uses the latest greatest technology.
- It is a heavily governed industry.
- There are more of advantages like comfortable, suit to meet your needs, excellent connectivity.
- Generating big and vast the scope of jobs

Weaknesses:

- It utilizes a lot of resources to do its thing. Fuel, rubber, metals, etc.
- It is getting too expensive for many airlines to afford newer aircraft and do maintenance on them.
- Contribution in air pollution.
- Increase in air traffic.

Opportunities:

- Opportunity to develop huge potential market.
- Opportunity to grow under penetrated market.
- Opportunity to develop untapped air cargo market.
- Opportunity to support consumer and tourist demand for local foods.

Threats:

- Infrastructure constraints
- Shortage of airport facilities
- Parking bays
- Air traffic control facilities
- Takeoff and landing slots.

Low cost carriers have reshaped the competitive environment within liberalised markets and have made significant impacts in the world's domestic passenger markets, which had previous ly been largely controlled by full service network carriers. In Europe, 14% of available seat miles are now provided by low cost airlines, with the two largest players easy Jet and Ryanair accounting for nearly 9%. These carriers have pursued simplicity, efficiency, productivity and high utilization of assets to offer low fares. (O'Connell and William). During the late 1990s andearly 2000s, Ryanair achieved a compound annual traffic growth rate of 30.5%. The company has set itself the target of becoming the largest airline in Europe with over 40 million passengers a year (Ryanair, 2002).

By the end of 2002, low cost carriers accounted for one-third of the total intra-European market involving the UK and Ireland. Between Ireland and the UK, low cost carriers accounted for 47.2% of the traffic (Aviation Strategy, 2003b).

Although low cost airlines are relatively new to Asia, they have already developed very strong low fare brands through strong advertising and clever use of the media. The wide perception of people in Malaysia, when acknowledging Air Asia, is that it represents low fares (O'Connell and William). Gilbert et al. (2001) argue that branding is becoming increasingly important as a means of product and service differentiation, and that the low cost airlines are building brand recognition to compete in such a competitive environment. Air Asia currently has a 30% share of the domestic Malaysian market. Since the airline's inception in December 2001, the market has grown from 9 million passengers annually to 13 million. Bankers are valuing the carrier between $750 million and$1.2 billion (Ionides, 2004).

Air transport market was fully liberalized on 1st April 1997, when the restrictions on the right to engage in cabotage were finally lifted (Szymajda, 2002).

Differences in the functioning of low-cost carriers and traditional airlines

	Low-cost carriers	Traditional airlines	Advantage of low-cost carriers
The use of the fleet	Short stops at the airport (approx 25 min)	Prolonged stops at airports because of the use of main, more congested airports (about 45 min)	Increased use of the fleet, reduced demurrage charges
Additional services	"no free goodies", "no frills", additional charges for catering, extra baggage, etc.	"Entertainment programs", quick checkin, paper tickets, business class, catering	Lower ancillary costs, low complexity of services, additional revenue
Airports	Secondary and regional airports	Main, international airports	Lower landing and airport fees
Fleet	Standardized fleet (only one type of aircraft), higher density seating (eg, Boeing 737-300: 148)	Different types of aircraft, lower density seating (Boeing 737-300: 128)	Lower maintenance costs, spare parts and training, easier exchange of the onboard crew, increasing the use of the capacity of the aircraft
Ticket sales	Direct sales channels, sales through agencies and travel agents only if the costs are minimal	The majority of tickets sold through agencies and travel agencies, and by the airlines themselves	Lower distribution costs, less complexity (no classes)
Connections network	Direct connections, nonstop, short routes	Long destinations and short indirect routes	Reduced complexity of networks, greater use of the fleet and the ability of carriers
Personnel	A large variation in salary (up to 26%), better use of airline capacity	High base salary (variation up to 11%), strong workers unions	Lower fixed costs of employing staff

Source: Skeels, 2004

Conclusion:

Price has always been a key competitive factor in Indian market. That has resulted in the success of LCC in Indian market. Low cost carriers focus on their competitive marketing and brand positioning, multi-channel strategies. Maintaining low air fares, in the extreme fuel challenging atmosphere has been a critical area for LCCs, yet they have shown remarkable improvisations and the outcomes have been productive. Next leap that these Indian LCC players are taking is the presence of these in the international market. Spice and Indigo have already started their international operations. This has given much broader reach for these players in their nascent stage. Cost in LCCs is incurred in form of aircraft fuel, labour, landing charges, en- route navigation, ground handling, financial expenses including depreciation.

For a market like India the biggest challenge lies ahead in form of retention of the existing offered prices, the initial competition of lowering the prices of air tickets is very much present with the players marginally beating their market rivals in terms of the ticket fares. The market may present a promising platform for these low cost carriers, but it should not be forgotten that the earlier discussed factors in the paper may be so crucial that ignorance of them may result in an inevitable fall as a major airlines like kingfisher had to suffer. Fixed Capacity, Ability to Segment Markets, Perishable Inventory, Fluctuating Demand, Low Marginal Sales Costs and High Capacity Change Costs are some of the appropriate situations for effective yield management application. These debacles stress on the need of continuous research and observance of trend in the aviation sector, the influencing policies, ageing fleet, customer preferences, global fuel prices, and so on.

References

Aviation Strategy, 2003 a. Asia's emerging low cost carriers, Aviation Strategy, May, 2-5.

Gilbert, D., Child, D., Bennett, M., 2001. A qualitative study of the current practices of 'no-frills' airlines operating in the UK. Journal of Vacation Marketing 7, 302-315

Gour C. Saha, Theingi, (2009) "Service quality, satisfaction, and behavioural intentions: A study of low-cost airline carriers in Thailand", Managing Service Quality, Vol. 19 Iss: 3, pp.350 - 372

Lonides, N., 2004. Man of the Moment, Airline Business, April, 27-29.

Natarajan R. N., Sridevi, V. (1991), Airlines in India - a strategic analysis

O'Connell, J.F., William, G. 2005 Passengers' perceptions of low cost airlines andfull service carriers: A case study involving Ryanair, Aer Lingus, Air Asia and Malaysia Airlines. Journal of Air Transport Management 11 (2005) 259-272

Ryanair, 2002. Annual Report and Financial Statement. Ryanair, Dublin.

Randall Whyte, Bruce Prideaux, Hana Sakata, (2012) "The Evolution of Virgin Australia from a Low-Cost Carrier to a Full-Service Airline - Implications for the Tourism Industry", Vol : 8,

Szymajda I. (2002), Konkurencja w transporcie lotniczym, prawo europejskie i problem dostosowania prawa polskiego, Liber, Warszawa.

Skeels J. (2009), Airport Operations Today - Clearing Confusions. The Low Fares Carrier Perspective, lecture presented at the: Airport Operation Conference, Brussels 27.10.2004, www.elfaa.com, as on 09/01/2009.

RURAL TOURISM; KUCHIPUDI DANCE - A CULTURAL HERITAGE

P. Siva Sankara Reddy

Principal, GVRS Govt Degree College, Dhone, Kurnool

P. Aparna

Associate Professor (English), GNITS, Hyderabad

Abstract: The objective of Rural Tourism is to showcase rural life, art, culture and heritage at rural stations and in villages, which have core competence in art and craft, handlooms and textiles as also an asset base in the natural environment. The development of a strong platform around the concept of rural tourism is useful for a country like India where 74% of the population resides in seven million villages. The potential of Rural Tourism has been harnessed as a strategy for rural development. Besides, increasing level of awareness, growing interest in heritage and culture and environmental consciousness is enabled by rural tourism. The X Five year Plan has identified tourism as one of the major sources of generating sustainable livelihoods and employment in India. Rural India has a rich tradition of art, craft and culture. Rural Tourism is therefore, seen as a major avenue for this endeavour and the Government of India has given a priority to tourism in the plan as it has great potential, particularly in rural areas, to create jobs and to ensure 'sustainable livelihood.' The Ministry of Tourism, Government of India has launched the Scheme for Rural Tourism in this X Five year Plan period in order to promote village tourism as primary tourism product to spread tourism and its socio- economic benefits in various geo graphical regions all over India. Under this Scheme, substantial funds also have been given to State Governments. The Rural Tourism project has also been taken up with United Nations Development Programme (UNDP) support under the Tourism Ministry's Endogenous Tourism Project with the local involvement of grass-root workers and village Panchayats. So far, 158 rural tourism sites in 28 States/Union territories have been sanctioned by the Ministry of Tourism including 36 rural sites where UNDP has supported for carry building. The scheme identified key villages with core competency in heritage, culture, handlooms and handicrafts, aiming to build unique experiences with infrastructure components of Rs.50lakh per village. The more significant aspect was the community participation, component of additional Rs.20lakh in each village to enhance the host community's tourism awareness, art, and skill development, training in visitor handling and gender sensitization. The projects are being implemented through local Non-Governmental Organizations (NGO) whose role is critical and significant. The implementation of this scheme has provided an opportunity to position the Indian rural tourism project as a unique tourism visitor experience in a low-impact setting. The primary target has been the low volume but high yielding visitor community experience.

Kuchipudi Dance -A Cultural heritage

Dance has been, from Ancient times the most effective form of expression of the joy of life. In India, the art had developed and acquired a refined technique as early as 500 B.C. The earliest treatise in this art is Nritya Sastra of Bharata a comprehensive codification of the general principles and technique as practiced all over India. In the course of time the art has developed into various forms and Kuchipudi is one of its forms. Andhra Pradesh has a glorious cultural heritage of performing arts. Kuchipudi dance takes its name from a village of the same name in Krishna district. It originally belongs to the Natyamela tradition and was practiced by the Brahmin Bhagavathas of Kuchipudi agraharam. They made this village their abode during 17th century. Siddhendra Yogi is the founder who trained the Brahmins of Kuchipudi in that medium. The performance usually begins with some stage rites, after which each of the character comes on to the stage and introduces him/herself with a daru (a small composition of both song and dance) to introduce the identity, set the mood, of the character in the drama. The drama then begins. The dance is accompanied by song which is typically Carnatic music. The singer is accompanied by mridangam (a classical South Indian percussion instrument), violin, flute and the tambura .The movements in Kuchipudi are quicksilver and scintillating, rounded and fleet-footed. Performed to classical Carnatic music, it shares many common elements with Bharatanatyam. In its solo exposition Kuchipudi numbers include 'jatiswaram' and 'tillana' whereas in nritya it has several lyrical compositions reflecting the desire of a devotee to merge with God - symbolically the union of the soul with the super soul. Beyond the stylistic differences of Kuchipudi and Bharatanatyam steps, there are certain types of dances that are unique to Kuchipudi. Specifically there is the Tarangam of Kuchipudi which is unique in that the dancer must dance upon a brass plate, placing the feet upon the raised edges. The dancer moves the plate with much balance as the individual is traditionally dancing on the plate with two diyas (small oil-burning candles) in his or her hands while balancing a "kundi" (small vessel) containing water on their head. At the end of the dance, typically, the dancer extinguishes the candles and washes his or her hands with the water from the vessel. There are also subtle differences in the costumes of both types of dances. Generally, Bharatanatyam dresses have three fans of differing heights that form the illusion of the spreading pleats of a sari. However, in Kuchipudi there is typically only one fan which tends to be longer than the longest.

A number of scholars who worked on the subject have not questioned the historicity of Siddhendra Yogi and accepted the tradition of Kuchipudi Bhagavathas and made through discussions on the period and likewise aspects of Siddhendra Yogi. Various scholars tried to fix his period in between 11th and 18th century. Machupalli Kafiyat states that kuchipudi Bhagvathas were honoured by Veera Narasimha Raya of Vijayanagara dynasty who ruled from 1502-1509. It is evident from this source that he belongs not later to that period. Ponanki Srirama Apparao opined that there is no reference about Kuchipudi Bhagvathas in Panditharadhya charithra and Basavapuranam of Palkuriki somnatha in the context of the reference to dance and dancers. As such they opined that the Kuchipudi Bhagvathas did not exist by then. In their opinion Siddhendhra Yogi lived after that period i.e.14th-15thcenturies. Not only Palkuriki Somnatha, Vinukonda Vallabhacharya while describing the dances and dancers no way referred to any Bhagvathas from Kuchipudi. By this also it can be derived that Kuchipudi Brahmanas did not take the dance as their profession by that period. Since Machala Devi that was described in Kridabhiramam is identified with her name sake referred to in the inscription dated 1437 A.D, it can be stated that until the second half of the 15th century the Kuchipudi Bhagvathas and their dance guru Siddhendra Yogi were not known. In the absence of any evidence of their existence prior to that period, scholars like Sistla Ramakrishna Sastry fixed a tentative 1450A.D.as the date of Siddhendra Yogi. Another scholar Vissa Appa Rao0 is of the opinion that the Kuchipudi Bhagvathas were there even during the Kakatiya Period. They are stated to have toured the village after the village by singing and dancing 'Satavidha Sivaleelas'. It is during the 17th century Siddhendra Yogi the disciple of Narayana Tirtha prepared Bhamakalpa, the story of Parijatapaharanam as a beautiful dance drama and made it to the Kuchipudi Bhagavatas. He also felt that Siddhenda Yogi received Kuchipudi as an agrahara from Abul Hasan Tanisha the sultan of Golkonda who ruled from 1672-1685A.D, through a copper plate record and gave it to the Bhagvathas of Kuchipudi, if this opinion of Vissa Appa Rao regarding the receipt of copper plate grant by Siddhendra Yogi from Tanisha of Golconda is correct, it is to be accepted without doubt that Siddhendra Yogi belonged 17th century. But no copper plate grant as such has come to the light of the day, and the grant of Kuchipudi as an agrahara is not confirmed in any of the evidence except in tradition. Since the existence of the Kuchipudi Bhagavatas during the period of Vira Narasimha, the brother of Krishnaraya of Vijayanagara is well evident by the Machupalli Kaifiyat, it is to be accepted that Siddhendra Yogi must belonged to 15th century.

Normally it is believed that the village Kuchipudi associated with Siddhendra Yogi and Bhamakalapa is no other than Kuchipudi in the Diviseema. But there are no evidences to accept it as a fact. We cannot say with certainty the antiquity of that village in Diviseema. A document of A.D. 1763 which mentions about the Dharmasasana or an agreement of fifteen Mahajana families is the only recorded evidence to that Kuchipudi. In that there is no reference about Siddhendra Yogi and Bhagavatas. Machupalli Kaifiyat states the location of Kuchipudi is one among the twelve samithis in the Kondavitiseema (dachina dhanambu vantidi Kuchipudi). Similarly a number of villages by name Kuchipudi are found in different areas. Near Repalle on the banks of Krishna, in the Podili division of Nellore District, near Kodada in the Nalgonda district, there are villages by name Kuchipudi. Out of all these only the Kuchipudi near Tenali had antiquity as noticed in the Kaifiyats. By this it can be understood that Bhagavatas originally had their base in the Palnadu area and in course of time gradually settled in the Krishna bank, and from 15th century it is from the period of Siddhendra Yogi became popular for their performance of 'Bhamakalapamu. With rich historical heritage, Kuchipudi village has high potential to grow as one of the Tourism destinations in the state of Andhra Pradesh.

Promotion of Kuchipudi through Rural Tourism

Among the six rural tourism sites identified in Andhra Pradesh by the Ministry of Tourism, Government of India, Kuchipudi village is well known for the dance form and is earmarked as one of the potential Tourist destinations. The proposed Kuchipudi village showcases the rich cultural diversity of Andhra Pradesh including its rural traditions besides a Museum and Library showcasing their Techniques, Costumes, apart from artist town ship, indoor/outdoor auditorium for stage performances, and dramas by the artists. The Ministry of Tourism, Government of India provides Rs.20 Lakhs for software programme i.e., sensitizing the local community for Rural Tourism awareness in Kuchipudi and the Government of Andhra Pradesh contributes Rs.50 Lakhs for hardware programme i.e., providing rural infrastructure like Tourist amenities, Natyasala-cum-interpretation centre and artist village. Government acts as facilitator and promoter and the driving force is the community through NGO to enable the development of infrastructure and tourism awareness campaign. It provides income generation and employment to the locals and at the same time preserving the art form.

Focal point - artists

The rural tourism programme aims to revive and sustain the dance form. As part of the Rural Tourism scheme, different workshops, seminars will be conducted to provide value addition to existing artist's skills. This has helped in exposing the dance form and overall revival of the rich heritage of the village. As part of Guru-shisya parampara programme, one of the ancient traditional schools of learning, wherein the pupils come and stay with the teacher to learn the education, the learner who is interested to know and to update the knowledge can also stay and learn the dance kills from the master and it provides opportunities to the artists in the country as well as in foreign countries enhancing the economic prosperity to the artists.

Creation of tourism infrastructure

The creation of common facilities has been given importance in the rural tourism scheme as it provides the local people a quality life and also helps in providing the satisfaction to the tourists. Creation of facilities like, Rest houses, drinking water, restaurant and improvement of pathways, refurbishing of monuments and landscaping will give facelift to the villages. With creation of common facilities, the environment in the rural tourism sites has become clean and beautiful. The development and improvement of infrastructure has benefited the village communities in projecting a good image of the rural areas and also enhancing the chances of providing the good infrastructure support to the tourists. Tourism is leading to assets creation and public amenities in rural villages and thereby benefiting the local residents.

Art museum serves to showcase the traditional materials created especially for the tourism development. Many of the treasures used by the people have been lost over the period of time and there manning could be seen in these museums .The Art museum serve the purpose of displaying the rare art, craft and artifacts of the region. The visitors obtain a wealth of information about the dance form thereby enriching their knowledge about the site. The idea of establishing the Natyasala cum interpretation centre is to showcase to the tourists, the history of dance form, Dresses and costumes etc.

Enhancing local community awareness

Systematic tourism development in rural sites through public participation has contributed towards the socio-economic development of the areas. Tourism has ensured that heritage, history and culture, both tangible and intangible is conserved in its right context and at the same time generates livelihood opportunities for the villagers. To achieve this output, creation of awareness about the importance of rural tourism among local community has been one of the most important tasks carried out in the villages. Villagers migrate to towns and cities looking for opportunities leaving behind traditions and cultures which are subsequently lost, while the younger generation loses pride in its culture and adopts urban ways of the cities. To address these issues, awareness was created among the younger generation, so that they start afresh on the work of their forefathers and infuse it with new designs and ideas. Alternative employment avenues as guides and cooks in the tourism sites have been adopted by the youth as alternative livelihood opportunities while continuing to practice their inherited Art.

Employment generation and income generation

Rural tourism sites create awareness about what the rural areas have to offer. Tourism supports direct or indirect employment opportunities in rural areas without adversely affecting agricultural workforce. Overall, its contribution to rural economy is considered to be substantial. It has helped in reducing the migration by providing employment opportunities in the villages by restructuring rural entrepreneurial system. It has been observed that rural tourism has become a source of income for rural communities. As we know that majority of activities in the rural tourism do not require advanced training; local residents with minimum training on skill development are capable of providing services like food serving etc. Since tourism is accepted as a legitimate form of economic development, it is serving as a vehicle for other types of business development opportunities for local communities. The overall goal of the rural tourism is to create a community managed rural tourism model by strengthening sustainable livelihoods of the local communities for the preservation and development of local heritage of the village. Due to the government initiative to promote rural tourism, a number of avenues for the employment of local population have opened up.

- o The employment of local youths as tour guides has given gainful employment to a large Number of unemployed in the village. The concept of home stays has potential of enhancing the income of the host population.
- o A large number of tea stalls, small restaurants, pan shops etc have started functioning due to the increase in flow of tourists, which has again enhanced the income of the local people.
- o As local resources (labour and material) have been used to construct the hardware structure under the rural tourism sites, a number of local people have got employed. Not only this, many of them will be employed to maintain the facilities and utilities being created in the village like sweepers, receptionists, watchmen, cook, guides etc
- o The revival of Tourism products like folk arts by formation of activity groups has helped the local population. These folk arts provide link with the past and bring to life ancient tradition and culture. They have also helped in perpetuating legacy for the future. The support to rejuvenate the folk art has lead to the revival of the folk arts and also providing livelihoods to the art practitioners.

Conclusion

It is important to note that rural tourism has enhanced the local quality of life and also supported local culture in rural areas by encouraging restoration of historic sites. With rich historical heritage, Kuchipudi village has high potential to grow as one of the rural

Tourism destinations in the state of Andhra Pradesh. One of the preconditions of sustainable tourism development is the consideration of long-term interests of local residents. Rural tourism cannot succeed without the participation of rural society. Under the rural tourism scheme, the rural tourism had the multiplier effect on rural society. It has developed the rural economy by improving the rural income by providing employment for people in the village, and supporting small businesses such as restaurants and art shops .A less obvious impact, but important over the long-term is the change in attitude towards sustainable tourism and its delivery by a large number of stakeholders who participated in consultative meetings and training. The participants achieved a substantive shift in their attitudes to rural tourism. The aim of rural tourism is to increase the net benefits to rural communities from tourism, and increase their participation in managing the tourism product. If more tourism can be developed in rural areas, particularly in a way that involves huge local participation in decisions and enterprises, then poverty impacts are likely to be enhanced. In broader context, tourism has brought a range of other benefits to rural areas, such as infrastructural development and spin-off enterprise opportunities. The project focused on creating community institutions, not just supporting individual entrepreneurs. Community associations are seen as the guardians of culture, the developers of the tourism resource, and the agents for community benefit. This is more in line with a development approach in rural areas than a typical small business approach. The project has focused on institution building of local communities as much as developing entrepreneurship, and it is still very early to make judgment with regard to acquisition of skills. The quality of micro-enterprises inevitably varies across the artisans depending on their capacity, as does their potential to diversify service provision .One of the most common features of rural tourism, as offered to local communities as an incentive to consider starting a tourism business, is its ability to generate an alternative income stream. This income can come at times that supplements income during seasonal fluctuations but local communities are looking for alternative income that does not impact or interfere with their 'real' business.

The actual level of income is not as important as the fact that they have an alternative source of income. Factors affecting income were room capacity, visitor numbers and price. It has been reported that low revenues from rural tourism will result in low room numbers and so many rural tourism activities may have difficulty securing sufficient tourist numbers to be financially self-sufficient. The employment theme is extended to include specific opportunities for young people within rural communities in the hope that tourism may provide an incentive for them to remain. The rural tourism has promoted an exciting and growing industry suited to the energies and enthusiasm of young rural people. Career options are enhanced with the opportunities for training and direct involvement in running tourism business.

To conclude, rural tourism in Kuchipudi is not only the end, but the means to stimulate economic growth, to increase the viability of underdeveloped location, and to preserve the cultural and traditional dance art form. Rural tourism scheme has been a valuable vehicle to bring the ultimate rural stakeholders in touch with tourism sector to increase employment. In order to make the scheme more meaningful, it is very important that the sustenance issues be discussed with the artisans and local communities before the start of the project and also aggressive marketing of the destinations be taken up with the local and international Tour Operators.

Bibliography

Annual Report of Ministry of Tourism 2009-10, Ministry of Tourism, Govt. of India New Delhi 2010

Explore Rural India, Book Prepared by Ministry of Tourism, Government of India, and UNDP, New Delhi 2009

"Community Based Rural Tourism in Andhra Pradesh", Ministry of Tourism, Government of Andhra Pradesh, Hyderabad 2010

P. Siva Sankara Reddy Paper on "Rural Tourism and Handicrafts" in Yojana, June 2007 Vol. 51, PP 29-32.

Kaifiyat of Machupalli, L. R 56,pp. 65ff

Bharati, January, 1960.

Vinukonda Vallabhacharya, Kridhabhirama, p.90 S.I.I.,Vol,no.773

Bharati, January, 1960 Ibid.,

Kaifiyat of Machupalli, L. R 56,pp. 65ff

Rural Tourism Project, Kuchipudi

Report of National Productivity Council, New Delhi, on "Guru-Shisya parampara" Report of the Task Force on Handicrafts for the VIII Five Year Plan

P. Siva Sankara Reddy Paper on "Rural Tourism and Handicrafts" in Yojana, June 2007 Vol. 51, PP 29-32.

"Community Based Rural Tourism in Andhra Pradesh", Ministry of Tourism, Government of Andhra Pradesh, Hyderabad 2010.

Ashwini Kumar Singh, "Rural Tourism: Tool for Rural Employment", in Kurukshetra, Vol 55, No.8, June 2007, PP 7-13.

Mohinder Chand & Ravi Bhushan Kumar "Rural Tourism: A new approach to sustainability", in SAJOSPS, Jan-June 2005

Annual Report of Ministry of Tourism 2009-10, Ministry of Tourism, Govt. of India New Delhi 2010, Also Explore Rural India", Book Prepared by Ministry of Tourism, Government of India, and UNDP, New Delhi 2009

TRAINING NEEDS FOR THE HOSPITALITY INDUSTRY A STUDY OF HOTELS IN RAJASTHAN

Parul Mathur

Director, Pacific Institute of Hotel Management, Pacific University Udaipur & Ahmedabad ,mathur.parul@rdiffmail.com

Puja Mathur

Assistant Professor, Pacific Institute Of Management & Technology Pacific University Udaipur, puja11@rediffmail.com

Abstract: In this study the main focus is upon harnessing the extent of relationship between training and services in the hospitality industry. Training offers great scope in strengthening the services rendered by the hotels. In thus age of cut-throat competition, training helps the companies to derive competitive advantage as service separates a great hotel experience from an average one. A well trained, professional staff can make each guest's stay a pleasant experience and not only ensures the same guest's return but also brings many new customers owing to favourable word of mouth publicity. The study revealed that services provided by the hotels influenced by training and also the management of hotels is unaware of the importance of training and its impact on services.

Keywords: Training, hospitality, services, professional.

Introduction

Hospitality industry is a part of large enterprise known travel and tourism industry. In present scenario, tourism has become a panacea especially for the economic foundation of many countries.

Every country is trying to grab a bigger share of world tourism may it be a developing country like India, who is able to capture meager share of less than 1 percent or it may be USA or France who are getting a bigger share of world tourist arrivals and receipts. The hospitality industry, world wide, prides itself on its customer focus i.e. to create and satisfy customers by providing necessary or desired services to travelers.

Services and tourism go hand in hand. Services require skills and well trained staff .It is true that tourism is labour intensive industry, which provides employment to skilled, semi-skilled and unskilled workers directly and indirectly. But it is also true that the services required in the tourism and hotel industry are highly personalized and no amount of automation can substitute for personal service providers. This is because of the basic features of services, which are very different from those of manufactured products. Cooper et. al.(1993) identify three characteristics which separate tourism as a service from manufactured goods and present these dissections in what is called a "goods and services continuum". It is shown in figure-

Goods and services Continuum

Services	Product
Intangibility	More Tangible
Perish ability	Often Separable
Inseparability	Standardizable

Source: Cooper et.al. (1993, P.231)

The success of any industry depends to a great extent upon the quality of human resource and tourism is not an exception. Training is an activity for the development of human resource to cope up with the changing scenario of tourism and hospitality sector. It is a key to enhance capability and efficiency of employee to show good performance in the hospitality sector. Training involves skill development, communication and managerial qualities etc. Organizations also get benefit out of it as they derive competitive advantage. Tessin (1978) has discussed the benefits of training to employees and the benefits to the individual which in turn ultimately benefit the organization.

With regard to inadequate training, Mahesh (1998) has very well expressed that, in many countries, the growth of tourism, as an industry is severely limited by the lack of adequately trained personnel. Where the industry has developed in spite of these constraints, the quality of services provided to the visitors has frequently been the causality. Inordinate delays at airports, horrendous experiences in rail road transportation, unpleasant stay in hotels are commonly attributed to inadequate system and facilities when the central problem is actually lack of professionalism in the approach to human resource development.

Rajasthan

The state of Rajasthan was formed by the merger of 19 princely states and three chief ships into the Indian republic on 30th March 1949.Rajasthan, the abode of kings, has been the home of the Rajputs, a group of warrior's clans, who have controlled this part of India for 1000 years according to the code of chivalry and honor. In olden times, the rulers often commissioned their greatest architectural monument -forts, palaces, temples and Baories (wells) to ensure employment, food and water for the public. So rich is the history of the land that every roadside village has its own tales of sacrifice and valour.

Tourism in Rajasthan

Today, Rajasthan is attracting tourists from all nooks and corners of the world as well as from all parts of India. Some of the tourism products of Rajasthan have become internationally famous and popular among the tourists such as Palace on wheels, Heritage on wheels, Heritage hotels, Camel safaris, Pushkar fair, Desert festival, Palace Hotels and Wild life Sanctuaries/national parks. Recognizing the potential attractions that Rajasthan has to offer to domestic and foreign tourists, tourism was declared industry in Rajasthan in the year 1989.

Table 1: Share of Rajasthan from Foreign Tourist Arrivals in India

1.	2001	7757217	608283	8365500	5.19	-2.38	4.60
2.	2002	8300190	428437	8728627	6.99	-29.57	4.34

3.	2003	12545135	628560	13173695	51.14	46.71	50.92
4.	2004	16033896	971772	17005668	27.81	54.60	29.09
5.	2005	18787298	1131164	19918462	17.17	16.40	17.13
6.	2006	23483287	1220164	24703451	25.00	7.87	24.02
7.	2007	25920529	1401042	27321571	10.38	14.82	10.60
8.	2008	28358918	1477646	29836564	9.41	5.47	9.21
9.	2009	25558691	1073414	26632105	-9.87	-27.36	-10.74
10.	2010	25543877	1278523	26822400	-0.06	19.11	0.71
11.	2010	27137323	1351974	28489297	6.24	5.74	6.21
12.	2012	28611831	1451370	30063201	5.43	7.35	5.52

The world famous "golden triangle"comprising of Delhi-Agra-Jaipur has put Jaipur on the world tourism map.60 % of international tourists visiting India, come to these places. Annual rate of growth for domestic tourists has been 7 percent and for international tourists has been 5 percent. This increase in tourist arrivals has resulted in an increase in complexity of tourism. This has lead to an awakening need for a better education and training in the field of tourism.

Hotel Industry in Rajasthan

The hotel industry in India is the largest and rapidly growing industry in India. It has provided employment to approximately 8.5 percent of the total work force of India.

Rajasthan has all kind of hotels to accommodate all kind of guests. All the prominent hotel chains of India, like Taj Group of Hotels. Oberoi group of hotels, ITDC, RTDC, Bharat Hotels are running their hotels. Among the international hotel chains, Hyatt, Leela, Radison, Quality Inn are having their hotels in important tourist cities of Rajasthan. If we look from the Hotel and Restaurant Approval and Classification Committee point of view, all categories of hotels ranging from one star to five star deluxe are operating in Rajasthan. With regard to heritage hotels, need not to say that these hotels are strength of tourism in Rajasthan. Also, three-fourth heritage hotels of entire country are based in Rajasthan. Then individual hotels -approved and unapproved, registered and unregistered are in abundance to cater the needs of various kind of tourists.

The most unfortunate part of it is that no agency, government or non-government is having records about these hotels (Singh, 2002)

However, the hotel industry is confronted with considerable challenges imposed by the rapidly changing external environment. Thus in order to continue the higher growth rate,the industry requires highly trained professionals. As per Anastassova and Purcell (1995) its success depends "on the social and technical skills of its personnel, their ingenuity and hard work, their commitment and attitude".

Research Methodology

The research was conducted with the objective to find out the extent of relationship between training and the services rendered by the hotel.

In an exploratory research design, 49 hotels, including each category, approved by HRACC, ranging from five stars deluxe to one star and heritage hotels were included in the survey. The chain hotels and independent hotels have also been considered in the above survey. After pilot study, well structured questionnaire was administered on Human Resource heads to find out the training scenario being practiced in hotels in Rajasthan. Then, to find out service satisfaction among visitors, another questionnaire was framed and administered on visitors of these hotels. The researchers contacted 750 tourists. Finally 735 responses (15 from each hotel), are used for analysis. In this questionnaire, questions were asked about their satisfaction from 29 services, covering entire hotel operation, viz. front office, housekeeping, food and beverage, other services and about staff.

Tourist's opinions were received in form of Likert type 5 point rating scale. This was given numerical scores, ranging from 5 marks to the highest to one mark to the poorest. The service satisfaction score was calculated by adding scores of all service statements replied by the visitors. A median value of 85 was calculated and service sore was categorized in 'good' and 'poor' categories. A score equals to median or higher than median was considered 'good service' and score less than the median was considered as 'poor service'. To check the validity of above categorization, test of difference between means of the two groups were calculated with the help of SPSS. Further, to check the dependence of service satisfaction on training, chi-square test has been applied.

Results and Discussions

Categorization of Guest Services: Good or Poor

As discussed above, that to measure the service satisfaction among visitors an instrument was developed and the aggregate score of the instrument was calculated by numerical values to the responses. This score was divided into two categories to determine good or poor service on the basis of median score. But the researchers were afraid of validity of the categorization, as whether difference between good and poor categories exists? Thus a null hypothesis was framed to check the differences in means.

H01: The mean scores of service satisfaction of 'good' and 'poor' categories do not differ significantly.

To test the above hypothesis, test of difference between means was performed using SPSS.

The results are as under in table - 3

Null Hypothesis	T-value-	df	Significance	Acceptance Status
H01	-49.306	733	0	Rejected

The above table depicts, the significance value of the hypothesis (H 01) is .00.This means that the null hypothesis "The mean scores of service satisfaction of 'good' and 'poor' categories do not differ significantly" is rejected. Hence, the categorization of service satisfaction scores 'good' and 'poor' is valid.

Dependence of service satisfaction on training practices

The categorization done earlier was used to check the dependence of the service satisfaction score on training practices, practiced in hotels in Rajasthan. The response regarding training practices was collected through another questionnaire designed for HR heads in form of 'yes' and 'no' and were give numerical scoures of one and two. The visitor service satisfaction score categorized in 'good' and 'poor' categories and training responses in 'yes' and 'no' ,both were taken together to check the dependence. Hence, another hypothesis was framed-both were taken together to check the dependence. Hence, another hypothesis was framed.

H02: Service Satisfaction scores are independent to training practices in hotels.

To test this hypothesis, chi-square test was used and the results are summarized in the table -4

Null Hypothesis	Chi-value	Significance	Acceptance Status
H02	158.765	.00	Rejected

The table depicts that the null hypothesis (H02) has been rejected. This means, that the visitor service satisfaction and training of hotel employees are not independent and the training influences directly to the guest services.

Training Practices in Hotels:

As mentioned above, the response regarding training practices was collected through questionnaire separately designed for human resource heads. Out of the respondent hotels, who have given affirmative response have been further asked about training assessment needs and type of training given to the employees. As per the results received from human resource heads, none of the hotel determines training need assessment to organize training programs for their employees. Further, with regard to training practices, only 30.61 per cent hotels have organized training programs for their employees, in last two years. Then, two types of training is being extended to the hotel employees (i) On - the - Job training and (ii) Off - the - Job training. On - the - Job training refers to the training provided an the methods applied at the workplace of the employee. Off - the - Job training methods are used away from the work place of the employee. Training techniques represent the medium of imparting skills and knowledge to employees.

Table -2 : Methods and Techniques Used for Training in Hotels in Rajasthan

S.No.	Training Methods	Training Techniques	Response
1	On - the -Job Training	Orientation, Job instruction Apprentice and Job Rotation,	100 %

2	Off - the - Job Training	Role playing, Lecture, Film/ Audio Video, Seminar/Workshops And Simulation	38.77 %

The data reveal that all the hotels which are conducting training programs are practicing On - the - Job training method for providing training to their employees. This is because of Job Instruction technique which is practiced by all the hotels. Other training technique used by hotels are orientation. This technique is also known as 'induction program'. Then,hotels use apprentice and Job rotation techniques also to train their employees.

With regards to off - the - Job training method, only 38.77 % hotels are practicing it. This method is used by chain hotels only. All the hotels that are providing Off - the - Job to their employees are using lecture method. The human resource heads also revealed that, subject experts, and psychologists are invited to deliver lectures. In lecture technique use of OHPs and LCDs is quite common. Now and then, purposive films are also shown, the workshop and seminar are also organized to develop skills as well as attitude. The hotels do not use vestibule, role playing and simulation techniques for training their staff in Rajasthan. The human resource heads, who were not in favor of conducting training programs, opines that-

1. Training and development is an expensive investment in employees.
2. If staff is going to leave anyway, it does not make sense to invest in their training and development.
3. Why to give enhanced skills to staffs, as it will make more attractive to other employers and encourage them to leave.

Conclusion

As stated earlier, this research paper has two broad objectives. The major finding with regard to objective no 1, is that the management of hotels are unaware of the importance of training and its impact on services. This is the reason that very few hotels are conducting training programs that too, they are only chain hotels like Taj and Oberoi Groups. The independent hotels may be a five star hesitates in organizing training programs.

The major finding with regard to second objective may be summarized as the services are highly affected by training. Employees become efficient after undergoing training and the chances of delivering poor guest services, damage and accidents are minimized. This eventually helps the organization to grow. The research findings are in agreement with the general notion that the trained personnel perform better.

A humble suggestion may be submitted through the above findings that Hotel And Restaurant Approval and Classification Committee can include 'number/s of training programs conducted by the hotels in a year' in their star categorization award list.

References

Anastassova, L. and Purcell, K. (1995), Human Resource Mangement in the Bulgarian Hotel Industry: From Command to Empowerment? Internation journal of Hospitality Mangement, Vol.14 no.2.

Albrecht, Karl & Zemke, Ron (1985), Services America! Doing Business in the New Economy, Dow-Jones-Irvin, Homewood.

Mahesh V.S (1998) Effective Human Resource Management: key to Excellence in services Organizations, Vikalpa 13(4).

Baum Tom and Mahesh V.S, (1992) Developing a system for competitor Analysis: In Managing Projects in Hospitality Organizations, (ed. Richard Teare, debra Adams and Sally Messenger), Cassel, London.

Copper et al, (1993,p.231.) Goods and Services Continuum, in Baum Tom, Managing Human Resource In European Tourism & Hospitality Industry, Chapman Hall, London.

Singh, Dr. Ashok, Destination India: Why Education precedes Marketing, India Management, December 2002.

Aswathappa K.(2005) Human Resource and Personnel Management, Tata McGraw-Hill publishing Company, New Delhi (4th Edi)

Subba rao Sriniwas P. (2008), Issues and Constraints in Manpower supply In India Hospitality Industry, IIMA

FHRAI Hotel Guide-2008

Tourist Statistics, Department of Tourism, Government Of Rajasthan,Jaipur.

Tessin, M.J.,"Once again, Why Training?' Feb 1978, In Aswathappa K.(2005) Human Resource and Personnel Management, Tata McGraw-Hill Publishing Company, New Delhi (4th Edi).

www.emraldinsight.com

www.tourism.gov.in

FLOURISHES THE TOURISM SECTOR AND ITS TRENDS IN STATE OF QATAR

Parul Mathur

Director Pacific Institute of Hotel Management Pacific Academy of Higher Education & Research University Udaipur-Rajasthan (India)

Daleep Kumar

Research Scholar of Hotel & Tourism Management, Pacific Academy of Higher Education & Research University, Udaipur-Rajasthan (India)

Abstract: The main purpose of this study is to examine that, is the tourism sector really flourishes in state of Qatar? What are the trends in the sector of tourism of the State of Qatar? Also to find that, is the state government really energetic in development of sector of tourism. Is there any five years plan made by govt. to develop the tourism sector in peninsula? What are the achievements of the govt. through the five years plans? What are the component/tools of tourism in the state? What is the growth of components/tools in the state? What is the contribution from components in the sector of tourism? What is the scenario of Foreign Tourist Arrival (FTA) and Foreign Exchange Earning (FEE) & Expenditures for tourism in the country? What is the percentage of occupancy in hotels and growth of hotels and rooms in the country? Finally put overall focus on Q2 of 2012 and 2013.

Keywords: State of Qatar; Tourism; Flourishes; Hotels; Components; Occupancy; Revenue; FTA; FEE.

An overview: Qatar's tourism sector grew 13% in the first quarter of 2013 compared to 2012, fuelled by a hotel boom. The hospitality sector plays a crucial role in the growth of tourism and Qatar's hotel sector is growing at an incredible rate - 110 hotels were under construction last year, which when finished will offer 19,931 rooms to visitors.

Introduction:

As we all are aware that Gulf Region/Middle East is known due to its Oil and Gas industry which is on boom right now and this is the main sources of income and economy of those countries. But along with this industry various sectors and small scale industry also grow up and flourish like real estate/construction and trading, food & beverages, meat & poultry, tourism and food and accommodation establishment, luxuries malls, entertainment establishments, banking & money exchanges etc. It is also true that tourism hold the second position in Middle East after oil and gas and its going to become an industry in that region. The income from tourism is also calculated for the development of the countries.

Here in this study we are focusing on "The Peninsula, State of Qatar" which comes under Gulf Corporation Council (GCC) in the Middle East. With strong economy this country is in boom due to its oil and gas industry. People from various countries like USA, UK, Australia, New Zealand and many more are investing in this country. Due to movement of people for business, sports, education, luxuries trips the country is becoming attraction place which we called as tourism. Means the tourism sector is flourishing in the state of Qatar.

The visitors start to arrive here after fully independent in 1971 of the state for the main business oil and gas before the people travel here for the daily consumable things on the base of exchange business related to food and cloths/trading purpose from India with ships. The Indian Rupee was in the use for trading purpose in the past decades. But after 1971 the economy of country starts to rise due to its main export of oil and gas. But bit by bit another additional business starts to rise in the country. The one main sector tourism starts to flourish in the country in various foams. Means the visitor's starts visits in the peninsula with various purpose and tourism like business, sports, climate/sunny and hot weather, peaceful gulf, culture, tradition, attractive beaches, fishing, wildlife and its marine.

Mainly tourism rise in the state due to the business and sports purpose. The sport activities start in Qatar in 2006 due it 15th Asian games, which is officially known as XV Asiad. Asia's Olympic sporting that was held in Doha-Qatar December 1 to 15-2006. Doha (Qatar) was the first city in its region and only the second in West Asia. In 2006 the arrival of tourist was 946,000, and in the year 2007 the number of visitors increased and the figure reach at 9, 64,000 which, the best deal in the sector of tourism and learn a lot regarding tourism sector. After this the country start the development programme related to infrastructure in the country like New Airport, Metro Rail, Road, Flyover/bridge, Star Hotels, Port, Water ways, Telecommunications, Hospitals, Water & Electricity supply etc. Now the number of arrival were 25, 27,000 in the year 2011. There was 15312 total no. of beds till the year 2011. Last year, hotels in Qatar had a total capacity of 13,407 rooms.

"It is not only the number of rooms that is important, but also the quality, eco-sustainability and the diversity of choices across all grades and price levels," Al-Mohannadi said.

The state allocated some $17bn for tourism development through 2014 most of which is going towards hotels, exhibition space and infrastructure under the five year plans 2008.

Currently there are 121 hotels and hotel establishments under construction and register to supply 20955 new hotels rooms and units. The details given below as per QTA report;

Hotels-75 and 46 Hotels Apartments, which is total =121

Hotels Rooms-15713 and Hotel Apartments Room-5242, which is total =20955.

Qatar is expanding the level, diversity and quality of its tourism offerings. While progressing to ensure a successful World Cup in 2022, the UNWTO partnership shall further ensure that Qatar has a well-planned, quality and reliable tourism industry meeting the expectations of the international travel trade.

While the country tourism sector thrives, QTA's agreement with UNWTO seeks to align the travel boom with Qatar's 2030 Vision, ensuring that tourism is also sustainable. Latest update from the country is that in the tourism sector the Metro Rail project started with estimated value of 3bn USD and already open first face of New Doha International Airport (NDIA) with the capacity of 24 million passengers.

Review of literature

Waleed Hazbun (1997), examine that in the Arab world today, while Western tourists still come in search of the region's past, many governments are feverishly promoting tourism as a means to build their own economic futures. The argument posed by tourism boosters such as state elites, private entrepreneurs and international bankers is that the Arab world's warm climates, sunny beaches, vast deserts, historical monuments, and native hospitality are some of the most valuable resources of the region and they should be exploited for the means of generating new sources of wealth. This industry has been touted as a means to help their developing economies adjust to the ever more competitive pressures of the global marketplace.

Abdulla M. Alhemoud (2003), Tourism is an increasingly important area of services trade. Every foreign visitor who spends money at a tourist resort contributes to an improvement in the balance of payments of the country to which this resort/destination belongs. With the value of the oil industry fluctuating, and given the vast natural resources and beauty offered by the Gulf Co-operation Council (GCC) states including Bahrain, Kuwait, Oman, Qatar, Saudi Arabia and the UAE, tourism services may well become a key GCC export factor. Within a few years, the GCC countries developed tourism festivals, which received a warm welcome by nationals but had little exposure to Western visitors. However, the literature on marketing and image of tourism in this part of the world is still in an infant stage. This research study presents a tourism-marketing plan that could be used by the GCC tourism bureaus in dealing with potential foreign consumers. The research also presents a model of perceived service quality and applies it to the Kuwaiti and other GCC countries' hotels seeking to accommodate foreign tourists. Finally, the researcher offers some recommendations pertaining to the marketing mix of the GCC tourism industry aimed at attracting the maximum number of foreign visitors, particularly during the festivals.

Issa bin Mohamed al-Mohannadi (2013), (Qatar Tourism Authority chairman) said that "QTA has been hard at work creating an ambitious strategy to solidify Qatar's position as a leading tourist destination and enhancing the quality and standards of international tourism for the nation. However, we are conscious of the importance of environmental sustainability for tourism development and as the regulator of industry standards and codes, we are taking the lead in ensuring sustainable growth and development of Qatar's fast-growing tourism sector."

Taleb Rifai (2013), (UNWTO secretary-general) welcomed the agreement as "an important step forward in developing Qatar's tourism policies, legislative framework and institutional capacities". He pointed out that the agreement reflected the strategic priority afforded by the Qatar government to tourism as a driver of socio-economic development.

QTA's (2013), overall tourism development strategy is aimed at lowering Qatar's carbon footprint, energy and water consumption, and so also at protecting Qatar's natural habitats, its wildlife and its marine reserves. "We see these natural assets as forming important future tourist attractions in a well regulated and professional industry," al-Mohannadi said.

Research methodology:

Data Collection:- The data and information collection is on the base of primary and secondary source. As per my stay in State of Qatar it is collected directly, for that a questioner was setup/ frame and with the help of Journal, News papers, Magazine, Barometers, Websites etc. For analysis the data the MS Excel was used so that the figures and tables can present all the information in well manner regarding the trends of tourism used in State of Qatar.

Limitations of the Study:-The main limitation of this study is that the same study is never done before by any author related to tourism of Qatar. The first time we are trying to produce the study in front of you with the help of limited sources like local news paper "Gulf News" and Qatar Tourism Authority as well as one website www.indexmundi.com. In this way we can say that, this is the special and unique study in sector of tourism of state of Qatar due to unavailable same study and paper in any journal in the education trends.

Need of the Study: - As the explanations in the limitation of the study that the same study is never done earlier by any author related to "Flourishes the Tourism Sector and its Trends in State of Qatar". Because the country comes under gulf region and Middle East and the economy is based on Oil and Gas. So people never think, neither aware about tourism of the state. As a researcher of this field (Tourism and Hospitality), after reading the local news paper, magazine and from local website of the state got a bit experiences about local tourism and also try to observe with the help of local internet websites, the views and comments of people related to tourism in the area that, is the people also taking interest and would they interested to know about the tourist arrival in the state for tourism or different purpose from where the traveller came, and when, what the activities they have done here, have they enjoy as a tourism purpose here. There are lot of question people would like to know and would like to see the growth of tourism sector in the state. So decide and make a plan to find/dig out and present the paper about the Tourism and its Trends in State of Qatar. As per my thinking this is more important and necessary to highlight all the things in well manner though this study, the need of all to know how the tourism sector is flourishing in peninsula with the business of oil and gas.

Scope of the Study:-After the need of the study it is very important for me to explain the scope of the study. Trying to produce various things through this study like arrival of visitors, purpose of visitors, number of visitor in the previous years and current, what is the percentage /change of tourist, foreign exchange earnings and expenditure in and by the state for tourism sector all the things comes under the scope of the study, which will be beneficial for all like researchers, academicians. Local people of the country those are interested to know the trends of the sectors also various division of the govt. of the state. Most important for local govt also so that it can take initiative in the growth and development of tourism and its trend in State of Qatar.

Tools of the Study:-

Figure: 1 Tools of the Study

Findings and results:

Table: 1

Foreign Tourist Arrival in State of Qatar

Years	No. of Tourist	% Change
2000	378000	-
2001	376000	-0.53
2002	587000	56.11
2003	557000	-5.11
2004	732000	31.41
2005	913000	24.72
2006	946000	3.61
2007	964000	1.9
2008	1405000	45.74
2009	1659000	18.08
2010	1519000	-8.43
2011	2527000	66.35

Sources: Indexmundi/UNWTO

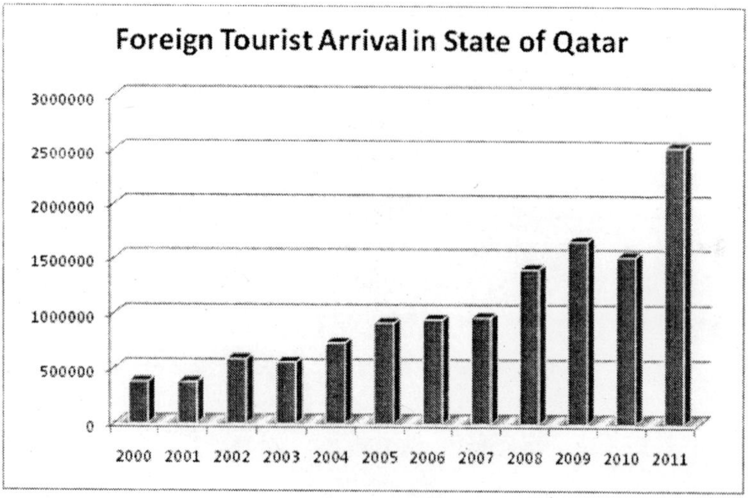

Figure: 2 Foreign Tourist Arrivals in State of Qatar during 2000 to 2011

According to Indexmundi and UNWTO the above table and figure is showing amazing growth in the Foreign Tourist Arrival (FTA) in State of Qatar during 2000 to 2011,which was 3,78,000 in the year 2000 in the mid of decade it was 9,13,000 for the year 2005 and the rapidly growth was seen in the year 2011 which was 25,27,000. In this way we can say its really a flourishes tourism in the State of Qatar.

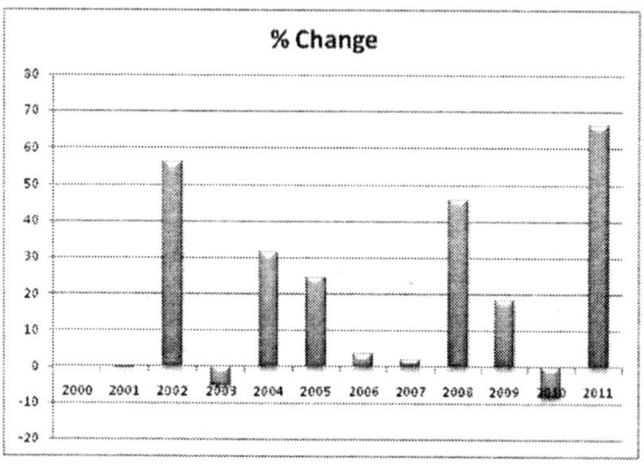

Figure: 3 Percentage/Change on arrival of Foreign Tourist in State of Qatar during 2000 to 2011

According to Indexmundi and UNWTO the above table and figure is showing the change /percentage on the bases of previous year in the Foreign Tourist Arrival (FTA) in State of Qatar during 2000 to 2011, which was -0.53 in the year 2001 on the base of 2000; It was the surprising result seen in the year 2005 which was positively change with 24.72 on the base of 2004 and it was rise in 2011 with 66.35 on 2010 which was in minus with -8.43 if compare with 2009

Table: 2

Foreign Exchange Earning and Expenditures Related to Tourism Sector of State of Qatar

Years	FEE in Million US$	Expenditure in Million US$
2000	128	307
2001	272	366
2002	285	423
2003	69	471
2004	498	691
2005	760	1759
2006	874	3751
2007		
2008		
2009		
2010		
2011	1170	7813

Sources: Indexmundi/UNWTO

Figure: 4 Growth of Foreign Exchange Earning (FEE) from Tourism Sector in State of Qatar during 2000 to 2011

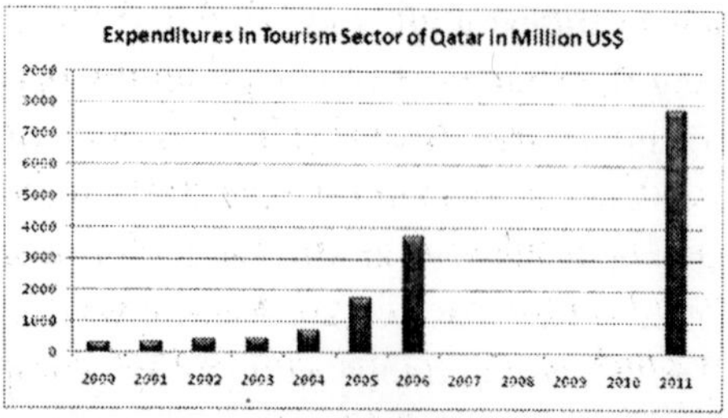

Figure: 5 Expenditures for Tourism Sector in State of Qatar during 2000 to 2011

According to Indexmundi and UNWTO the Foreign Exchange Earning (FEE) was 128 million USD for the year 2000 and it rise rapidly in the years 2002, 2003, 2004, for 2005 it was 760$ million, it was 874$ million for the year 2006. Finally it was 1170$ million in 2011. Really it was the amazing result in the sector of tourism of Qatar which is shown in the above table-2 and figure-4.

According to Indexmundi and UNWTO the expenditures on tourism sector by Qatar govt. was 307million USD in the year 2000 after this it was increased and in the last 2011 which was 7813USD showing in the above table-2 and figure-5.

Table: 3

Hotels Occupancy Rates Q2

Q2	2012	2013
April	64%	69%
May	58%	67%
June	52%	64%
Average	58%	67%

Sources: Gulf Times/Qatar Tourism Authority

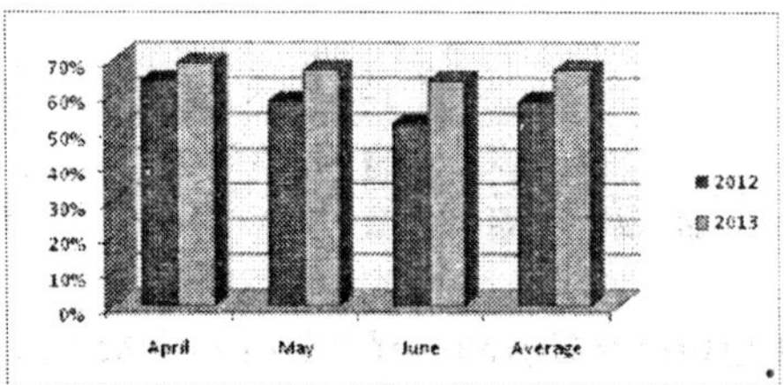

Figure: 6 Hotel Occupancy Rate and Average Rate in State of Qatar for Q2 of 2012 & 2013

The above table and figure is showing the average rate of hotels occupancy was 64% in April-2012 which was 58% and 52 % for May and June 2012, finally the average occupancy was 58% of Q2, 2012. The average occupancy was 67% after 69% of April and 67% -64% for May and June of Q2 of 2013 according to Gulf News and QTA.

Table: 4

Revenue of Q2 from 4 Star Hotels in Qatari Riyal

Q2	2012	2013
April	60826213	63614419.93
May	65244081	64289552.15
June	53104604	57174882.81
Total	179174898	185078854.9

Sources: Gulf Times/Qatar Tourism Authority

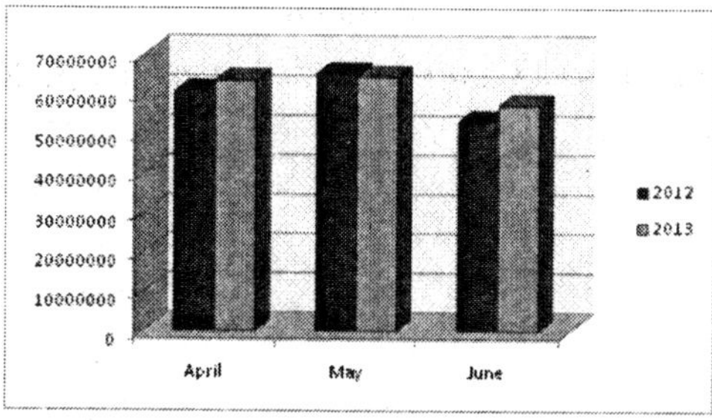

Figure: 7 Revenue from 4 Star Hotels in Qatari Riyal for Q2 of 2012 & 2013.

The above table and figure is showing the revenue from 4star hotels in Qatari Riyal which was total 179174898 RQ for Q2 of 2012 and it was total 185078854.9 RQ for Q2 of 2013 according to Gulf News and QTA.

Table: 5

Revenue of Q2 from 5 Star Hotels in Qatari Riyal

Q2	2012	2013
April	216579755	265327006.9
May	232382980	267671449.8
June	166813044	233596515.2
Total	615775779	776594971.9

Sources: Gulf Times/Qatar Tourism Authority

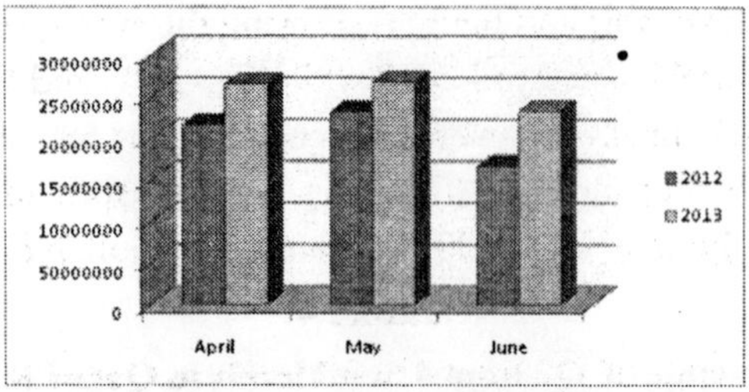

Figure: 8 Revenue from 5 Star Hotels in Qatari Riyal for Q2 of 2012 & 2013

The above table and figure is showing the revenue from 5 star hotels in Qatari Riyal which was total 615775779 RQ for Q2 of 2012 and it was total 776594971.9 RQ for Q2 of 2013 according to Gulf News and QTA.

Table: 6

Tourist from Gulf Cooperation Council (GCC)

Countries/Years	2012	2013
UAE	24215	28712
Bahrain	23984	26433
KSA	119008	144491
Kuwait	12556	14757
Oman	23052	24569
Total	202815	238962

Sources: Gulf Times/Qatar Tourism Authority

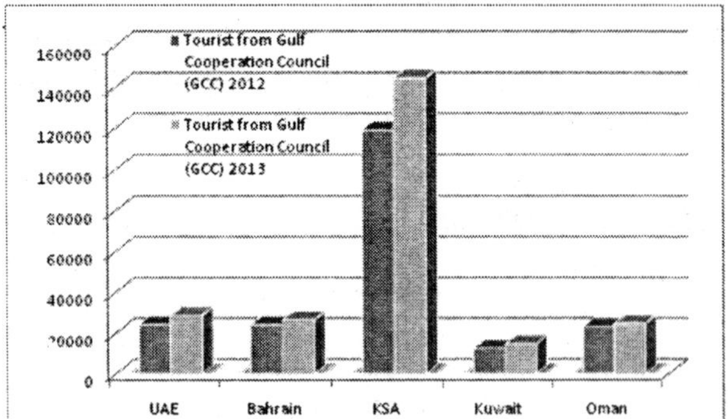

Figure: 9 Tourist from Gulf Cooperation Council (GCC) in 2012 & 2013

The above table and figure is showing the arrival of tourist from Gulf Corporation Council (GCC), which was total 202815 numbers for the year 2012 and 238962 numbers for the year 2013

Table: 7

Travellers Arrival in Q2 for Tourism and Business Purpose in State of Qatar

	(April - June 2012)		(April - June 2013)	
Countries	Tourist	Business	Tourist	Business
Australia	40	211	76	220
Asia	7837	25639	9199	28905
Africa	477	705	447	634
Arab	3329	6465	3206	6450
South America	842	272	878	171
North America	117	1185	895	991
Europe	3807	6376	3581	5719
Others	13	19	16	18

Sources: Gulf Times/Qatar Tourism Authority

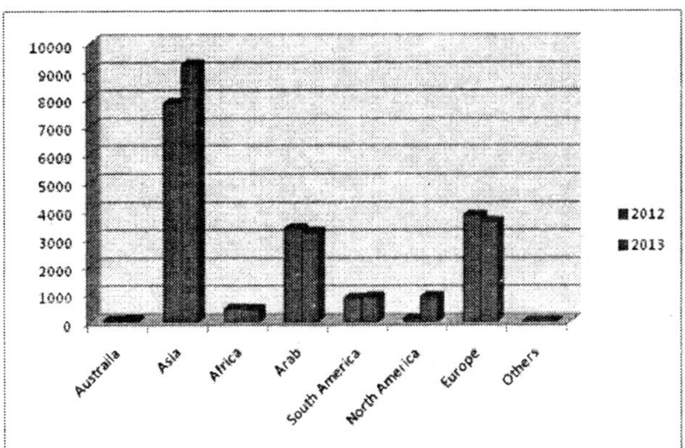

Figure: 10 Traveller Arrival for Tourism Purpose in Q2 of 2012 & 2013 in State of Qatar

The above table and figure is showing traveller arrival for tourism purpose in Q2 for the year 2012 and 2013, which was highest numbers of arrival 7837 from Asia reason for 2012 and it was 9199 in 2013. After this on second position hold by Europe the number of arrival for 2012 is 3807 and for 2013 is 3581 according to Gulf news and QTA.

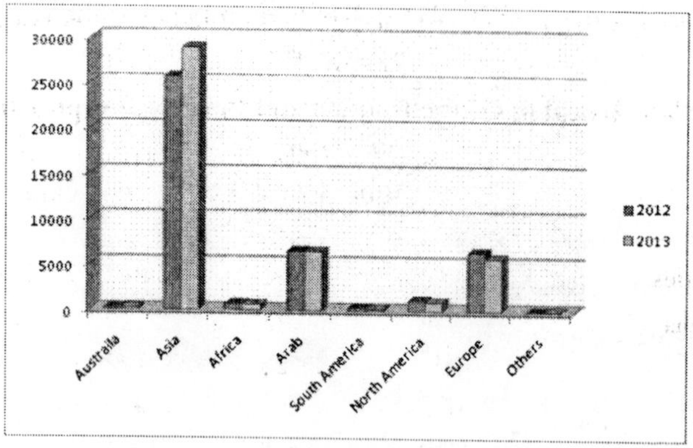

Figure: 11 Traveller Arrivals for Business Purpose in Q2 of 2012 & 2013 in State of Qatar

The above table and figure is showing arrival of visitors for business purpose in Q2 for the year 2012 and 2013, which was highest in numbers 25639 from Asia reason in 2012 and numbers 28905 in 2013. Arab comes on second position with number of arrival 6465 in 2012 and 6450 in 2013.

Conclusion

Finally can say it is true that the tourism sector is flourishing in the State of Qatar. The government is working on various projects on broad level in the country. There is five years plan system adopted by the govt. The state govt. focusing on the tourism attraction places developing the infrastructure like Education Institutes/Universities, New Airport, Metro Rail, 4 and 5 star Hotels, Hospitals, Road, Flyover/bridges, Stadiums for sport tourism coming in 2022 and many more to keep in mind about vision2030.

Bibliography:

An Overview

1 Qatar Tourism Authority (16 Jul-2013), "Gulf Time"

Introduction

2 Al-Mohannadi (16 Jul-2013), Qatar Tourism Authority, "Gulf Time"

3 Five Years Plan,

http://en.wikipedia.org/w/index.php?search=qatar+tourism&button=&title=Special%3ASearch

4. Qatar Tourism Authority (16 Jul-2013), "Gulf Time"

5. ibid

6. ibid

7. Infrastructure

http://www.infoqat.com

Review of Literature

Waleed Hazbun, "The Development of Tourism Industry in The Arab World"

http://hazbun.mwoodward.com/Tourism_in_the_Arab_World.pdf

Abdulla M. Alhemoud (2003), "A Tourism Marketing Plan for Kuwait and other GCC Countries", Journal for International Business and Entrepreneurship Development, ISSN online: 1747-6763, ISSN prints: 1549-9324, Vol. 1, Issue 1, pp. 52 - 57.

Issa bin Mohamed al-Mohannadi (16 Jul-2013), "Qatar Tourism Authority & Gulf Time News".

Taleb Rifai, (16 Jul-2013), "Qatar Tourism Authority & Gulf Time News"

Issa bin Mohamed al-Mohannadi (16 Jul-2013), "Qatar Tourism Authority & Gulf Time News".

Finding and Results:

Foreign Tourist Arrivals in State of Qatar and Percentage/Change on arrival of Foreign Tourist in State of Qatar

http://www.indexmundi.com/facts/qatar/international-tourism

Foreign Exchange Earning and Expenditures Related to Tourism Sector of State of Qatar

http://www.indexmundi.com/facts/qatar/international-tourism

Hotel Occupancy Rate and Average Rate in State of Qatar for Q2 - 2012 & 2013, (29Jul-2013), QTA Report published by "Gulf Times".

Revenue from 4 & 5 Star Hotels in Qatari Riyal for Q2-2012 & 2013, (29Jul-2013), QTA Report published by "Gulf Times".

Tourist from Gulf Cooperation Council (GCC) -2012 & 2013, (29Jul-2013), QTA Report published by "Gulf Times"-

Traveller Arrival for Tourism Purpose in Q2 in State of Qatar -2012 & 2013, (29Jul-2013), QTA Report published by "Gulf Times".

Traveller Arrivals for Business Purpose in Q2 in State of Qatar-2012 & 2013, (29Jul-2013), QTA Report published by "Gulf Times".